T0328360

FACETS OF POWER

FACETS OF POWER
Politics, Profits and People
in the Making of Zimbabwe's
Blood Diamonds

edited by

Richard Saunders

and

Tinashe Nyamunda

Published by
Weaver Press
Box A1922, Avondale, Harare, Zimbabwe
<www.weaverpresszimbabwe.com>
and in South Africa by

Wits University Press
1 Jan Smuts Avenue
Johannesburg, 2001
www.witspress.co.za

First published in 2016
© Each individual chapter, the author, 2016
This compilation, the editors, 2016

Maps on pages x and xvi by Street Savvy, Harare
We are grateful to the following for permission to use their photographs:
Tsvangirai Mukwazhi (photos i and iii on the back cover and on pp. 69,
116 and 158); Panos and Robin Hammond (pp. 95 and 111); Avi Krawitz
and Rapaport USA (p. 47); Annie Mpalume (p. 128); Clayton Masekesa
and *The Zimbabwean* (p. 173, top); Melanie Chiponda (p. 173).
Every effort has been made to identify the source of the other photographs.
Any information subsequently received about these will be acknowledged
in future editions.

Cover Design: Danes Design, Harare
Typeset by Weaver Press
Printed by Directory Publishers, Bulawayo

ISBN: 978-1-77922-288-6 (print) Weaver Press
ISBN: 978-1-77922-289-3 (digital) Weaver Press

ISBN: 978-1-86814-975-9 (print) Wits University Press
ISBN: 978-1-86814-976-6 (digital) Wits University Press

For the people of Marange,

who have endured the most and gained the least from their rich lands

and

Edward Chindori-Chininga (1955-2013)

who knew these stories.

The country is starving, civil servants are going on strike, hospitals have no medicine, agriculture have no chemicals and schools have no books. We cannot continue to be playing around like you guys are doing... Are our diamonds meant to benefit certain individuals, or are they intended to benefit the nation?

– Edward Chindori-Chininga, MP*

---

* Statement by the Chair of the Parliamentary Committee on Mines and Energy, in response to a government witness during proceedings of the Committee, Harare, February 8, 2010.

IN A COUNTRY RIDDLED WITH WIDESPREAD AND CHRONIC ABUSE of authority and breakdown of law and order, Marange's diamonds stand out as an emblem of the toxic mix of state power, poor governance and private greed. This book shines a light on both the murky dynamics of Marange's exploitation and the underlying political and legal order which enabled and encouraged them. An important contribution to the documentation of the full range of rights abuses of recent years – and to making a way forward from them. Beatrice Mtetwa, Human Rights lawyer.

NOT ONLY DOES THIS VERY NECESSARY BOOK examine Zimbabwe's new and unsavoury political-economic networks of accumulation and power in ever widening circles around its diamonds, but it illuminates with great clarity and sophistication the complexities of local and global responses to this elite predation, state repression – and ruling party attempts to regain slipping hegemony. As such Facets of Power *raises important questions about the possibilities of forging 'post-nationalist' political forms in the Zimbabwean state-society complex and further afield. Even better, this book introduces some very sharp new minds to Zimbabwe's critical mass of public intellectuals and young academics: a huge bonus in itself.* – David Moore, Professor of Development Studies, University of Johannesburg

CONTENTS

Acronyms

ACR	African Consolidated Resources plc
AMV	African Mining Vision
CCDT	Chiadzwa Community Development Trust
BICC	Bonn International Centre for Conversion
CIO	Central Intelligence Organisation
CNRG	Centre for Natural Resources Governance
CPHT	Carats per hundred tonnes
CRD	Centre for Research and Development
CSO	Civil Society Organisation
CSOT	Community Share Ownership Trust
CSR	Corporate Social Responsibility
CSU	Counselling Services Unit
DA	District Administrator
DMC	Diamond Mining Corporation
DRC	Democratic Republic of the Congo
DRI	Directorate of Revenue Intelligence, India
EMA	Environmental Management Agency
EPO	Exclusive Prospecting Order
GNU	Government of National Unity
HRC	Human Rights Commission
JOC	Joint Operations Command
JWP	Joint Work Plan, Kimberley Process
KP	Kimberley Process Certification Scheme
LFP	Local Focal Point
MDC	Movement for Democratic Change
MMCZ	Minerals Marketing Corporation of Zimbabwe
MZCT	Marange-Zimunya Community Trust
NANGO	National Association of NGOs
PAC	Partnership Africa Canada
RBZ	Reserve Bank of Zimbabwe
SRSDIL	Surat Rough Diamond Sourcing India Limited
WDC	World Diamond Council

WGM	Working Group on Monitoring, Kimberley Process
ZANU-PF	Zimbabwe African National Union – Patriotic Front
ZELA	Zimbabwe Environmental Law Association
ZIMRA	Zimbabwe Revenue Authority
ZLHR	Zimbabwe Lawyers for Human Rights
ZMDC	Zimbabwe Mining Development Corporation
ZNA	Zimbabwe National Army
ZRP	Zimbabwe Republic Police

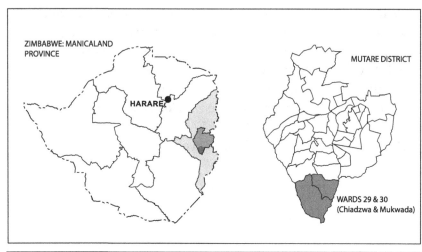

ZIMBABWE: MANICALAND PROVINCE

HARARE

MUTARE DISTRICT

WARDS 29 & 30
(Chiadzwa & Mukwada)

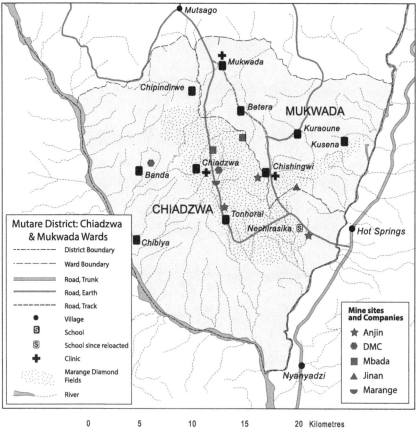

Mutsago

Mukwada

Chipindirwe

Betera

MUKWADA

Kuraoune

Kusena

Chiadzwa

Chishingwi

Banda

CHIADZWA

Tonhorai

Nechirasika

Hot Springs

Chiblya

Nyanyadzi

Mutare District: Chiadzwa & Mukwada Wards

- – – – – – – District Boundary
- – – – – – Ward Boundary
- Road, Trunk
- Road, Earth
- – – – – Road, Track
- ● Village
- Ⓢ School
- Ⓢ School since reloacted
- ✚ Clinic
- Marange Diamond Fields
- River

Mine sites and Companies

- ★ Anjin
- ⬣ DMC
- ◼ Mbada
- ▲ Jinan
- ⬯ Marange

0   5   10   15   20 Kilometres

CONTRIBUTORS

Melanie Chiponda is the Co-ordinator and a founding member of the Chiadzwa Community Development Trust, a leading community organisation working on behalf of the residents of diamond mining-affected areas in Marange. She holds an MSc in Development Studies from the Women's University in Africa, Harare. Her research and advocacy work in Zimbabwe engages with global extractive industries from the perspective of mining communities, and is embedded in a participatory action research approach. Overarching themes of her research include land rights, social justice and the emancipation of women in rural areas.

Crescentia Madebwe has a DPhil in International Population Migration from the University of South Africa, MSc from the University of Zimbabwe and BA from Fourah Bay College, University of Sierra Leone. She is a Senior Lecturer in the Department of Geography and Environmental Studies at Midlands State University, Gweru, Zimbabwe. Her research interests range from population migration to issues of sustainable development, gender and development, urban poverty, and environment and food security.

Victor Madebwe is a Senior Lecturer in the Department of Geography and Environmental Studies at the Midlands State University, Gweru, Zimbabwe. He has a PhD in Hydrogeology from Midlands State University, an MA in Environmental Policy and Planning and a BSc, both from the University of Zimbabwe, and a Bsc in Geology and Geography from the University of Sierra Leone. His research and teaching interests focus on environmental issues, including environmental pollution and control, water resource use and management, and environmental impacts and assessment.

Farai Maguwu is Director of the Centre for Natural Resource Governance, a leading organization working to improve participation in and management of extractives Zimbabwe. He has extensively researched the illicit diamond trade in Marange, and has been a key figure in documenting and campaigning around diamond-related human rights abuses. In 2010 he was charged and detained for 40 days by the Zimbabwean authorities as a result of his work to expose rights abuses in Marange. The following year, Human Rights Watch honored him with the Alison Des Forges Award for Extraordinary Activism in recognition of his work on Marange. He is currently a PhD candidate at the School of Developmental Studies, University of Kwazulu Natal, South Africa.

Alan Martin is Director of Research at Partnership Africa Canada, a Nobel Peace Prize-nominated organization which works to improve the governance and trade of high value and conflict-prone minerals. Born and raised in Southern Africa, he trained as a journalist and worked for more than a decade as an editor and reporter in sub-Saharan Africa, Canada and the UK, before obtaining an MA in conflict and development from the School of Oriental and African Studies at the University of London. He has taught international journalism at Carleton University's School of Journalism in Ottawa, and has travelled to diamond producing areas around the world as a member of the Kimberley Process Certification Scheme's Country Monitoring teams.

Alois Mlambo is Professor of History at the University of Pretoria, South Africa. He has published widely on Zimbabwe's social and economic history. His recent books include *Becoming Zimbabwe: A History from the Pre-colonial Period to 2008*, co-edited with Brian Raftopoulos (2009); and his 2014 monograph, *A History of Zimbabwe.*

Shamiso Mtisi is a lawyer with 15 years experience working on mining, environmental and natural resources law and justice issues in Zimbabwe. He is a founding member of the Zimbabwe Environmental Law Association, Harare, where he is Head of Programmes. He holds an LLB Degree from the University of Zimbabwe and is currently pursuing an LLM in Constitutional and Human Rights Law with Midlands State University. Mtisi has researched, published and campaigned on diamond mining and elimination of the global trade in conflict diamonds, and works more broadly on mining's impact on communities in Zimbabwe. He is a member of the Kimberley Process Certification Scheme's Civil Society Coalition, and since 2010 has served as Co-ordinator of the Coalition's Representatives in Zimbabwe.

Tinashe Nyamunda obtained a PhD in Africa Studies from the University of the Free State, South Africa, and a BA and MA from the University of Zimbabwe. His research is focused on the effects of financial policy on colonial and postcolonial Zimbabwe's economy and the financial dimensions of the informal economy. He lived and worked in Manicaland in the early phases of the Marange diamond rush, later publishing accounts of artisanal diamond mining, cross-border business networks and the informal economy associated with that period. He is currently a Post-Doctoral Fellow in the International Studies Group, Centre for Africa Studies, University of the Free State.

Mathew Ruguwa received his BA Honours from the University of Zimbabwe and a Diploma in Education from Mutare Teachers College. In 2015 he commenced graduate studies for a Masters in History at Trent University, Canada, where his research focuses on the impact of diamond mining on villager displacement in Marange. While teaching at one of the secondary schools close to the Marange diamond fields during 2006-2008, he participated in the diamond story as both diamond digger and cross-border trader.

Richard Saunders is Associate Professor in the Department of Political Science, York University, Canada, where he teaches African political economy and development. His current research focuses on the political economy of extractive resources, including issues of governance, participation and empowerment, and the potential for resource-fuelled 'developmental states' in the Global South. He has published widely on contemporary Zimbabwean politics, including *Dancing Out of Tune: A History of the Media in Zimbabwe*, and *Never the Same Again: Zimbabwe's Growth Towards Democracy 1980-2000*.

ACKNOWLEDGEMENTS

This book has its origins on the sidelines of a civil society workshop marking 10 years of the Kimberley Process, held in Johannesburg in 2013. The meeting undertook to review the successes and failures of the KP's first decade, with Zimbabwe and the Marange debacle featuring importantly in much of the discussion. In the course of the gathering several of the contributors to this collection, including the editors and a number of chapter authors, met informally for the first time and arrived at a similar observation: despite Marange's importance – for Zimbabwe's political economy, the lives of those communities most directly affected and the future of ethical alluvial diamond mining – a comprehensive account of what had transpired there did not exist. That would still be the case if it were not for the commitment of time, enthusiasm and not least funding, by several individuals and institutions, without whom this book would not have been possible.

An initial authors' workshop was held at the University of the Witswatersand in September 2013, and was ably co-organised and hosted by Dr. Obvious Katsaura of the Department of Sociology, a valued early collaborator in this project. Generous financial support provided by Vice Chancellor and Rector Professor Jonathan Jansen of the University of the Free State, and Professor Ian Phimister of UFS' Centre for Africa Studies, enabled workshop attendance by an impressive range of scholars and peer reviewers and set the book on a path forward. We are particularly grateful to Ian Phimister for his enthusiastic, unwavering support. Warm thanks go to those scholars who participated in the first stages of the project and presented at the Wits workshop, including Obvious Katsaura, Shumirai Nyota, David Towriss and Prosper Chitambara; their shared insights contributed to the broad perspectives of the final product. We also wish to acknowledge our workshop peer reviewers and their thoughtful and incisive inputs, and hope they will see the fruits of their contributions in the final versions of chapters here; sincere thanks to David Moore, Trevor

Maisiri, Piers Pigou and Venitia Govender for their assistance.

We appreciate as well the very helpful feedback provided by colleagues and informants as the arguments in this book were developed and refined; thanks to Melanie Chiponda, Violet Gonda, Tony Hawkins, Godfrey Kanyenze, Farai Maguwu, Alan Martin, Derek Matyszak, Shamiso Mtisi, Tony Reeler, Mathew Ruguwa, Sasha Smith and Peta Thornycroft, and to those who prefer to remain anonymous.

The final stages of editing and publication of this book were made possible by generous support from ActionAid International Zimbabwe, and the Faculty of Liberal Arts & Professional Studies, York University, Toronto. We are thankful for their enabling contributions.

Finally, very special thanks to our publishers, Weaver Press, and Irene Staunton and Murray McCartney, for their admirable patience, professionalism, and abiding good humour and support for this project. This book would be nothing like it is without their deft touch. We are grateful for their enduring commitment to publishing quality alternative scholarship in Zimbabwe.

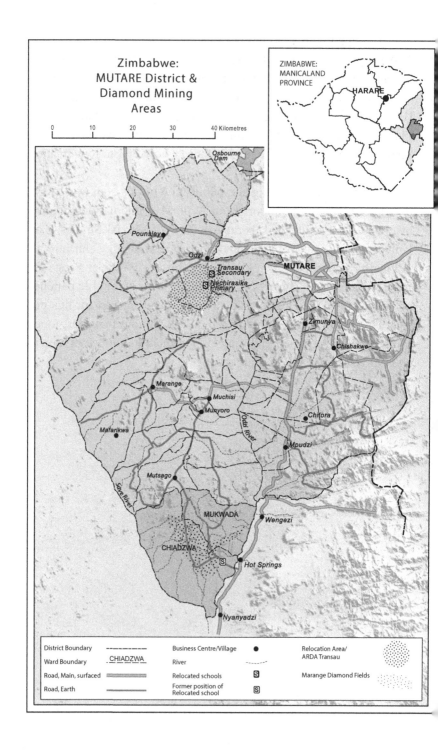

Zimbabwe:
MUTARE District &
Diamond Mining
Areas

0   10   20   30   40 Kilometres

ZIMBABWE:
MANICALAND
PROVINCE

HARARE

Osbourne
Dam

Pounsley

Odzi

Transau
Secondary

Nechirasika
Primary

MUTARE

Zimunya

Chishakwe

Marange

Muchisi

Munyoro

Chitora

Matarikwa

Odzi River

Mpudzi

Mutsago

Sava River

MUKWADA

Wengezi

CHIADZWA

Hot Springs

Nyanyadzi

District Boundary	-----	Business Centre/Village	●	Relocation Area/ ARDA Transau
Ward Boundary	CHIADZWA	River		
Road, Main, surfaced		Relocated schools	S	Marange Diamond Fields
Road, Earth		Former position of Relocated school	S	

FOREWORD

by

ALOIS MLAMBO

In its first decade of independence, Zimbabwe seemed pregnant with the promise of a better life for a people who had endured nearly a century of European colonial rule, culminating in a fratricidal armed conflict pitting white and black Zimbabweans against each other. But the euphoria of independence soon ebbed, sobered by the tragedy of Gukurahundi's mass killings and the more enduring abandonment by the ruling elite of the liberation struggle's goal of a popular democratic, more equitable Zimbabwe. In the 1990s mounting economic crisis and hardship, elite predation and intolerance, and, finally, the militarisation of politics in the face of widespread challenge from the people, shredded the popular mandate of the ruling party. A new social and political movement led by the trade unions and civil society catalysed and brought into stark relief the wholesale crisis of the old order. A besieged ZANU-PF leadership responded by realigning with 'war veterans', youth militias and other elements of violent coercion to systematically target and chaotically restructure the country, starting with the state and then continuing with the dominant sections of the economy; most famously and recklessly, attacking the commercial agricultural sector, dealing an economic blow from which the country has yet to recover.

At the dawn of the new century, the old nationalist order was bankrupt: economically, politically, ideologically. Its standard-bearers survived primarily by coercion while the economy under their management plunged precipitously. It seemed the deepening and inescapable crisis of economic viability would bring Zimbabwe to a new fulcrum point of political transition and change in the face of the opposition's insistent if bloodied challenge. It was at this critical moment that a new player slipped into the political arena to alter the dynamics of conflict. In 2006, during a period of severe economic contraction and spiralling social tension, alluvial diamonds were discovered at Chiadzwa in Marange District of Manicaland Province in eastern Zimbabwe. Among the economically hard-pressed general Zimbabwean public, there was suddenly hope that this new resource would not only turn the country's economic fortunes around but would also usher in an age of prosperity for all – it was, after all, one of the largest alluvial reserves in Africa, according to experts.

As is now well known, this hope was grossly misplaced. While it now seems clear that fortunes were made by the ruling elites and their foreign allies, the generality of the Zimbabwean population gained next to nothing from the exploitation of Marange's stones. Companies working the area remitted very little of their earnings to the public coffer in taxes and shared profits, while large quantities of diamonds were smuggled out of the country and traded surreptitiously, entirely evading state regulation in what amounted to a wholesale looting of a national resource. Meanwhile, the local population in and around Marange was ruthlessly and repeatedly brutalised by state security forces and diamond gangsters alike. Invasion, threats, violent abuse and forced relocation; the prey of diggers, traders and mining companies, and the victim of state agencies meant to be their protectors: this was the reality of Marange's diamond wealth for those who had been their unknowing custodians for centuries.

Facets of Power: Politics, Profits and People in the Making of Zimbabwe's Blood Diamonds traces the troubling trajectory of the Marange diamond mining saga by providing multiple complementary views of its dynamics. Its collection of essays makes powerful linkages between national political struggles and elite formation on the one hand, and new iterations of local poverty and marginalisation on the other; between international predation and criminal networks, and local collaborating interests in the public and private spheres; between international organisations charged with ensuring transparency in the global diamond industry, and the murky world of the international diamond trade they are ostensibly meant to be supervising.

The book is a major and welcome contribution to the study of recent Zimbabwean economic history. *Facets* is the first comprehensive set of scholarly studies focused on the Marange diamond controversy and is, emphatically, a must read for anyone who wishes to obtain insight into how Zimbabweans were once again short-changed by their self-interested rulers. It illuminates the challenges faced by the country's public institutions in managing both the elites that dominate them and the crises they have done so much to generate. In different ways, the book reveals how a key national resource was privatised for the benefit of a few, enabled by the direct collusion of the international community. But it also sheds light on multiple forms of resistance – local, national, regional and international – which were driven by demands for social justice, and which resulted in the elaboration of new notions and strategies for minerals-fuelled development. Here, *Facets* is exemplary as an engaged account of contemporary history. Its authors offer visions for new ways forward, taking stock of the hard-earned lessons from Marange's tragic recent past. And therein, perhaps, lies the book's most enduring contribution to the living history of Marange, and the continuing search for justice and development in the diamond fields of the east.

1

INTRODUCTION:
THE MANY FACETS OF MARANGE'S DIAMONDS

Richard Saunders

The Modern Face of Conflict Diamonds

In 2006 major new alluvial diamond deposits became known in Chiadzwa, in the Marange District of Manicaland Province in eastern Zimbabwe. The discovery coincided with a dramatic and worsening economic and political crisis which posed a growing challenge to the governing ZANU-PF party of President Robert Mugabe. Out of these circumstances a new case of 'blood diamonds' emerged by 2008, in which control over the extraction and black market trading of rough diamonds was accomplished through widespread violence and secretive, irregular state intervention. Local communities, informal miners and commercial mining title holders were displaced, deprived of protection by the law and subjected to a range of rights abuses at the hands of government, and notably, the state security agencies. Faced with mounting pressure from international diamond regulatory organisations and donors, government moved in 2009 to formalise mining in the alluvial sector. However, this restructuring was orchestrated in a manner which facilitated the preservation of power by elite interests who had earlier emerged as key players in Marange: after formalisation, mining continued to disproportionately benefit private and unknown interests to the detriment of the state treasury, national development and local communities in diamond-bearing areas. Moreover, far from solving the problems of violence, rights abuses and criminality which characterised Marange before 2009, the reforms appeared to entrench, extend and institutionalise them, generating new forms of tension and struggle.

In important ways, Marange represents the modern face of conflict diamonds. This is a more nuanced and complex situation than earlier cases in which high-value minerals contributed to militarised conflict by helping to fund armed groups, or by serving as objects of contestation among weaponised interests. In the 1990s, wars in Angola, Sierra Leone and the DRC brought notoriety to diamonds for their role in enabling and sustaining hostilities which resulted in social and economic devastation. The term 'blood diamond' was coined to identify the linkages between violence-tainted mining in Africa and global consumer markets, and became part of a campaign to establish mechanisms for preventing the flow of conflict stones into the global trade. One outcome was the establishment in 2003 of the Kimberley Process (KP) Certification Scheme, an international agreement bringing together governments and civil society from diamond producing countries and representatives of the industry, to establish minimum standards and monitoring procedures for the diamond industry.[1] Given the context of the 1990s, the KP defined 'conflict diamonds' as those whose proceeds contributed to fuelling organised, weaponised or militarised challenges to legitimate regimes. While this approach was successful in slowing the flow of diamonds from Angola, Sierra Leone and other war-affected areas, its effectiveness was soon brought into question by the changing environment of alluvial production. In the 2000s, governments and state based officials – not rebel armies, or other non-state weaponised actors – would emerge as key perpetrators of violence and rights abuses in the alluvial sector, and prominent players in smuggling and parallel trading networks. For many observers, Marange soon became emblematic of the new order.

While the Marange story was a Zimbabwean one, it echoed broader trends in which Africa's alluvial diamonds sector became embedded in complex new ways in the matrices of elite governing interests and private sector power, fomenting heated contestation among a range of stake-

---

1   Bieri (2010) provides a comprehensive account of the KP's origins and early experiences.

holders. Changing regulatory conditions and expectations in the world diamond trade were important factors in this reconfiguration of power; so were neoliberal reforms, particularly through their impact on state capacity and autonomy. These dynamics intersected with parallel elite initiatives aimed at capturing sections of the state in pursuit of wealth accumulation, to yield a new, problematic model of alluvial diamond management. In Zimbabwe, the formalisation of mining in Marange in 2009 marked the establishment of this highly functional, lucrative regime. On the one hand, regular access to international diamond markets was secured via a degree of legalisation which met the KP's minimum standards; on the other, the process of mine licensing created opportunities for elite predation by various means, including the establishment of stealth partnerships in mining ventures, participation in parallel markets and multiple forms of tax evasion. High levels of state secrecy around Marange – reflected in government's refusal to disclose the contents of its contracts with mining companies, its declaration and enforcement of Marange as a security-protected no-go zone, and its resistance to providing a full accounting of Marange revenues – provided a protective cocoon for this mining regime, steeled by the backing of state security agencies and hardened by a combative, hostile rhetoric from senior ZANU-PF officials.

These new dynamics raised crucial questions about the relations among the state, commercial and criminal interests in Marange's management, and the enabling role of some in the international diamond industry and donor community. At the same time, Marange brought renewed attention to the role of civil society and its demands for greater participation and strengthened transparency, particularly in the ambiguous context of neoliberal 'democratisation'. Despite constitutional and statutory provisions for community participation in resource governance, and government's undertaking to consult and partner with civil society in the formulation and implementation of policy for the burgeoning diamond sector, civil society organisations and local mining communities were frequently targeted by government for attack. In contrast, mining companies in Marange were often shielded by senior state officials from civil society requests for information and governance cooperation; and from local communities' demands for mining firms to meet their agreed commitments to provide compensation and community investment.

More broadly, Marange posed important challenges for those in the KP and other international bodies who sought to strengthen the barriers to exploitative diamond mining, and improve the developmental impacts of alluvial production on local communities and states. During the informal mining phase of 2006-2009, Marange fostered heated debate within the KP over the organisation's definition and mobilisation against human rights abuses, amid assertions by one KP founding member that Marange represented the 'return of the blood diamond'.[2] After 2009, many saw Marange as an important litmus test of the KP's viability as an effective supervisory watchdog in a complex and changing global industry; others viewed Zimbabwe's new alluvial diamonds regime as a laboratory of sorts for developing new national strategies from below, and international schemes from above, to contain minerals-fuelled conflict and persistent elite predation. In this context, this book argues that both the struggle over Marange's riches and the lessons learnt from from their destructive exploitation had wide-reaching consequences, extending from rural Manicaland through the national political terrain into the heart of global institutions regulating the diamond trade. The multiple, overlapping and contradictory facets of power underlying the consolidation of these linkages are the starting point for the authors in this collection.

Marange: A perfect storm and a changed landscape

The confluence of extraordinary conditions – a once-in-a-lifetime diamond strike; a state characterised by militarised partisan control, elite predation and withered professional capacity; and the presence of willing partners in a shadowy international trade – cast Marange's diamond fields into the centre of politically inflected, violent and ultimately destructive struggles for control over extractive resources. Marange ranked as one of the world's most important sources of diamonds and the largest find in Africa in a century; some estimated the deposit represented as much as 20-30 per cent of the world's rough diamond supply. In 2010 one Belgian diamond expert predicted annual production of as much as 30-40 million carats, with projected annual sales of almost $2 billion based on per carat averages at the time.[3]

While the extent of Marange's accessible stones was considerable,

---

2   Global Witness (2010).

3   'Marange diamond output could reach 40 million carats', *Mining Review,* 1 September 2010.

precise data on the total volume and estimated value of the deposit were unclear. In 2009, independent private sector and KP assessments predicted a 20-year mining life; five years later, concerns were raised that those initial assessments were too optimistic. What is known is that in the intervening period, at the height of Marange's boom – from the commencement of widespread artisanal, unregulated and mostly illegal exploitation in 2006-2007, to government's establishment of large-scale formal mining in 2009 through the licensing of companies hand-picked by the mining minister – diamonds contributed far less than anticipated to the national fiscus. These sharp contrasts – of high expectations and disappointing outturns, of vast potential for new public resources and their actual privatisation through stealth – reflected Marange's location at the centre of intense contestation among a range of stakeholders and fuelled growing distrust of government and its regime of diamond governance.

Politics and geology provided critical contexts for the emergence of Marange's skewed political economy. State capture by elements of the ZANU-PF and security elite in the early 2000s helped to erode the state's administrative autonomy and injected partisanship into decision making, setting the stage for erratic and politically expedient interventions.

The allure of enormous mineral wealth incentivized secretive, irregular and predatory behaviour by elites with access to the resource via the state. Geology provided an additional catalyst. As alluvial deposits, Marange's diamonds were located near the surface and spread over extensive swathes of terrain. Unlike kimberlitic deposits, which can be effectively secured given their relatively small mining footprint, alluvial diamonds are typically more difficult to police in light of their widespread surface distribution, and the relative ease with which they can be accessed by means of manual digging. By extension, alluvials' geographical dispersion and the difficulties of securing diamondiferous fields in remote rural areas facilitated significant leakage of alluvial rough stones into informal trading markets.

Another enabling factor in the consolidation of illegal smuggling networks was the international diamond trade, an industry notorious for the scale of unaccounted revenues due to smuggling, corruption and undervaluation of stones – as much as $2 billion between 2008-2012.[4] For

---

4   Martin and Taylor (2012).

Zimbabwe's state-based elite in 2006 – embattled by a strengthening political opposition, undercut by a mounting economic crisis and starved of foreign exchange and investment flows – Marange's diamonds presented unprecedented opportunities for the partisan monopolisation of wealth and, by extension, the strengthening and reassertion of political power.

Informal mining commenced in Marange in 2006 under chaotic circumstances, after news emerged of a significant diamond strike by African Consolidated Resources, a British company which had only recently been licensed to operate. By mid-2006 government had withdrawn the company's permit, marking the start of an ill-fated legal battle to restore its claim. Meanwhile, senior state officials publicly encouraged artisanal mining, leading to waves of informal miners invading the diamondiferous areas and effectively displacing the title holder in what became known as the 'free-for-all' phase of development in Marange. Unregulated extraction blossomed along with significant leakages of rough stones into international smuggling networks. The local economy around Marange also exploded, evidence of the substantial trickle-down wealth generated by the local stones. Diamond wealth also surfaced in other parts of the country. As signs of a flourishing parallel diamond economy grew, interests linked to state security agencies and ZANU-PF became intertwined with the hidden accumulation streams flowing from Marange. A series of violent and legally questionable interventions by state security forces, ostensibly undertaken to contain and establish state authority over the booming artisanal sector, were key in consolidating a controlling stake in the Marange trade.

By 2008, major security operations had sealed off access to the fields and made state security personnel the primary gatekeeper of mining activity, controlling and supervising – but not eradicating – informal digging and the murky parallel markets. The violence deployed in the process of containment resulted in episodes of horrific human rights abuses – most notoriously in late 2008, when more than 200 miners and local residents were killed by security forces.[5] Paradoxically, an unintended consequence of this onslaught was rising pressure on the state to move towards the formalisation of mining: the extent of the 2008 violence, together with anecdotal evidence of the vast scale of illegal mining activity and thriving black market, prompted the KP to investigate. In the

---

5   Human Rights Watch (2009).

face of intensive government lobbying, a ban on rough diamond exports was implemented and minimum conditions were specified by the KP for Zimbabwe's return to legal trading.

Government's response to the KP's ban marked a new phase in Marange's development, while preserving the power of key interests through the restructuring of their access to the diamond fields. Formalisation of mining operations in 2009 saw leading ZANU-PF officials in the Government of National Unity (GNU) strike secretive deals with mining entities whose common feature appeared to be linkages to the party of President Mugabe. On the one hand, this restructuring went some distance in meeting the KP's minimum standards for secure, regularised legal mining; on the other, it helped shield Marange's production from accountability. It also helped perpetuate low revenue flows and unsteady fiscal management. Government's restructuring exercise had deep flaws, including partisan contracting that was prejudicial to the state's fiscal interest, enabling of continuing abuses in diamondiferous areas and resistance by officials to access to information. Together, these weaknesses provided the grounds for concerted lobbying against the lifting of the KP's ban on Zimbabwe's rough stones. The legitimacy of the new mining regime orchestrated by senior ZANU-PF officials became a key point of contention, echoing the broader stakes and underlying array of forces during the 2009-2013 life of the GNU. As an icon of wealth during a period of political and economic crisis, Marange became a lightening rod for demands and grievances under the new political dispensation.

The problem of fiscal transparency and predation, coming amid demands on government for economic and social recovery, placed alluvial diamonds at the centre of multiple struggles within the state, and between the state and other stakeholders. Within government, competing institutional claims over diamonds, and factional competition among elite interests, pitted revenue generating entities like the Zimbabwe Mining Development Corporation (ZMDC) and Minerals Marketing Corporation of Zimbabwe (MMCZ) against the Ministry of Finance, Zimbabwe Revenue Authority (ZIMRA) and Parliament. These differences were exacerbated by power sharing, such as it was, during the GNU. By 2011, the MDC-controlled Ministry of Finance fought openly with ZANU-PF run Ministry of Mines and Mining Development over the value of diamond production and revenues delivered to the treasury. Irregular, poorly documented and hard to trace fiscal flows from Marange generated confusion and tension inside government over the actual financial benefits accruing from diamonds, and the extent of companies' compliance with government's fiscal regime.

With the resumption of KP-approved exports in late 2011, the negative impacts of government-company collusion in Marange became even clearer; for example, through revelations concerning the undervaluing of rough diamond exports, and evidence of transfer pricing and fraudulent contracting, including at government's wholly-owned Marange Resources mining operation where government would order a forensic audit in 2014.[6] Rising tensions within government over accountability for Marange revenues were also reflected in the work of the Parliamentary Portfolio Committee on Mines and Energy. In a path-breaking investigation on the diamond sector in 2009-2013, the Committee reported widespread irregularities in the formalisation and supervision of diamond mining under the ZMDC and Ministry of Mines; and inconsistencies, confusion and critical information gaps with regard to the monitoring and management of diamond revenues. It recommended enactment of a comprehensive taxation law for the sector to clarify ministerial and supervisory discrepancies and improve fiscal efficiency. But the paralysis resulting from GNU partisanship ensured little was done to implement the report's recommended reforms; within months, national elections brought the GNU – and internal state pressure for reform at Marange – to an end.

Beyond struggles in the state and political party arena, Marange was also the subject of intense engagement among a range of interests which were sometimes complementary but often competing and contradictory, including donors, international industry players and not least, civil society and local communities directly affected by the diamond rush. During the GNU, government's re-engagement with the donor community saw the latter making claims for fiscal transparency and accountability, and influencing debates over the mobilisation and deployment of diamond revenues. There was renewed attention on the discrepancies between diamond production and fiscal outturns at Marange, particularly as diamond

---

6   Assessing substantial and inexplicable shortfalls in revenue, audits commissioned by civil society revealed instances of chaotic management and administrative irregularities; see, Sibanda and Makore (2013) and Sibanda (2014).

revenues disappointed and began to fall after 2012, and government made little progress in strengthening fiscal accountability and transparency. Government's failure to deliver on promises of stronger revenue flows was exacerbated by its parallel, mostly unrealised commitments to funding recurrent budget items and new development spending out of diamond income. The actual developmental impact of diamonds appeared to be especially elusive and difficult to trace, apart from limited flurries of Corporate Social Responsibility spending by some mining companies in Marange. But with the rapid contraction of production, softening of prices and slowing of operations in 2013-5, Marange's 'development dividend' appeared to vanish entirely – raising new questions about government's development performance, and the actual beneficiaries of diamond wealth.

Civil society was also catalysed by Marange and its diverse members became forceful, key activists on issues of transparency, local development and rights violations, their voices amplified further during the GNU years. Membership in the KP proved a particularly important point of civil society leverage. In 2009-2010, widespread debate within Zimbabwe around rights abuses in Marange was matched by a period of intense contestation within the KP, during which civil society members effectively challenged the Zimbabwe government and allied international interests, winning a ban on rough diamond exports that lasted until November 2011.

Inside the country, civil society and community actors helped expand the scope of discussion beyond issues of transparency to include questions of environmental threats, mining's risks to human and social rights, and local and traditional authorities' participation in resource governance. If civil society activists pointed to inexplicably low royalties paid by Marange's mining companies and poor rates of dividend declaration and remissions to government by the ZMDC and MMCZ, they also identified the lost opportunities these shortfalls represented for community development and national benefit from diamonds, and called for a more transparent, formalised and developmental approach to diamond management. Issues of community benefit and participation in resource governance would become an enduring civil society focus, making non-governmental actors' relations with government and miners ambiguous and sometimes hostile. If Marange opened the door to new roles for civil society in resource management, it also laid risks on the winding and uncertain path towards stronger social participation.

Assessing the Meaning of Marange: Multiple facets, greater clarity

Marange's diamonds are of multiple significance: a key component of government, elite and international trade accumulation schemes; a source of renewed disruption and dislocation in Zimbabwe's rural areas; a test case for new international approaches aimed at preventing conflict-generated human rights abuses; and, a litmus test for democratic and development-oriented transitions in countries emerging from deeply embedded political disputes. The contributions in this collection aim to capture from different perspectives the complexity and diversity of Zimbabwe's alluvial diamonds experience. The authors draw on, engage with and help to extend an emerging body of research on conflict minerals and accounts of blood diamonds in Africa, while underscoring the need for more rigorous, nuanced understandings of the conceptualisation of African resource conflicts in the twenty-first century.

Until recently, much of the scholarly literature on resource-linked conflicts in Africa was grounded in the experiences of the 1990s. The focus of analysis was typically on intrastate or civil wars, and the impact of high-value mineral resources as enabling tools in the hands of dissidents, rebel movements, criminal elements and other weaponised interests.[7] In the case of countries like Angola and Sierra Leone, relatively direct causal linkages were sometimes drawn between mineral resources and sustained political violence.[8] A diverse set of analyses emerged gradually in the 2000s, and contributed to the building of a broader political economy approach to conflict diamonds. Notions of the 'resource curse',[9] 'global governance'[10] and 'greed and grievance'[11] provided overlapping assessments of the volatile dynamics of the high-value minerals industry in poorer mineral-rich countries, and some international comparative studies expanded the debate by explicitly framing minerals manage-

---

7   See for example, Le Billon (2001), Samset (2002) and, Lujala et al (2005).
8   See for example, Smillie (2014, 2010a).
9   Lujala et al (2005). An engaging critical assessment of 'resource curse' arguments is Rosser (2009).
10   Duffy (2005).
11   See Collier and Hoeffler (2004) and Berdal (2005).

ment experiences in the context of social development outcomes.[12] But few writers focused directly on the post-2000 turn of alluvial diamond production and the emergence of hybrid forms of non-militarised, administrative and economic disputes – for example, forced displacement, revision of traditional cultural rights and the private capturing of public revenues.[13] Fewer still studied the destructive social and economic turbulence of diamonds on local mineral-rich communities, including the shredding of the social economy of formerly productive, stable societies by legal, 'legitimate' violent extractivism;[14] this remained an area of focus in which key contributions would come from engaged civil society organisations.[15] Similarly, the shortcomings of international regulatory bodies in coming to terms with new anti-developmental models of extraction led by 'legitimate' governments were under-researched, particularly in the wake of the increasing prominence of such weaknesses within organisations like the KP.

This collection aims to contribute to the growing literature on African alluvial conflicts by expanding the focus of analysis beyond the frame of weaponised violence and intra-state clashes, to include a range of contestations among multiple interests. As the authors here illustrate in multiple ways, the absence of war and resource-fuelled political violence does not suggest the absence of conflict – or for that matter, that the conditions for resource-based 'development' are in place. The militarised disputes of the 1990s do not serve are a useful benchmark for understanding the conflicts of the 2000s, or for defining and achieving the objectives of diamond sector progress in the future.

The studies here seek to identify, trace and understand new dynamics of conflict around alluvial diamonds and development in a period where predatory interests are enabled and protected by rights of legitimacy, or by rules and institutions put in place to engage with previous forms of violent predation. In different ways, contributors explore the evolving,

---

12   See for example, the collection of comparative studies in Hujo (2012).

13   For an interesting case study from Botswana, see Taylor and Mokhawa (2003).

14   A recent useful survey of African diamond experiences is found in Cleveland (2014).

15   For example, the Diamond Development Initiative (http://www.ddi-global.org/) and Southern Africa Resource Watch (http://www.sarwatch.org/).

porous nature of boundaries separating key players in resource govern-ance and the diamond industry – for example, between diamond mining operators and those charged with regulating, managing and supervising them in local, national and international contexts. Importantly, this re-search illuminates the critical and malleable linkages between the realm of minerals, markets and accumulation, and the securing of political pow-er and 'legitimacy' on the terrains of national politics and international business and diplomacy. The richly diverse accounts of the Marange story found here point to the need for a wide-ranging political economy of conflict diamonds in Zimbabwe – one that explains the struggles by which the balance of forces, power and social interests surrounding Ma-range are mediated, and interrogates the strategies and outcomes of key players. The authors in this collection acknowledge and are animated by the importance of developing such a critique, and contribute important evidence towards its elaboration.

The first two chapters chart and assess the political and economic ter-rain of Marange diamonds from the first public revelation of their exist-ence through to their exploitation by artisanal and mechanised mining. In the opening discussion, Saunders explores how diamonds became inter-woven with national political economic struggles as a result of their coin-cidental discovery at a time of worsening crisis of accumulation and po-litical crisis of legitimacy associated with the ruling ZANU PF and state. The processes by which management of Marange evolved institutionally, legally and politically to meet the contradictory and changing needs of government, political elites and the international diamond industry form the basis of the chapter's arguments about diamonds and their role in helping to shape the prospects for Zimbabwe's political transition during the GNU of 2009-2013. In Chapter 3, Martin goes beyond the realm of the national political economy to trace the international networks that have financed and enabled the emergence of a substantial and irregu-lar international trade in Marange's rough diamonds. Following the flow of funds and diamonds into international networks, Martin exposes the global dimensions of greed and corruption surrounding Marange. De-ploying the notion of 'legal thieves,' the chapter demonstrates the limits and loopholes in the 'legitimate' global diamond industry and its local actors in Marange.

The global dimensions of the Marange case – in all its opportunities and obstacles – are accounted for in Chapters 4 and 5, which are focused on the problematic engagement of the KP by authors who have both been active in the KP's Local Focal Point group of civil society organisations working on the Marange issue. Shamiso Mtsi's contribution rethinks the KP's involvement in Zimbabwe in terms of its underpinning strategic agenda and eventual outcomes, and poses the challenging question of whether the organisation has been an enforcer of best practices in the diamond trade – or an enabler of rogue, politically aligned producers and the politics they sustain. Mtsi explores Marange's role in provoking new, important debates within the KP around the need to redefine conflict diamonds in light of the changed circumstances of human rights abuses, of which Marange was exemplary. Here, he traces the trajectory of the difficult and contentious negotiations between Zimbabwe and critics in the KP, leading to the country's re-certification and the resumption of legal trade from Marange in 2011. Mtsi demonstrates that while the KP remains relevant and necessary, its Marange experience points to areas in which the organisation needs to improve in order to become not just relevant, but more credible and effective as a global governance organisation. The KP's governance failures from a local perspective are witnessed in Farai Maguwu's chapter. Maguwu, a leading Zimbabwean diamond rights activist, provides a first-hand account of his encounter with the KP's power dynamics against the backdrop of challenges to the Zimbabwean state over transparency and accountability in Marange. From his unique perspective as head of a leading investigative civil society organisation working in Marange, Maguwu details the legal and extra-legal efforts of government to undermine independent research and advocacy around diamonds, notably in exposing gross human rights violations in Marange in 2008 and beyond. His gripping account also reveals the sometimes problematic contradictions within civil society itself, generated by divisions and weaknesses which risk corrosion of the power and presence of popular voices in resource governance advocacy.

The last four contributions of the book speak to the local experience of Marange: first, during the 'free-for-all' period of 2006-2008, which saw tens of thousands of artisanal and informal miners descend on Marange's diamond fields and the growth of an extensive and lucrative informal diamond economy alongside international networks of criminal smuggling; and thereafter, during the development of mechanised, commercial mining, which led to new forms of disruption and chaos in the form of displacement of villagers through forced relocation, increasing environmental damage and continuing social and economic disruption of local livelihoods. In Chapter 6, Tinashe Nyamunda charts the rise and fall of the 'free-for-all' economy beyond the edges of state regulation and control. Nyamunda recounts the growth of informal business and local accumulation on the basis of first-hand testimony from those who actively participated in the wave of economic activity, and undertakes a comparative assessment of the differential local distribution of economic benefits during the earlier and later periods of diamond extraction. He argues for the need to reconsider the appropriateness of different forms of mining in terms of their decisive impact on local communities and economies in mineral-rich areas.

In Chapter 7, Mathew Ruguwa undertakes a case study of mining's impact on schools and education outcomes in the areas most-affected by diamond mining in Marange District. He argues that the chaotic disruption of local society was evident in the impact on the local educational system, during both the informal and formal periods of mining. The emptying of schools as teachers and students sought fortunes in the diamond fields; the widespread disruption of communities by the invasion of diggers; the turbulence resulting from the activities of state security forces and their clean-up operations; and new forms of dislocation with the onset of formalised mining: all combined to negatively and seriously undermine education in Marange, a tragic and seemingly embedded reality that has been reflected in school performance outcomes in worst-affected areas.

The last two chapters provide accounts of the forced relocations of villagers from Marange mine sites during the formalised period of mining after 2009. In Chapter 8, Crescentia and Victor Madebwe interrogate the promises and realities surrounding the first wave of relocations of families from Marange by government and mining companies in 2011. The Madebwes raise questions about the management and execution of the first stages of the relocation process, and the social and economic impact of removals on the first households affected. The problems identified in Chapter 8 are further explored in Chapter 9, where Chiponda and Saunders follow the trajectory and growing fallout of household relocations. They explore the emergence of community resistance, advocacy and widespread activism, in the wake of disappointment and anger at the loss of homes, communities and livelihoods. At the centre of their case study is the Chiadzwa Community Development Trust, a local organisation which came to have an international reach. The Trust's experiences in engaging government, mining companies and other stakeholders demonstrate the multiple opportunities for and constraints on local advocacy. In a sobering assessment, Chiponda and Saunders argue that locally-driven agendas for community development are at increasing risk of being displaced by policy initiatives championed by the state on behalf elite and private sector interests.

2

GEOLOGIES OF POWER: CONFLICT DIAMONDS, SECURITY POLITICS AND ZIMBABWE'S TROUBLED TRANSITION[1]

Richard Saunders

In 2006, major new alluvial diamond deposits became known in Marange District in eastern Zimbabwe. The discovery coincided with a dramatic and worsening economic crisis of accumulation and a political crisis of legitimacy for interests associated with the ruling ZANU-PF party and state. The result by 2007 was a new case of 'blood diamonds', whereby state security forces secretly oversaw the extraction and criminal smuggling of rough diamonds – in the process, violently displacing local communities, informal miners and legal title holders, and depriving the national treasury of significant new revenues and foreign exchange earnings. Unlike other infamous cases such as Sierra Leone and Angola, where the illicit trade in diamonds helped fuel armed rebellion, Zimbabwe's conflict diamonds came to pose a threat to legitimate government from within. Following the 2008 national elections and the subsequent formation of a Government of National Unity (GNU) in 2009, corruption and criminality associated with Marange diamonds negatively inflected

1   This chapter is a slightly modified and updated version of my 'Geologies of Power: Blood Diamonds, Security Politics and Zimbabwe's Troubled Transition,' *Journal of Contemporary African Studies*, Vol. 32, No.3 (2014) pp.378-394, DOI: 10.1080/02589001.2014.956501.

the trajectory of Zimbabwe's fragile national political transition. The GNU, inaugurated in February 2009, brought ZANU-PF together with two opposition parties, the Movement for Democratic Change-Tsvangirai (MDC-T) and Movement for Democratic Change-Mutambara (MDC-M). Soon, however, the convergence of political need and elite accumulation opportunities in Marange's alluvial diamond geology came to pose a direct challenge to the viability of the new 'unity' government. The challenge of transparency and accountability within the GNU around Marange quickly emerged as a stark litmus test of the new government's success.

In Zimbabwe, the consolidation of criminalised networks spanning political, security and business elites – and national borders – raised important questions about the shape of and prospects for transitions to post-nationalist political orders in southern Africa. After the decades-long establishment of thickly-woven political-security-business networks, cemented through corrupt forms of accumulation, it was unclear whether heavily circumscribed political transitions and the weakened state forms they produced were sufficient to deliver new kinds of participatory politics and economies. Would states already weakened by neoliberal reforms be capable of mounting challenges to embedded elite interests, particularly when the latter included elements from the official and unofficial securitocracy? In more profound terms, was a post-nationalist political and economic order possible?

Marange's blood diamonds provide a lens into the dynamics, extent and wider implications of criminalised political-cum-business accumulation networks in southern Africa. The minerals sector is a particularly important point of investigation given both its comparative productive value in several countries of the region and the latter's documented involvement in illegal trading networks.[2] Mining also reflects the ambiguous and complex interface between local governments and elites, and international markets and regulatory institutions such as the Kimberley Process (KP) Certification Scheme, the worldwide association of government, industry and civil society interests established in 2003 to develop, monitor and enforce standards for the mining and export of rough

---

2 Zimbabwe, Angola, Botswana, the Democratic Republic of the Congo, Namibia, South Africa and Zambia, have substantial precious mineral deposits, and many of these countries have featured as locales or transit points for the burgeoning illegal trade in diamonds and gold.

diamonds. If, as the Zimbabwe case suggests, key levers to encourage transparency, equitable participation in production and the rule of law may be frequently weak or unreliable, then more critical perspectives are needed for assessing and combating entrenched, criminalised and elite-driven politics.

Mining, Politics and Power in Zimbabwe

Zimbabwe's minerals sector has been an important source of capital accumulation, political contestation and policy intervention by the state since the first years of independence. Mining's unique production characteristics set it apart from other leading sectors like manufacturing, where structural adjustment devastated local businesses in the 1990s, and commercial agriculture, which was transformed by ZANU-PF's militant project of 'fast-track' land reform in the 2000s. In mining, a different set of factors has been crucial to the development of the industry: the availability of comparatively large sums of investment capital, access to foreign exchange for inputs, spares and skills, and support from surrounding infrastructure. While other key economic sectors suffered during the structural adjustment years of the 1990s, mining experienced growth fuelled by a resurgence of exploration and investment led by international companies. By the end of the 1990s Zimbabwe seemed poised to become a significant force in African mining. New gold sector investments lifted the country into third place among African gold producers and into the world top ten, and a US$500m investment in platinum led to a major new foreign currency exporter. Other mining sectors, including ferrochrome, coal and nickel, were also resurgent.

As other productive sectors were rendered unstable for the acquisitive, faction-ridden and internally competitive political and business elite, minerals emerged as a central point of contention. Not only did large-scale mining, dominated by gold and increasingly by platinum, offer high foreign-currency denominated returns; it also figured centrally in factional struggles for political ascendancy within ZANU-PF, serving as a barometer of sorts of the sway of different factions of the party hierarchy in struggles to amass political and economic capital. However, the first years of the 2000s saw the collapse of most large-scale mining, notably the crucial gold sector, as shortages or inconsistent supplies of foreign currency, fuel, electricity and spares led to dramatic scale-backs of production and, in many cases, mothballing and effective closure of primary production.[3] The decline of the gold sector was emblematic of the difficulties faced in the wake of production constraints and increasingly chaotic government administration of the sector. In 1999-2001 fifteen gold mines were closed or mothballed, and gold exports and earnings dropped off sharply.[4] By 2003 gold production, at 12.5 tonnes, was less than half of what it was in 1999 and by 2008 most commercial operations had stalled, with output falling to 3.5 tonnes, the lowest levels since before independence.[5]

Meanwhile, a rapid erosion of bureaucratic professionalism and authority within government underscored a wider deterioration of the rule of law. The ruling party leadership came under the growing influence of a security-led political strategy rooted in militarist and commandist management of government, and state institutions were increasingly subordinated to more partisan considerations.[6] Disjointed, unpredictable and often contradictory regulations and announcements by different state agencies and officials signalled growing competition around policy-making by interests inside and outside designated regulatory institutions. In mining, key players affected included the Reserve Bank of Zimbabwe (RBZ) and the state's primary mining-related institutions: the Zimbabwe Mining Development Corporation (ZMDC) (the state's mine operator), the Minerals Marketing Corporation of Zimbabwe (MMCZ) (the agency in charge of minerals sales and exports), and ministerial departments concerned with issues of 'indigenisation' or black economic empowerment. These state mining structures were directly drawn into intense factional struggles within the ruling party, deeply eroding coherence in formal policy making processes.[7]

The imposition of sanctions by the European Union, USA and most western donor nations. Sanctions targeted leading figures in ZANU-PF and the security forces, and businesspeople who had been implicated in political violence, human rights abuses and the rigging of the 2002 presidential election. Following the suspension of lending by key international financial institutions and donors in 1998 and the ensuing shortages of foreign exchange, the sanctions of 2002 effectively cut off much

3   Saunders (2008).
4   BusinessMap (2001: 30).
5   Chamber of Mines (2009: 23-25).
6   Hammar et al. (2003); Raftopoulos (2009); Saul and Saunders (2005).
7   Saunders (2007, 2009).

of the political and business elite from external sources of financing and sharply undermined their trading and cross-border commercial activities. So while many established mining houses looked to sell their Zimbabwe investments in an environment of stalled production and uncertain long-term property rights, the opportunities for local mining takeovers were sharply limited by shortages of hard currency needed to sustain production, and threats of diminished market access for exports. Targeted sanctions, which included the ZMDC, further weakened ZANU-PF's mining restructuring options, and the attraction of international financial support for locally-driven mining house takeovers became nearly impossible.

These constraints opened the way for new foreign players with the political and financial resources needed to ensure investment security; namely, investors based in southern Africa (and later, China) with links to regional political interests supportive of ZANU-PF. New mining investors were led by prominent South African Black Economic Empowerment activists, including Mzi Khumalo, Bridget Radebe and Patrice Motsepe; and by politically-linked regional entrepreneurs like Mwana Africa.[8] Investors also included South Africa's Implats and the global conglomerate Anglo-American, both of which aimed to secure new investments by means of 'empowerment credits' negotiated with government. So while ZANU-PF's assertive nationalist rhetoric facilitated significant ownership transfer to blacks – 'indigenisation and economic empowerment' in the terminology used by government – paradoxically, in the first years of the 2000s those empowered were largely expatriate Africans. There were few positive examples of new black Zimbabwean mining houses and ZANU-PF-linked businesspeople taking stakes; indeed, the leading black Zimbabwean mining entrepreneur of the late 1990s, Mutumwa Mawere, fell out with the ruling party, suffered the seizure of his assets through 'specification' by government and went into exile in South Africa. At the same time, the arrival of southern African investors laid the groundwork for closer regional integration of mining entrepreneurs with complementary linkages to powerful political and security constituencies in neighbouring countries. These dynamics in Zimbabwean mining – the frustrated accumulation ambitions of elites amid their rising needs and moribund if not declining output, and the emer-

---

8   Saunders (2008).

gence of nascent cross-border business networks – were dramatically transformed by the discovery of substantial new mineral assets in 2006.

Marange Diamonds: A new political geography over old fault lines

In 2006, significant deposits of alluvial diamonds became known in Chief Chiadzwa's area of Marange District, in eastern Zimbabwe.[9] The public revelation of easily accessible surface diamonds that could be retrieved through non-mechanised mining (including hand-digging and panning) presented opportunities for important new mining ventures at low cost. Soon, a diamond rush had descended on Chiadzwa. But this rush was not spontaneous. While a broad range of interests sought their fortune through diamonds, the Zimbabwean government and elite political interests manoeuvred to manage both the legal and illegal diamond trade. As state security agencies moved in late 2006 to impose control over illegal informal mining and diamond trading, it became apparent that the aim was not to *eliminate* the black market trade, but rather *facilitate and incorporate* it within a mining regime dominated by elements of ZANU-PF's security and political leadership. A secretive alliance of political and economic interests soon converged around Marange's resources: soldiers, policeman and low-level security officers on the ground; ranking security and political officials; informal miners; local and expatriate black market traders and diamond exchanges; and state mining operators. From the start of the diamond rush, therefore, diamonds and national politics were inextricably linked in a bloody cocktail of economic and political power.

Diamonds represented a potential windfall for those who controlled access to them, creating a dynamic of conflict and competition among a variety of actors. These included the legal titleholder to the Chiadzwa claim from April 2006, African Consolidated Resources plc (ACR), a British-registered company led by mostly white Zimbabwean nationals; state regulatory and producer structures, such as RBZ, ZMDC and

---

9 Diamonds had been discovered in eastern Zimbabwe at least three years before their presence was made publicly known in 2006. As noted by Mines minister Obert Mpofu and others (Mpofu, 2010; Nyamunda and Mukwambo, 2012), prospecting by South Africa's De Beers had earlier identified diamondiferous deposits in the Marange area. However, De Beers, in search of more lucrative kimberlite structures, had estimated the yield from Marange to be of low grade, and abandoned its claims to the area in 2006.

MMCZ; leading state security agencies, including the Zimbabwean National Army (ZNA), the Zimbabwe Republic Police (ZRP) and the Central Intelligence Organisation (CIO), which were soon tasked with securing the diamond fields; political and allied local business elites; informal or 'illicit' miners (known as '*magweja*'); and the profoundly impoverished rural communities located around the diamond-bearing areas.[10] ACR had staked a claim to the mining title for an important section of the fields, pegged off and fenced a test mining section and begun preliminary surface operations by mid-2006. But the company's control over the fields was soon cast in doubt by the dynamics of a volatile political environment.

Marange's deposits represented a critical opportunity for government and key state institutional players to reassert ministerial political control over an unquantified resource and re-establish political influence in a region where the opposition MDC-T was prominent. At the same time, state security agencies soon came to recognise the diamonds' value, whether they were mined legally by the ZMDC with security provide by state agencies, or illegally by syndicates and panners with the frequent collusion of security personnel. Beyond state interests, Marange held the promise of rapid accumulation in hard currency for local business and community elites beset by deepening economic crisis. Meanwhile, thousands of small-scale diggers, along with traders and vendors who serviced them, saw the black market trade as a critical source of household income amid wider economic crisis.

In the context of contested legal claims, weakened state regulatory agencies and growing recognition of economic opportunities, government officials intervened in a succession of linked moves to assert control over Marange. First, the erstwhile title-holder, ACR, was displaced by legal and political manoeuvres, and the resulting chaos provided government with an opportunity to forcefully 'restore order'. In September 2006, Deputy Minister of Mines Tinos Rusere visited the area, announced that ACR's claim was invalid and invited informal miners to work the land, as long as they sold their rough diamonds to the parastatal MMCZ. This ignited a massive and increasingly chaotic diamond rush.

---

10 For a critical disaggregation of the diverse actors and interests who became enmeshed in struggles for access to and control over the mineral assets in Chiadzwa district, see Nyamunda and Mukwambo (2012) and Towriss (2013).

Some reports[11] suggested that by October as many as 20,000 informal miners had descended on the diamond fields, fuelling a thriving black market for stones which rapidly eclipsed the state's own buying agent, the MMCZ, which was cash-strapped and unable to offer competitive prices. Government soon seized on the chaos and reasserted its control in the name of protecting a strategic national resource. Thus began three years of cyclical violence in the diamond fields perpetrated by state security agencies.[12]

In November 2006, the first of several military-style interventions in Marange was launched. Operation 'Chikorokoza Chapera' ('End to Illegal Panning') saw approximately 600 ZRP officers brutally evict diggers and impose a seal on the area, while forcing ACR to abandon its preliminary mining operations. More than 22,000 people were arrested nationwide – 9,000 or more in Marange alone – though many had no connection to the diamond trade, and were rather involved in artisanal gold mining and sales to parallel gold markets.[13] Allegations soon emerged that police personnel were working with illegal miners in the secured zone by permitting access through bribes and commissions, and even digging for themselves. Senior government and military people also were implicated in diamond dealing.[14] One commentator wrote in 2007 of the manipulated chaos: 'our government will console itself with the thought that diamonds extracted from Marange have not been used to finance conflict. That does not make them clean because the gems have become a means by which senior government officials and their cronies have continued to acquire illicit wealth.'[15] The source of the diamond fields confusion, the writer continued, was government itself, and if the state had 'mobilised to clean up the mess in an exercise meant to portray government as working for the betterment of the country', it was a situation of its own deliberate making, enabling a solution of a decidedly self-interested and lucrative kind.

Growing awareness of Marange's value ignited intense competition within state structures as well. Jurisdictional claims by over diamonds

---

11 Including Hawkins (2009: 14).

12 See Human Rights Watch (2009); Partnership Africa Canada (2009a); Zimbabwe Lawyers for Human Rights, et al. (2009); Global Witness (2010).

13 Human Rights Watch (2009: 19).

14 Saunders (2007).

15 'Comment', *Zimbabwe Independent*, 2 March 2007.

led to battles among government departments and state institutions, drawing in political-cum-business factions of the ruling party for which some government agencies appeared to be proxies. The conflicts primarily involved struggles over access rights, rather than the matter of regularising Marange production to render it more efficient or transparent. For example, the RBZ challenged (ultimately unsuccessfully) the mining and indigenisation ministries' capacity to manage production and exports, and warned of large losses of potential income to the national treasury. Meanwhile, the mining ministry sought to expand its authority in Marange via its control of the ZMDC and MMCZ, arguing that professional management of the new resource should be centred in the ministry. At the same time, the ministry's claims to jurisdictional rights were undercut by emerging evidence of widespread smuggling and criminal activity, sometimes involving senior officials connected to the state security sector. Among those arrested and charged with smuggling were a government department director (since deceased) and the son of the CEO of Zimbabwe Defence Industries, a security-dominated firm active in the DRC and allegedly involved in illegal resource exploitation there.[16] By mid-2007, the foundations of a new and increasingly shadowy regime of Marange management were in place under the control of security-linked networks. The state security forces' key role was underpinned by Chiadzwa's listing as a 'restricted area' under the Protected Places and Areas Act, with the ZRP given chief responsibility for securing the diamondiferous areas. Meanwhile the mining ministry moved to block ACR's legal challenge over its title claims, and ramp up production through the ZMDC.

This new management order was consolidated through renewed violence by state security forces. Successive waves of attack in 2007-08 led first by the police and later involving the ZNA and CIO subjected thousands of community members, local residents, informal miners, buyers and ordinary merchants and traders to severe legal and extralegal violence. A strategic aim of these attacks was not to stop the illegal trade, but rather to bring it under the control of the political and security leadership. In this way, networks of security-linked trading 'syndicates' emerged involving illegal miners, traders and security personnel. This arrangement

16 'Diamonds seized from ZDI boss's home', *Zimbabwe Independent*, June 2007.

seems to have been extraordinarily productive and lucrative: by 2008 Marange diamonds were appearing on markets as far-flung as Guyana, Sierra Leone, Dubai and India, and independent research suggested diamond syndicates were being consolidated and strengthened under the government's watch.[17]

Election Panic and Violent Consequences

The wider political significance of Marange's booming trade only became clear at the time of the 2008 national elections. Having lost the 29 March parliamentary elections (and the first round of the presidential vote) to the MDC-T, ZANU-PF chose to fight its way back from the brink of political defeat through the use of extreme violence directed at both the opposition and traditional ZANU-PF constituencies which had broken rank with factions headed by Robert Mugabe.[18] This path required both the loyalty of the active agents of ZANU-PF's political violence – the security forces, police, youth militias, 'war veterans' and others – and funding to facilitate their activities. Chiadzwa diamonds represented a key source of concealed cash financing and payment-in-kind for the security agencies.[19] Marange's location in hotly contested Manicaland (which voted overwhelmingly for the MDC-T in the March elections) provided additional incentives for renewed action.

The immediate outcome was a series of deadly new interventions in Marange. The waves of violence unleashed in 2008 against informal miners, traders, local communities, opposition supporters and activists and others had a double objective: to undermine electoral support for the MDC in the June round of voting, and to consolidate control over diamond field revenues that were needed to secure the instruments of partisan political violence. Therefore, the 2008 elections were a benchmark in the comprehensive politicisation of Marange diamonds against the backdrop of organised political violence. 'Operation Restore Order,' launched by the ZRP after the 29 March poll, claimed to target illegal miners and traders, and seek re-establishment of 'government' control in Marange. But the scope of violence was much wider. Thousands of local inhabitants were victimised in state-led violence, resulting in a cas-

---

17   Partnership Africa Canada (2009a; 2009b).
18   Solidarity Peace Trust (2008), Human Rights Watch and International Crisis Group (2012b).
19   Global Witness (2012b).

cade of serious human rights abuses including murder, severe beatings, rape and irregular detention.[20] Violence associated with 'Restore Order' peaked before the June run-off vote but continued to simmer for months, and certainly well past the September 2008 signing of the Global Political Agreement (GPA), the political settlement establishing the GNU involving ZANU-PF and the MDC formations.

Reports of continuing illegal mining and human rights abuses by the ZRP placed new pressures on – and elicited divergent responses from – the fragile GPA. ZANU-PF, which retained unilateral control of government ministries until February 2009, intensified its militarised involvement in the diamond fields by unleashing a new and profoundly violent assault on informal mining in late October 2008. This time the ZNA led the attack. 'Operation Hakudzokwi' ('You Will Not Return') culminated in unprecedented numbers of deaths and human rights abuses in Chiadzwa and surrounding areas. The ZNA's deployment of three brigades led to massive violence against miners, traders and rural folk, and occasionally even involved skirmishes with members of the ZRP. Independent reports documented the shooting of informal miners from military helicopters and systematic illegal abductions, rapes and beatings by army personnel. During the three-week period when the ZNA was solely in control of Chiadzwa, one influential report noted, 'thousands of gross human rights abuses occurred' and at least 214 civilians were killed. By government's own account, tens of thousands of illegal miners were chased off the fields, and more than one thousand arrested.[21] However, the ZNA's tightened security regime in Chiadzwa failed to meet its officially stated goal of stopping the illegal trade, and instead institutionalized and consolidated illicit mining under the control of the security forces and ZANU-PF sections of government – a grim reality later confirmed by documents leaked from the ZNA regional command.[22]

Widespread outrage following the revelation of gross human rights abuses under 'Operation Hakudzokwi' – especially as it occurred after the promise of shared power under the GPA – and led to new MDC and civil society calls for the demilitarisation, depoliticisation and regularisa-

---

20 Zimbabwe Lawyers for Human Rights et al. (2009: 26-32).

21 Human Rights Watch (2009).

22 'Brief for Sub-National JOC by Assistant Commissioner Mawere N. on Operation Hakudzokwi Phase VII on 07.05.2010'. May, 2010. Leaked and published on numerous Zimbabwe-focused websites.

tion of Marange diamonds. But dislodging the shadowy trading networks faced steep challenges in the context of 'shared power'. While the GPA promised greater transparency in government, it simultaneously created new incentives for entrenched political, security and business elites to defend their lucrative and strategic interests in Marange by undermining transparency and blocking accountability in government's management of the diamond trade.

The GPA and Stalled Transitions: Conflict diamonds in the time of democratisation

The GPA introduced a new dynamic into the political-economic matrix of Marange's management. On the one hand, the MDC's arrival in government diminished ZANU-PF's unmediated access to the state, and notably state finances;[23] on the other hand, this loss of access forced President Mugabe's party to defend existing, and seek out new, off-budget sources of funding to help sustain partisan security-based interests, which had been key in retaining the presidency for ZANU-PF in 2008 and leveraging the negotiations leading to the GPA. A stark contradiction soon took root: the spirit and letter of the GPA came to stand as a primary challenge to the partisan illegal accumulation nexus at Marange, while the violent political strategy fuelled by its diamonds placed in doubt the GPA's goal of a political transition founded on a new democratic constitution and legitimate free and fair elections. ZANU-PF's continued political and economic profiting from diamonds *required* power-sharing to be undermined. Marange diamonds therefore emerged as a key 'litmus test' of the new GPA: if politicised illegal diamond networks could not be dislodged by the unity government, and there seemed little hope for the wider 'normalisation' of the national political economy.[24]

The initial results were not encouraging. Soon after the GPA was signed in September 2008, violence and rights abuses perpetrated by state security agencies under 'Operation Hokudzokwi' signalled an im-

---

23   The appointment of the MDC's Tendai Biti as the new Minister of Finance proved significant not only in the increased supervision of and transparent control over regular state finances including foreign donor flows, but also in the marginalisation of RBZ Governor Gideon Gono, who had previously played a central role in sustaining ZANU-PF's agenda through erratic ad hoc monetary and lending policies.

24   Saunders (2009).

mediate challenge to the fragile political accords. The MDC was mostly silent on the issue, occupied as it was until early 2009 with negotiations over the distribution of posts and power under the GPA. In this critical period leading up to the MDC's assumption of cabinet seats in February 2009, ZANU-PF used its control over the security forces and the mining ministry to seal off illegal diamond activities from wider GPA scrutiny and intervention and shut down the flow of information from the fields. This situation persisted after the formation of the GNU when ZANU-PF strategically demanded and retained control of the mining ministry under Minister Obert Mpofu, along with key security ministries.

Political management of Marange continued to be characterised by secrecy and ministerial commandism. Through a series of measures the party and its senior leadership further instrumentalised the once-respected state mining bureaucracy – and more widely, the GNU 'partnership' itself. Minister Mpofu invoked ministerial discretion to impose personnel, plans and targets on ZMDC and MMCZ without consulting MDC partners in government; the judicial system was deployed as a means of asserting ministry claims around ACR's title (and was ignored when unfavourable decisions were rendered); and information flows to, and collaboration with, other government ministries under MDC control were blocked. Longstanding requests from the mining industry for Marange production figures remained unanswered. Others seeking information on diamond operations, the role of the security forces and related rights abuses, including local and international civil society organisations, were challenged, threatened, attacked and denied access to Marange. Even parliamentary structures were interfered with on Minister Mpofu's instruction. As late as April 2010, fact-finding investigations by Parliament's Portfolio Committee on Mines and Energy were blocked, and its members repeatedly prevented from visiting Chiadzwa. The Minister cited spurious 'national security' concerns as the reason.[25]

The extent and effectiveness of ZANU-PF's tight grip on Marange's management and the negative consequences of the MDC's marginalisation from decision-making within the GNU were drawn sharply into focus when the government confronted a growing challenge from the KP. Marange had been a cause for concern within the KP beginning with the first stages of the diamond rush. As early as December 2006, important

---

25   'Mines committee barred from Chiadzwa again', *The Standard*, 25 April 2010.

players within the KP, such as the World Diamond Council, had raised flags about the irregular nature of production and legal title management in Chiadzwa. Initially, the focus was on the government's dispute and refutation of ACR's legal claim to title. But once reports of human rights abuses became known the KP expanded its investigation to include these as well. However, mining ministry officials deftly handled a KP Monitoring Working Group country review mission that was dispatched in May-June 2007. The visiting team barely touched down: it overflew the Chiadzwa fields in a Zimbabwe Defence Forces helicopter, and met with few witnesses who were not arranged by the ministry. The outcome was a report that gave a clean bill of health to a manifestly unhealthy situation.[26] The firm and unobstructed hand of ministry and state security officials proved effective in blunting the KP challenge, partly enabled by the KP's own internal weaknesses including lack of transparency, accountability, good faith and consensus among a diverse collection of industry, government and civil society members.[27]

But the tide of international criticism following Hakudzokwi's excesses in 2008 reignited KP concerns over smuggling, illegality and rights abuses. A new KP country review team visited Zimbabwe in mid-2009 and produced an interim report which was unusually harsh in its criticisms of government. The review team's confidential report called for the immediate demilitarisation of the diamond fields, the appointment of a Special Rapporteur to investigate allegations of human rights abuses, and the suspension of Marange diamond exports pending improvement of the situation.[28] But these potentially disastrous recommendations were kept under wraps, thanks in part to generous cooperation from ZANU-PF's erstwhile political ally, the government of Namibia. Bernhard Esau, Namibia's Deputy Minister of Mines and the KP Chair, oversaw a long delay in the publication of the review mission's interim report; and when it was leaked to the local media, he went to unusual lengths to blunt its sharper recommendations. Esau also helped set the stage for further manipulation of KP discussion of Marange in the lead-up to the organisation's annual plenary in Namibia in November 2009.[29] Consequently,

---

26 Kimberley Process (2007); Ziyera (2007).

27 Smillie (2010 b).

28 Kimberley Process (2009).

29 Human Rights Watch (2009); 'Kimberley Process Chair Defends Recent Decision Not to Suspend Zimbabwe', *Voice of America*, 20 November 2009.

the impact of the team's findings was severely undermined.

The new challenge mounted in 2009 by the KP under pressure from its business and civil society members demanded a new strategy from government to prevent Zimbabwe's suspension from the rough diamond trade. ZANU-PF developed a multi-pronged approach. In addition to lobbying regional KP member governments for support, it clamped down on information gathering and lobbying activities of civil society; and more importantly, moved to restructure mining in Marange in ways that lent the appearance of 'normalisation' – or at the very least, 'legality' in terms of compliance with the KP's minimum standards for diamond trading. ZANU-PF government officials mobilised the state media and security apparatus – also retained under ZANU-PF ministerial control in the GNU – to threaten key civil society organisations and individuals who had provided critical evidence to the KP mission. Minister Mpofu questioned the political motives of local groups, accusing NGOs of being 'deranged and requiring psychological examination'.[30] State-controlled media served up warnings against future 'unpatriotic' activity, and local community leaders including Chief Newman Chiadzwa, who had been an impressive witness for the KP mission, were publicly harassed and accused of involvement in the illegal diamond trade.[31]

Importantly, Minister Mpofu also took steps to regularise production at Marange through the introduction of new commercial joint venture mining operations. Again, ZANU-PF's unilateral control of ministry structures enabled opaque partisan management of this process of 'transition' to commercialisation. In mid-2009, Mpofu secretly approved concessions for two new companies in Chiadzwa, Mbada Diamonds and Canadile Miners. Both involved joint ventures between the ministry's ZMDC and South African-based parent companies; they were presented with fanfare at the KP's November plenary as a reflection of government's attempt to bring Chiadzwa operations into compliance with KP standards, and won a favourable response from most KP members.

---

30   'Zim diamond ban "unlikely" as gov argues lack of evidence', *SWRadioAfrica*, 4 November 2009.

31   In Chief Chiadzwa's case, this intimidation allegedly led him to write a retraction of evidence he had supplied to the KP mission in June 2009 'CIO wants me silenced at KP summit', ZimOnline. 5 November 2009; 'Zimbabwe Delegation to Kimberley Meeting in Namibia Said to Threaten NGOs', *Voice of America*, 3 November 2009.

It was only after details of the joint venture deals emerged that new questions were raised about the motivation for, and beneficiaries of, the partnerships. The Mbada and Canadile concessions had troubling features in common: neither company was an experienced miner, let alone in the diamond sector, and both had direct links with Zimbabwean state security agencies and, by extension, ZANU-PF.[32] Neither South Africa-based enterprise had been in a transparent process or undergone due diligence by the ZMDC in advance of their signing on with the Zimbabwean partner; indeed, by the ZMDC's own account, neither would have been likely with such a tendering process. Moreover, while Minister Mpofu argued that the deals were rushed through because government had been in urgent need of foreign exchange, there was little evidence that revenues had ended up in government's coffers – a situation which would become chronic by 2012, by which time it was reported that hundreds of millions of US dollars in proceeds due to government from Mbada and other new miners had not been deposited with the treasury.[33] In reality, then, Mbada and Canadile reflected a strategic double-move by ZANU-PF to deflect KP criticisms of illegal mining and rights abuses by normalising the institutional arrangements of Marange mining, without derailing the politicised administration and skewed financial benefits derived from it. Later concessions to mining firms in Chiadzwa would reflect a similar process of partnering with foreign politically aligned interests, typically using opaque shareholding arrangements featuring offshore shell companies with hazy links to

---

32   The ZMDC's partner in Mbada, the New Reclamation Group (Pty) Ltd (through its Mauritius-based subsidiary Grandwell Holdings), was focused on scrap metal operations. Its head and board member, Robert Mhlanga, was a retired Zimbabwe Air Force pilot and was known to be close to Air Marshall Perence Shiri. Canadile's private sector partner, Core Mining and Minerals (Pvt) Ltd, was unknown in mining circles in its South African base. Included in its senior structures was retired ZNA soldier Lovemore Kurotwi, considered close to the current ZNA senior ranks. Other reports suggested that Minister Obert Mpofu was linked in business to ZDF Chief General Constantine Chiwenga. Media speculation was rife that the two companies included the prominent participation of known diamond smugglers and drug dealers. See Global Witness (2012a, 2012b); Partnership Africa Canada (2012); Sibanda (2010); 'Police join diamond rush', *Zimbabwe Independent*, 29 April 2010; 'Israeli funding Zim diamond mining', *ZimOnline*, 20 April 2010; 'Parliamentary Committee ignores abuse and theft at diamond fields', *SWRadioAfrica*, 16 March 2010.

33   Partnership Africa Canada (2012).

interests with security backgrounds.[34]

These combined ministerial interventions succeeded in blunting and finally overcoming the threat of KP sanctions, aided in part by the weak and uncertain positions of ZANU-PF's GNU partners.[35] At the KP's annual plenary in November 2009 calls for Zimbabwe's immediate suspension were turned back. Zimbabwe agreed to a compromise, a Joint Work Plan and the appointment of a KP Monitor to assist the government in achieving KP certification compliance. NGO and media reports noted the role of Namibian, South African, Congolese, Tanzanian and Russian delegates in defusing the threats to Marange production, and indicated that the 'farcical' decision on Zimbabwe was causing a crisis of confidence in the KP for some of its key members.[36] Mpofu's spirited defence of the mess, backed by political allies in the region and industry voices keen to see the diamonds on international markets, deflected debates onto the KP and its criteria and practices, and away from the demonstrably irregular situation in Zimbabwe – even as new revelations seemed to confirm that ZANU-PF and its security and business allies' quest to lock down control over Marange's riches continued unabated in the wake of sustained criticism and KP threats.[37]

At the same time, criticism mounted within the KP in 2009-2010

---

34   See Alan Martin's chapter in this volume for detailed discussion of security links to Marange's mining companies.

35   The blundering presence of then-MDC Deputy Minister of Mines Murisi Zwizwai at the KP's Namibia plenary highlighted the MDC-T's inconsistent position on the question of diamonds, sanctions and legality, and underlined the ambit of Minister Mpofu's power. Zwizwai initially parroted Mpofu's view that there was no evidence of military involvement in illegal mining and rights abuses. MDC Prime Minister Tsvangirai was later forced to rebuke his colleague, but the damage had already been done. Zwizwai was shuffled out of the mining ministry in June 2010.

36   'Zimbabwe escapes 'blood diamonds' ban', *Daily Telegraph*, 5 November 2009; 'Diamond Monitoring Body's Failure to Suspend Allows for Sale of "Blood Diamonds"', Human Rights Watch Press Statement, 6 November 2009.

37   For example, media reports in early 2010 revealed that the police services, which were not part of the existing joint ventures, had applied to Minister Mpofu for a mining concession (see Sibanda, 2010). In late 2010 a corruption scandal broke at Canadile, resulting in the arrest of some of the company's executives, and the wholesale restructuring of its ownership and management, bringing it more firmly under the control of the ZMDC. See also 'Zimbabwe Activists Pressure Harare for Accountability on Diamond Operations' *Voice of America*, 14 May 2010.

about the Marange situation, with Zimbabwe becoming a central focus of deliberation and heated conflict. The 'regularisation' of production at the Mbada and Canadile joint ventures through commercialisation failed to disguise a deeply troubling pattern of military and ZANU-PF partisan involvement. Independent research published in 2010 by KP founding members Global Witness and Partnership Africa-Canada documented ZANU-PF and security links to the Marange miners, highlighted the low flows of diamond revenues into public coffers,[38] and repeated calls for Zimbabwe's suspension from the rough diamond trade. The KP Monitor for Zimbabwe appointed in early 2010, Abbey Chikane of South Africa, was also drawn into the fight. He ignored evidence of continuing rights abuses and irregular military involvement in mining – including from authenticated reports from the ZNA itself – and officially recommended in June 2010 that Marange diamonds be given the KP seal of approval for export.[39] As a direct result of his engagement with local civil society researchers, moreover, the leading diamond research organisation working on Marange and a KP civil society member organisation, the Centre for Research and Development, was severely harassed. Its director, Farai Maguwu, was irregularly detained and harshly treated. The uproar that followed at the KP's semi-annual meeting, where Chikane's report was discussed, placed Chikane's own future as Zimbabwe monitor in jeopardy, and led to new calls by civil society partners and some member governments in the KP for reform and recalibration of the organisation's criteria for assessing the 'cleanliness' of rough diamond production. In the short term the KP maintained its overall suspension of Marange diamond exports; but in the longer term the combined and complementary forces of economic interests, political allegiances and administrative authority overwhelmed voices in the KP calling for greater transparency in Marange. Meanwhile, voices in the GNU challenging the murky man-

---

38   The ZMDC's Chief Executive Officer testified before the Parliamentary Portfolio Committee on Mining and Energy in 2010 that his parastatal had declared no dividend to government for more than twenty years. As some observers argued, since ZMDC had sole jurisdiction over Marange from 2006 until the Mbada and Canadile joint ventures in 2009, it was not clear where revenues due to the ZMDC through its joint venture with Mbada and Canadile had gone – and why the ZMDC had not taken action to ensure their transparent transfer to the MDC-controlled Ministry of Finance. See for example Global Witness (2012) and Partnership Africa Canada (2012).

39   Chikane (2010).

agement of the Marange trade were blunted by ZANU-PF's unilateral engagement of the KP and its refusal to divulge information on Marange to its 'partners' in government.

In 2010 the KP allowed two significant allotments of stockpiled Marange diamonds to be sold overseas; by mid-2011, concerted government lobbying at the KP and the chairing of the organisation by the ZANU-PF ally of the DRC government, saw new moves to unban rough diamond exports – first via an irregular decree of the KP's DRC chair; later, at the annual meeting of the KP, by consensus. In November 2011, the KP's ban was lifted on the sale of existing tainted stockpiles of diamonds and by implication, future production. With the unblocking of international sales, a flood of stones – and poorly monitored revenues – ensued, although evidence soon emerged to suggest that government had overseen significant exports of non-compliant rough diamonds while working to lift the KP's sanctions. Exasperated at the failure of the KP to stand up to Zimbabwean officials and their industry and political allies, and noting the institutionalisation of security and partisan political interests responsible for past rights abuses within the recently commercialised diamond mining sector, some KP members, including founding member Global Witness, quit the organisation at the end of 2011.[40]

If Zimbabwe represented the 'new face' of conflict diamonds – in which the main perpetrators of diamond-fuelled human, social and economic rights abuses were governments and their allies, not armed rebels – it seemed clear that new thinking, regulatory criteria and enforcement measures were needed to combat the changed dynamics of conflict.[41] Unlike other notorious cases such as Sierra Leone and Angola, where diamonds fuelled anti-government rebel groups, Marange diamonds helped generate dissent from *within* a legitimate government. Confronting instances of illegal trade would therefore mean confronting influential government members of the KP itself who benefited from such illicit activities. It also implied a challenge to the political security of those interests within the Zimbabwean government who professed the ideals of unity, power-sharing and reconstruction, while actively pursuing the partisan ends of unilateral power and secretive wealth accumulation.

---

40   Global Witness (2011).
41   Saunders (2010); Vircoulon (2010).

Hard, Enduring and Costly: Diamonds and political transitions

As the GPA came to an end in mid-2013, Marange's diamonds presented a sobering illustration of the emergence of politically-linked elite business and security networks of accumulation in Zimbabwe. The illegal diamond trade became inextricably bound up with Zimbabwe's troubled transition to a more democratic, inclusive and stable political dispensation: failure to introduce transparency and accountability to the diamond sector implied a parallel defeat of democratic forces within the GNU. The political and economic autonomy afforded some sections of the security forces and ZANU-PF by their privileged access to Marange diamonds nurtured the foundations of a parallel, shadow axis of power within the fragile GNU. Included within that politically-led alliance were a range of interests with complementary power assets, notably state security forces and factions of the ZANU-PF elite. Also included in the alliance were party-linked business entrepreneurs, bureaucrats and officials in state-based mining agencies, diamond traders and dealers based in black markets, regional businesses (including some with links to political and security interests in their home countries), informal and artisanal miners and traders, and some sectors of local communities in the diamond bearing areas. The combined capacities of this coalition were anchored in the brutal disciplining and monitoring power of the security agencies, and the political, administrative and legal authority of the mining ministry. But they also included political support from powerful regional business and political allies.

The illegal trade especially strengthened militarised interests which fell under, but were not entirely accountable to, the charade of a 'unity' government. Diamonds injected new elements of violence into a fragile political dispensation by sustaining partisan capacities for violence. Indeed, Marange's partisan exploitation *required* the continued disruption of democratic administration, transparency and rule of law. According to some reports which documented the labyrinth of overlapping holding companies with securocrat and ZANU-PF connections, Marange's off-budget revenues effectively financed a parallel government enabled by the strategic protection of ZANU-PF-controlled sections of the GNU, whose two primary objectives were the safeguarding of access points to both secretive elite accumulation and state power.[42] As it happened, that

---

42   Global Witness (2012b).

strategy proved successful: in the July 2013 national elections, ZANU-PF swept to victory and regained majority control of parliament, while President Mugabe retained the presidency.

Looking back, a core contradiction remained unresolved throughout the life of the GNU and was episodically highlighted in fights involving control over Marange: it was not in the strategic interests of ZANU-PF and its business-security allies to implement a power-sharing agreement that might have enabled a transition leading to free, fair and decisive elections – which ZANU-PF would very likely have lost. A dysfunctional GNU was *required* for secretive accumulation – and the electoral politics of violence and intimidation that depended on it – to succeed. At the same time, strategic access to the 'legitimate' state of the GNU, notably its security, mining and information agencies, was needed to defend and expand political-economic claims by ZANU-PF and displace opposing interests. Analysts who called for sustained support for the GNU due to the absence of 'alternatives' failed to acknowledge that unwavering MDC participation served to undermine that party's own legitimacy, as well as the health of those sectors subjected to looting and attack by ZANU-PF partisans: compliance with uneven unity arrangements both rewarded partisan behaviour and undermined the prospects for recovery and democratisation in the run-up to the 2013 national elections.[43] For some critics, this one-sided entrenchment of militarised politics under the auspices of 'inclusive' government was a model to be *critiqued*, not *celebrated*; and the rescuing of the democratic transition project required *more* pressure on, and confrontation with, partisan militarised interests, not appeasement through concessions like the dropping of sanctions on rights abusers and perpetrators of political violence.[44] The poignancy of this critique was amplified by the manner of the GNU's eventual passing in 2013: re-legitimised and re-energised, ZANU-PF had used the period of the GNU to replenish its political capital, starve the opposition of new minerals-derived fiscal resources, and maintain unilateral control over the timing, agenda, and organising of the next national elections in order to win them.

The MDC's marginalisation from decision-making around diamond policy since the first days of the GNU had raised early alarms about the GNU's political coherence, democratic content and overall legitimacy. For

43   Solidarity Peace Trust (2010); Pigou (2010).
44   Research and Advocacy Unit (2010).

example, there was little response to reports in 2009 that criminal smuggling syndicates operating in collusion with the ZNA continued unabated, and that coerced labour, violent assault and torture, extralegal detentions and forced relocation of Chiadzwa communities persisted in the diamond fields. The Joint Monitoring and Implementation Committee – the structure set up under the GNU to monitor its implementation and address issues of human security and rights abuses (among others) – was effectively silent on the Marange chaos, and wholly irrelevant in addressing the complaints of civil society and rights organisations. Meanwhile, the MDC-controlled Ministry of Finance complained openly and fruitlessly about its inability to obtain basic data on diamond production revenues from the ZANU-PF controlled ministry of mines, and about the negative impacts of diamond revenue shortfalls on efforts to finance upcoming elections in the short term, and a reconstruction and development programme in the longer term. By 2013 it was revealed by the finance ministry (and subsequently confirmed by the ZANU-PF-led Parliamentary Portfolio Committee on Minerals and Energy) that only a fraction of diamond earnings due to government were actually deposited in the national treasury: for example, of the US$117m which Mbada claimed to have paid to government in dividends in 2012 only US$41 was recorded by the Ministry of Finance as having been deposited. Moreover, additional fees, duties and taxes reported by Mbada were not registered at all as having arrived at the treasury.[45] Just as shocking was the Portfolio Committee's revelation that it had been banned from visiting the Marange fields for more than two years, and that official requests for information and testimony from the ministry and public institutions under its control, and all diamond mining houses apart from Mbada, were met with concerted obstruction by means of silence, harassment, non-cooperation and, occasionally, criminal misrepresentation in the content of the information provided. The pall of secrecy, corruption and suspicion surrounding Marange only thickened when Edward Chindori-Chininga, the ZANU-PF MP and Chairman of the Portfolio Committee, was killed in a mysterious car crash one week after tabling his Committee's damning report in Parliament and amid well-sourced evidence that he would not be permitted by his party to stand as a candidate

---

45   MDC (2013); Parliament of Zimbabwe (2013).

in the upcoming 2013 elections.[46]

In this context, the political economy of Marange diamonds can be seen as a microcosm of the challenges posed by the overlapping political, economic and security networks which were cemented by ZANU-PF in the 2000s. Greater accountability and transparency at Marange implied a restructuring and rebuilding of the GNU state itself, including the reform and re-professionalisation of state agencies, and the institutionalisation of open and accountable systems of administration and management. 'Democratising' government was not primarily a matter of redressing the excesses of corruption, patronage and partisanship entrenched under years of single-party rule, as some MDC officials including Morgan Tsvangirai appeared to suggest in their continuing frustration at the slowness of change under the GNU.[47] Rather, it required the exposure and confrontation of embedded economic interests that had been nurtured and accommodated in the years of state capture by ZANU-PF, and efforts to disentangle them from key state institutions. Here, Marange diamonds demonstrated the risks of not securing institutional autonomy for public sector agencies critical to state elites' continued accumulation. While black market production flourished under the watch of security forces and mining ministry structures, the GNU failed to confront the matter of who in the state was profiting from the diamonds, their linkages to and engagement with the broader political terrain, and the consequences for the stability of the GNU itself.

The results of the GNU's Marange 'litmus test' were both sobering and instructive. After the July 2013 elections and the return of single-party rule, transparency and accountability in Marange's diamond sector scarcely improved. Basic information on Marange's production and financial benefits, which was key to the transparent management of the resource, continued to be difficult to access. Government's operating agreements with Marange's mining companies remained confidential, along with the complete record of taxes, fees, shares of profit and other income received by the state. There were no comprehensive and reliable accounts of valuations of diamond production, exports and foreign earnings, or of the investments which had been made by the state and

---

46   'ZANU-PF diamond whistleblower Chindori-Chininga dies in car crash', *SWRadioAfrica*, 21 June 2013; 'Chindori-Chininga family insist fatal "accident" was murder', *SWRadioAfrica*, 27 June 2013.

47   Tsvangirai (2010).

partnering companies in the diamond fields. While international donors returned to re-engage government and insisted on greater transparency over diamond revenues as a condition for expanded assistance, there was little evidence of substantial progress. Government's Diamond Policy of 2012, which elaborated a framework for managing diamonds and ensuring transparency, accountability, security and maximisation of value and beneficiation,[48] remained idle, with no enabling legislation developed or expected in the near term.[49] Meanwhile, as international prices for rough stones slipped in 2014, Marange miners faced with the prospect of paying unmet tax bills declared that the resource was running out and they were trimming back production. Marange's diamond rush would prove short-lived, its promises short-changed. Left behind was considerable environmental destruction, thousands of displaced lives, very little traceable revenue and productive investment – and a derailed transition to a more accountable, sustainable, developmental dispensation. If the lessons from Marange were mostly disheartening ones, they also pointed to the urgent need for more effective strategies for managing public resources, and mounting democratic challenges to the elites whose power was sustained by preying on them.

---

48 Government of Zimbabwe (2012).

49 Dhliwayo and Mtisi (2012).

3

REAP WHAT YOU SOW: CORRUPTION AND GREED IN MARANGE'S DIAMOND FIELDS[1]

Alan Martin

'What worries me most is that whoever speaks loudest about mining has not contributed a penny to the mining sector...They all complain about mining saying it is not giving much to the economy. You cannot reap where you have not sown.'
Minister of Mines Obert Mpofu dismisses calls for accountability of diamond revenues, July 26, 2012[2]

The Marange diamond fields of eastern Zimbabwe could have been the country's salvation. Often described as the biggest diamond discovery of a generation,[3] Marange undoubtedly put Zimbabwe on the diamond map.[4] Managed better, its diamonds could have been the transforma-

1   This chapter is an abridged and updated version of *Reap What You Sow*, a Partnership Africa Canada report published in November 2012. The primary focus of the original paper fell on trade irregularities and the lack of transparency of diamond revenues, and ZANU-PF's interactions with the global diamond industry before, during and after the KP imposed an embargo on Marange stones in 2009.

2   'Shut up on diamond money', *NewsDay*, 28 July 2012.

3   Minister Mpofu estimated Marange comprised 25% of the world's global rough diamond production, worth as much as $2 billion a year to the national fiscus. See CNN, 'Inside the Marange Diamond Fields', a documentary broadcast on March 16, 2012.

4   'Zim poised to be second largest diamond producer', *NewsDay*, 24 August 2012.

tional vehicle through which the country turned around its failing economic fortunes, while also serving as an example to other African countries blessed with mineral riches.

But since its discovery in 2006, Marange's potential was overshadowed by violence, smuggling, corruption, and most of all, lost opportunity. For most of this time, the chief political custodian of this precious resource was Obert Mpofu, the country's Minister of Mines until his demotion in the cabinet shuffle of September 2013. After President Robert Mugabe, whose office is vested with the ultimate authority over the country's natural resources, Mpofu was the gatekeeper and arbiter of mineral exploitation in Marange. In practice, however, he deferred many of these responsibilities to the country's military chiefs. On his watch, the world saw perhaps the biggest single plunder of diamonds since Cecil John Rhodes – a plunder which has not ceased with his successor, Walter Chidakwa, a nephew of the President.

The scale of illegality was breathtaking. One confidential report cited by the August 2010 Kimberley Process Review Mission to Zimbabwe claimed that 'in excess of 10 million carats have been removed by artisanal effort over the last three years' – an amount worth almost $600 million at current depressed prices for rough diamonds. The Review Mission also estimated illegal mining at 60,000 carats a month, ranking the illicit Marange trade at between seventh and tenth largest by volume in world diamond production.[5] It is now apparent that hundreds of millions of dollars due to Zimbabwe's treasury were lost in both illegal and legal trades.

Determining the actual amount has been impossible, but even official reports suggest large sums. The February 2011 fiscal update of former Finance Minister Tendai Biti complained that $300 million[6] collected by the Zimbabwe Mining Development Corporation (ZMDC) and the Mineral Marketing Commission of Zimbabwe (MMCZ) – two parastatals under Minister Mpofu's remit – had not reached the state's coffers.[7] Such complaints have spanned the partisan divide, with Biti's successor – a ZANU-PF hardliner no less – continuing to question the whereabouts of

---

5   Report of the Follow-Up Review Mission to Zimbabwe, Kimberley Process, 9-14 August 2010, p. 15.

6   All figures cited are in US dollars.

7   'US$300 million from Zimbabwe diamond sales missing', *Mining Review. Africa*, 17 February 2011, http://www.miningreview.com/node/19120

expected diamond revenues in 2013.[8] Questions also remain surrounding the mysterious whereabouts of a 2.5 million carat stockpile which apparently disappeared following the controversial 'Kinshasa Agreement' of the Kimberley Process in November 2011, a move which temporarily and irregularly lifted the ban on rough diamond exports from Marange. The stockpile in question – conservatively valued at almost $200 million – is widely believed to have been secretly traded during the embargoed period without yielding revenue to the state.

Taken together – the missing stockpile, known illicit trades to South Africa and Dubai, and Finance Ministry figures and industry assessments such as the ones above – it can be conservatively estimated that Zimbabwe lost at least $2 billion in potential diamond revenues between 2009 and 2012.

Concerns about lack of revenue transparency around Marange diamonds go to the heart of the country's compliance with the Kimberley Process (KP) Certification Scheme's minimum requirements. Missing revenues point to systemic breaks in the country's internal controls, and provide compelling evidence that an illegal, parallel trade is well underway – a trade which has thrived with the full knowledge and complicity of officials in the Ministry of Mines, ZMDC, MMCZ and the Zimbabwe security forces. In assessing how Zimbabwean military and political elites plundered Marange it is important to recognize that they could not have done it without the aid and abetment of industry insiders, compliant governments and amoral companies which ensured the illicit passage of diamonds into the legitimate supply chain.

While the mismanagement of Marange remains primarily a Zimbabwean problem, the global dimensions of the illegality have metastasized over time to compromise most of the major diamond markets of the world. In the early days following the KP's November 2009 export ban on Marange stones, most of the illegal trade primarily affected South Africa, Mozambique, UAE (Dubai) and India. Two years later, by the end of the embargo, however, there were few trading centres that had not dealt with these illicit stones.

This chapter explores how Zimbabwe's political and military elite established and consolidated their control of the production and trade of Marange diamonds, and the web of linkages to regional and global

---

8   'Diamond revenue missing: Chinamasa', *Daily News*, 6 November 2013.

networks of the diamond trade – both legal and illegal. These linkages have benefitted from secrecy in both the diamond industry and off-shore banking jurisdictions, making transactions largely untraceable or beyond reach of national regulations or the supervisory measures of the KP Certification Scheme that regulates the trade and production of rough diamonds. In addition to representing a new face of conflict diamonds, Marange underscores the anti-development challenges faced by many African countries with artisanal mining deposits.

A Trade Emerges in the Shadows

In July 2012, the violent death of Harare businessman Allan Banks sent ripples through both the legal and illegal Zimbabwean diamond industry. Not only was the manner of Mr. Banks's death shocking for a relatively crime-free Harare – his bloodied body was found in the trunk of his car, a plastic bag over the head – it also signalled that despite government pronouncements to the contrary, the illicit trade of Marange diamonds was alive and well.

Up until two weeks before his death, Banks and his associates had been given regular and exclusive access to Marange diamonds, which they would then smuggle to diamond dealers in South Africa and Namibia, for onward transit to foreign destinations. Banks, who owned a chain of grocery stores, got involved in the trade in 2010 after members of the battle-hardened One Commando Regiment[9] approached him to sell stones they had acquired during their rotations in Marange. Banks was struggling financially at the time and perhaps reckoned that the side business could help pay some debts.

What began with a few soldiers offering stones for sale soon escalated to Banks's being granted privileged access to diamond vaults – allegedly arranged with the high level collusion of officials in the Ministry of Mines, ZMDC, MMCZ and the Zimbabwe National Army (ZNA). Before long, Banks and his associates were in over their heads – at one point dealing parcels of diamonds worth millions of dollars, according to a source with first-hand knowledge of the trade.

Banks was not the only one to be given unofficial access to Marange diamonds. Consider the case of Shmuel Klein, an Israeli pilot arrested in

---

9   This is a special forces unit based in Harare. It was formerly known as One Commando Battalion and before Independence as the Rhodesian Light Infantry. It has had a constant presence in Marange since 2008.

March 2012 at Harare airport in possession of 8,486 carats worth $2.4 million as he was about to board a plane to South Africa. The stones, worth an average of over $280 a carat, were very good gem quality. In his court deposition, Klein claimed he was employed by Masri Diamonds, and intended to fly that night to Tel Aviv to hand deliver the parcel to owner Nisim Masri.[10]

Legal observers believed his arrest was probably a mistake by a junior customs official and pointed to several facts that suggest Klein received preferential treatment with the help of some very powerful people. For example, when he was arrested Klein did not have any paperwork, including KP certificates, RBZ export approvals or any other documentation which proved who he had bought the stones from, at what price, and whether taxes had been paid. His passport had no entry stamp, suggesting he had been accorded VIP treatment in circumventing immigration officials upon arrival. Moreover, Klein's brief trial was 'a classic case of a prosecution deliberately set to fail',[11] according to a top Harare lawyer. Under normal circumstances the case would have been tried before a High Court judge, not a junior magistrate. Klein was granted bail on the day of his arrest, an almost unheard of practice for a case involving significant quantities of diamonds and a foreigner at high risk of flight. In such a circumstance, the government would usually invoke its right to appeal, asking for a custodial stay of seven days – yet this was not done. The case ended up in acquittal and the whole issue was reduced to a simple immigration matter, punishable with a fine.[12]

Both cases – and there are other examples – illustrated a troubling reality at play in Zimbabwe. While the government had won praise from some quarters for 'regularizing' operations in Marange by bringing in new joint venture partners starting in 2009, there continued to be an entirely unrecorded, parallel trade of diamonds which was not only known to, but condoned by, those senior government officials.

---

10   'Israeli pilot pleads not guilty to diamond possession', *The Herald*, 30 March 2012.

11   Personal interview with author, Harare defence lawyer, 8 May 2012.

12   Klein's acquittal mirrored a case involving two former Canadile directors, Komilan Packirisamy and Viyandrakumar Naidoo, who were arrested in Marange in February 2010 in possession of diamonds worth $28,000 they had smuggled out of the mine site. Their arrest was interpreted by many as a warning, perhaps for trying to cut out their government 'partners' from the plundering.

At the heart of this trade was Zimbabwe Defence Industries (ZDI), a government procurement agency linked to Anjin, whose former CEO, Tshinga Dube, now runs Marange Resources. ZDI trades diamonds and other commodities primarily through two companies, Nkululeko Rusununguko Holdings and Impetus Capital, based in Clarion House on Sam Nujoma Street in Harare. In 2013 they traded an average of approximately $50 million worth of diamonds per month, with the main beneficiaries being members of the Joint Operations Command (JOC), the top echelon of Zimbabwe's military establishment.[13] Sources suggest that for several years the ZDI traded gem quality Marange diamonds – in parcels sometimes worth millions of dollars – directly from the MMCZ to dealers in Johannesburg, who would later traffic them to Dubai. This practice changed in March 2012, when a foolhardy white Zimbabwean courier, aligned to the late General Solomon Mujuru, reportedly short-changed his military bosses by switching the high value gems for lesser stones.

Until his death in August 2011, Mujuru had been an army general, businessman, and influential senior ZANU-PF politician. His widow, Joice, served as the country's vice-president from 2004 to 2014. At the time of his death Mujuru was in a bitter dispute with Adel Abdul Rahman al Aujan, a Saudi billionaire with whom he co-owned River Ranch, a diamond mine in the south of the country that has since filed for bankruptcy.

Aside from the high level collusion, these stories have raised additional questions, particularly in the context of the KP and its deliberations. Calls for greater revenue transparency have been dismissed within the KP – by governments and industry alike – as something that never was, nor should be, considered relevant to a country's compliance with KP minimum requirements. Civil society groups have seen it differently: diamonds leaking out of any country in such a fashion not only represent a loss to the national treasury and public good, they are the ultimate expression of a systemic failure of a country's internal controls. Their subsequent 'clean' trading makes a mockery of the KP's Certification

---

13 The JOC included Defence Minister Emmerson Mnangagwa; General Constantine Chiwenga, Commander of the Zimbabwe Defence Forces; Air Marshall Perence Shiri, Commander of the Air Force of Zimbabwe; Lt. General Philip Sibanda, Commander of the Zimbabwe National Army; Augustine Chihuri, Commissioner General of the Zimbabwe Republic Police; Major General (Rtd) Paradzai Zimondi, Commissioner General of the Zimbabwe Prison Service; Happyton Bonyongwe, Director General of the Central Intelligence Organisation; Gideon Gono, Governor of the Reserve Bank of Zimbabwe.

Scheme and the diamond industry's own System of Warranties, an honour system that promises diamond shipments are untainted by violence and traded in conformance with KP requirements.

While the full scope of the plundering will likely never be known, examples point to a substantial and continuing theft of stones. The previously mentioned mystery regarding the whereabouts of an estimated 2.5 million carats stockpiled following the November 2009 KP embargo of Marange diamonds underscores the reality that the smuggling of Marange stones was not a trickle, but a flood. As they were secured in company and RBZ vaults, it is inconceivable they could have disappeared without the full knowledge of senior officials in the Ministry of Mines or the Reserve Bank.

The trading of this stockpile was especially problematic. Some of the stones were unquestionably mined during episodes of gross human rights violations (which resulted in their initial quarantine by the KP). Their disappearance amounted to a massive breach of KP compliance. How, for example, did such a quantity of stones pass through the international diamond supply chain unnoticed, without legal KP certificates? Which members of the diamond industry took receipt of these stones, without concern for their illegitimacy? Why did the KP, when it had a chance in 2011, never fully investigate this stockpile or insist that Zimbabwe dispense of it in an orderly and legal manner?

More broadly, it needs to be asked: Where have Marange's promised riches gone? And how have they failed to deliver on expectations? While the illicit parallel trade has undoubtedly been responsible for the biggest diversion of diamond revenues, part of the answer lies in the legal trade, and the numerous unmet public expectations of it.

Legal Thieves

In 2010, leading industry insiders, including Filip van Loere, a Belgian diamond expert working for the Government of Zimbabwe, estimated annual production of 30-40 million carats if KP export restrictions were lifted.[14] At the conservative average price of $60 a carat, the low end of that estimate would have realized annual sales of almost $2 billion. Several other equally well informed sources have stated that Marange's deposits could represent as much as 20-30% of the world's rough dia-

14   'Marange diamond output could reach 40 million carats', *Mining Review*, 1 September 2010; personal email with industry expert, 4 June 2010.

mond supply[15] – a figure Obert Mpofu repeatedly cited as proof that legal diamond sales were capable of lifting Zimbabwe's ailing economy. With these projections and average sale prices, former Finance Minister Tendai Biti based his 2012 Budget on projected diamond revenues of $600 million. But in June 2012 he announced a projected shortfall of $244 million.[16]

Obert Mpofu, Minister of Mines (2009-13) holding Marange diamonds at Blue Star factory in Surat, India.

15   See for example, presentation by Chaim Even-Zohar on Marange to the 2010 Kimberley Process Intersessional, June 22, 2010.
16   'Anjin remits US$30m to fiscus', *The Herald*, 28 June 2012.

Of all the mining companies, Anjin came under the most scrutiny for its apparent lack of remittances to the national treasury. Between November 2011 and May 2012 Anjin is believed to have sold approximately $78 million worth of diamonds but, according to Biti, failed to remit any taxes or royalties. In June 2012 Anjin refuted this and claimed it had paid $30 million in royalties, but was under no obligation to pay taxes until it had recouped the capital costs spent setting up their operations – an amount claimed to be $400 million, a figure regarded as a significant overestimation by most industry experts.[17]

*President Robert Mugabe with officials at launch of
Anjin Mine*

Writing off capital costs is a common accounting practice of extractive companies, and widely accepted by revenue agencies worldwide. However, the disconnect between what the Finance Minister believed the treasury was owed and what the companies actually remitted raised several concerns. The most notable was that critical details of all joint venture agreements, including ownership structures, were withheld from high-level government ministers and officials other than a small clique inside the Ministry of Mines, the Ministry of Defence and the ZMDC. The opaque nature of the agreements – all personally approved by the Minister of Mines – led critics to question whether each company operated according to tailor-made terms; and whether the terms were geared in favour of the Zimbabwean public good, or rather, and more likely, in favour of the private sector partners with close links to ZANU-PF loyalists. Fears concerning these secret contracts were only heightened with

17   Ibid.

revelations that the joint ventures were not legally binding agreements.[18]

The process by which individual concessions were awarded, and, in some cases, taxes were collected, highlighted an uneven and subjective policy making system. Technically, the tax and royalty structure in Zimbabwe required mining companies to pay 15% royalties, plus an administration fee of 0.875% to the MMCZ prior to export. All other taxes (corporate and withholding taxes for example) were only due at the end of the fiscal period, after calculating a company's net profit. All told, deductions would amount to approximately 33%.[19] The reality of payments and collection has been far more opaque. There has been confusion, for example, over Mpofu's repeated use of the term 'dividends' when referring to revenues from mining. For example, he told CNN in March 2012: 'In terms of royalties… [the companies] are actually making major contributions. In fact, these companies are declaring dividends on a monthly basis to the national fiscus. So, it is quite substantial.'[20]

A high-level source, however, claimed this was not entirely the case. Instead Mbada, Canadile, and now Marange Resources were reportedly 'coerced' into paying advances on later taxes as a kind of a 'gentleman's agreement' to assist the government in dire need of cash. DMC also made these payments out of fear of losing their concession. There was, however, no legal basis for such payments. Anjin, insulated from such pressures by the political support of Beijing, refused to pay these advances, thereby solidifying the perception that it was short-changing the treasury.

Mpofu's observations on dividends therefore raised a troubling question: if no other taxes were due the fiscus until the end of the fiscal period, what monthly dividends were companies paying, and to which government institutions? Moreover, if the MMCZ collected the initial 15% tax, why did Minister Mpofu – the minister responsible for that parastatal – deny it was his responsibility to collect mineral revenues?[21] More to the

---

18   KP Monitor's report to the Working Group on Monitoring, Washington, D.C., 4 June 2012.

19   A breakdown of the taxes and royalty structure is laid out in 'KP Monitoring Team on Marange: Q1 Report on Marange, November 2011-January 2012', Abbey Chikane and Mark Van Bockstael, p. 5.

20   'Inside the Marange Diamond Fields', CNN documentary, 16 March 2012.

21   'I am Minister of Mines not Minister of Revenue. If revenue has not been collected it is not our fault. ZIMRA collects the revenue. Ask me about mining issues not revenue issues and I will explain.' Comments attributed to Obert Mpofu, remarks to Centre for Public Accountability, Harare, 11 June 2012.

point, where were the tax revenues and the wider Marange profits going, if not to the treasury?

In this context, 'following the money' flowing from the diamond fields proved difficult for those seeking transparency and clarity around mineral revenues. Key obstacles were the tight cohesion of the small group of ZANU-PF loyalists in control of the diamonds, and the near complete opacity of offshore banking practices and corporate structures related to the diamond mining companies. That evidence which was available only skimmed the surface. At the same time, however, an understanding of how ZANU-PF had operated in previous cases of asset-stripping and illegal acquisitions hinted at some likely conduits of revenue flows from Marange. Here, most observers discounted the notion that a single pot of diamond money was established from which ZANU-PF drew to fund its priority projects; for example, electioneering or voter intimidation campaigns. It was seen as more likely that most diamond proceeds were disbursed among a small group of individuals with access to either hard currency or anonymous off-shore bank accounts. While it seems certain that a wider group of politically connected but essentially mid-tier individuals received personal beneficiation, it also appears to be the case that the smaller group administered the wider proceeds on behalf of the party. When funds were needed for a particular party cause, the group, individually and as a collective, was called upon to deliver the needed resources.

An important criticism of the monitoring undertaken by the KP was its selective focus on technical aspects of mine operations, while ignoring deeper examination of the suitability of the companies or individuals behind the winning concessions – and their performance in delivering revenues to government. Canadile's board, for example, included a convicted Israeli diamond smuggler (Yehuda Licht), a former South African mercenary (Adrian Taylor) and an alleged drug dealer (Subithry Naidoo). Despite having full knowledge of this, Obert Mpofu granted Canadile a concession and the KP Monitor to Marange declared it 'compliant', with little thought to how such individuals might have negatively affected Marange's governance. But the problem went beyond the murky biographies of individual company executives. Many industry commentators noted, for example, that none of the mining companies in Marange had demonstrated relevant mining experience prior to being awarded their concessions in a process which was tainted by ministerial interference, according to ZMDC officials testifying before Parliament in 2009. Moreover, extensive research by civil society organizations into the corporate ownership of Mbada and Anjin, both of which were registered in off-shore jurisdictions in Asia and the Indian Ocean, concluded that the companies were structured to hide not only profits but also the identities of the main shareholders, the latter including some individuals with links to the Zimbabwean security establishment and human rights violations.[22]

Mbada, Marange Resources and Anjin are not the only companies to have had due diligence processes circumvented by political connections. Imad Ahmad, the principal player behind Diamond Mining Corporation (DMC), is linked to several businesses – Pure Diam and Sabi Gold – which traded Marange diamonds as far back as 2009, often purchasing gem quality stones from Marange Resources at lower prices than it paid for industrials.[23]

Until recently, close relations of Ahmad ran one of the biggest buying offices across the Mozambican border in Vila de Manica. In April 2010 this author visited their office posing as a seller looking to get diamonds to Western markets. An immediate offer was made to purchase whatever stones he had, and he was told they had $4 million cash on hand – an enormous sum for a small town in rural Mozambique. After insisting that he wanted to keep the fictitious diamonds, the author was offered courier services 'anywhere in the world' ranging from $1-$10 a carat, depending on the quality of the diamond. As Mozambique is not a member of the KP, and therefore not able to issue KP certificates, the export of these diamonds to any KP member country would have been entirely illegal.

In 2011 it was learned that the extended Ahmad family was under investigation by at least one law enforcement agency for suspicious diamond trading activity spanning Angola, Belgium, Central African Republic, Lebanon and UAE (Dubai). This included concerns about their involvement in tax fraud, money laundering and smuggling.[24] A well informed source also confirmed that the Ahmad family which operated in Mozambique was the same one named in a 2005 Partnership Africa Canada report for fraudulently exporting $3 million worth

---

22   See for example, Global Witness (2012a) and (2012b).
23   See for example, copies of Sabi Gold Mine Invoice number PD002/02/09 and Marange Resources invoice dated 02/05/2009, included in Ernst & Young (2010).
24   Personal interview, Belgian law enforcement official, 21 November 2011.

of diamonds from Brazil.[25]

Funds generated from the family's illicit business in Manica were almost certainly used to raise the $50 million capitalization needed to secure the concession DMC operates in Marange[26] – an example of how dirty Marange money gets recycled through other 'legitimate' businesses. Other conditions of their partnership with the ZMDC have proven more flexible, like creating a joint board of directors. Months after being approved, neither side had bothered to appoint a board, leaving Ahmad and his nephew Ramzi Malik at liberty to run operations as they saw fit. The absence of ZMDC board members raised questions about what oversight role, if any, the parastatal has had in the running of that operation, most importantly in ensuring the government gets its fair share of DMC's earnings.

The Ahmad family were not the only ones to have engaged in recycled illegality on both sides of the Zimbabwe-Mozambique border. In 2008, Canadile directors Komilan Packirisamy and Viyandrakumar Naidoo registered Saman Incorporated, a mining and mineral export company based in Manica, with Mozambican authorities.[27] The only purpose for this company appears to have been maintaining a presence in Manica's then lucrative and wholly illegal diamond trade.

In each of these cases, due diligence undertaken by the KP would have exposed the problematic processes and structure of the diamond concessions awarded unilaterally by the Ministry of Mines beginning in 2009, and anticipated the negative outcomes. By limiting the scope of monitoring and reporting only to matters occurring inside fenced concessions and by not evaluating Marange companies holistically, the KP avoided acknowledging and confronting many of the root causes of Marange's bad management. Consequently, the severely negative outcomes of mismanagement for public revenue, economic development and indeed the wider political fabric of the country remained obscured in the KP's assessment of Marange diamonds' broader impact.

Marange Globalised: International conduits of criminality

Marange has always had international dimensions to its illegality. In the early years after discovery, Mutare and Manica – towns on either

---

25 Partnership Africa Canada (2005, 2006).

26 DMC documents provided to the Kimberley Process.

27 *Boletim de Republica*, Publicação oficial da república de Moçambique, 4° Suplemento, III Serie, No. 32 12/08/08.

side of the Zimbabwe-Mozambique border – were overrun with dealers and hucksters from other lawless outposts, including veterans of diamond-fuelled wars in West Africa. Those of Lebanese origin were the most conspicuous by their numbers and enthusiasm, although several Mutare residents, most notably Bothwell Hlahla,[28] ran lucrative businesses driving diamonds across the border for everyone from military and police-led syndicates to those involved with Mbada and Canadile.

While South Africa was, and remains, the principal gateway for smuggled Marange goods, it was in the Democratic Republic of Congo where people first noticed something amiss.[29] Large quantities of bottle-brown, mostly industrial stones – typical of those found in Marange – were turning up in comptoirs in Kinshasa where they were issued Kimberley Process certificates for onward travel to Dubai and, finally, the cutting and polishing factories of Surat, India. While some Congolese nationals were arrested for trading Marange stones in both Zimbabwe and Kinshasa, the bigger fish were nearly always considered to be Zimbabweans with senior military connections. In the late 1990s President Mugabe had sent troops to the DRC to help then President Laurent Kabila fend off military attempts by Rwanda and Uganda to remove him from office. What followed was 'Africa's First World War' in which as many as six neighbouring countries took sides, while simultaneously plundering high value minerals in eastern DRC – a problem that continues to frustrate peace efforts there. For many senior Zimbabwean soldiers the military intervention created networks in the DRC through which they would later smuggle Marange diamonds.

Since the publication of *Diamonds and Clubs* in 2010 by Partnership Africa Canada, the sophistication and global reach of illicit diamond trade activity has become increasingly apparent. It has also been clear that this shadow trade has come to involve some of the more established players in the diamond industry; the Marange illicit trade is not simply confined to small-scale entrepreneurial or opportunistic activities, as

---

28   Hlahla died in August 2011, the result of a car accident. There was initial speculation his death was somehow related to the assassination four days later of General Mujuru, who owned River Ranch, a diamond mine near Beitbridge. Witnesses, however, attribute Hlalha's death to human error after Nilson Lennard from Harare failed to stop at an intersection. See also Hlahla's obituary, *Manica Post*, The Weekender, 19-25 August 2011.

29   See Kimberley Process Review Mission Report to DRC, Final Report, 9-14 March 2009, especially pp. 58-59.

it has sometimes been portrayed by government officials. Indeed some of the biggest smuggling in Marange today happens *inside* the confines of the legal KP system. Consider this: the average price of legal Marange diamonds dropped from $80-90 per carat in 2011 to $40-50 in late 2012. Some of this easing of prices may be legitimately explained by the worldwide drop in rough prices, yet the same goods have been noted miraculously exiting Dubai trading houses for sister-owned factories in Surat with an average price of $100-105 per carat. This constitutes a massive loss to the Zimbabwean treasury, but it has also helped to underscore a sophisticated price manipulation scheme perpetrated by (mostly) Indian buyers and their Zimbabweans allies with whom they are believed to share the spoils.

The extent of Marange's riches and the opportunities for manipulating transaction costs provided important incentives for a range of international diamond interests to subvert transparent trading. Industry insiders may not originally have known the full extent of Marange's diamond potential but most credible experts agreed it was extraordinary. Its carats per hundred tonnes (CPHT) – one measure by which the lucrativeness of a deposit is typically quantified – were judged to be very high, with some samples reaching as much as 4,000 CPHT, over 80 times more than in a normal artisanal deposit.[30] At the same time, rising demand for rough stones from a number of competing global diamond trading centres in the 2000s provided many opaque conduits for Marange's production.

The diamond industry has been loath to talk about 'good' and 'bad' diamonds, but the debate within the KP on Marange made that distinction hard to ignore. Dubai has become the principal destination of laundered illicit Marange goods – and indeed those from many other problematic areas in Africa. In recent years it has earned a reputation as the place where dirty diamonds – and gold as well – go to get washed. The reasons why are many, but much is due to an aggressive business strategy to dislodge Antwerp as the world's main trading centre. Currently Dubai is in third place (after Antwerp and Switzerland) but it has exploded into the diamond world, trading some $40 billion in 2011, double its 2009 figures – a remarkable feat for a country that had essentially no diamond industry at the launch of the KP in 2003.

Dubai's meteoric rise has been mostly related to its offering gener-

---

30   Personal interview, industry source, 8 August 2012.

ous tax holidays to companies that open an office in the Almas Towers, housed within the Dubai Multi Commodities Centre (DMCC) – the first step in creating a playing field Antwerp can never compete on. This has been no small factor in an industry obsessed by profit margins. The reality, however, was that the Almas Towers often served as little more than a mailing address for sister companies in other jurisdictions seeking to mask their business relationship to countries or individuals with questionable track records.

Dubai has gone out of its way to court African producers, irrespective of their human rights record or compliance with KP minimum standards. This has been done in a number of ways, from appointing African government officials to the board of the DMCC (including Prince Mupazviriho, a former Permanent Secretary of Mines in Zimbabwe), to thwarting KP action against non-compliant countries or blocking any reform, however modest, within the KP that might require more of participant governments or industry.

During the Marange embargo period, Dubai took receipt of several parcels of Marange goods that were either in outright contravention or fell in a grey area following a unilateral, unsupported and temporary decision in March 2011 by the then KP Chair, the DRC, to lift the embargo. The decision was made out of frustration at the political impasse within the KP on how to deal with Zimbabwe, but as every decision in the KP has to be made by consensus, and none was given, the order was immediately overruled. That did not stop Dubai from accepting at least five shipments from Marange and capitalising on the brief window of confusion. Throughout the embargo there were many more packages of Marange stones slipped by smugglers from third countries into Dubai's legal system the old-fashioned way – with a little grease or deception. For smugglers, getting a parcel into the legitimate supply chain somewhere spells the end of their difficulties, as the stones are then remixed with others and sent on (usually to their real owners) for manufacture or re-sale. Once repackaged, they are given a KP certificate that lists their 'origin' as that of the last place of transit (i.e. Dubai), thereby making it almost impossible to identify their true origins.

Dubai also has played a key role for those looking to evade Western sanctions against politically exposed individuals or organizations in Zimbabwe. American sanctions were far more onerous than the European ones which were retired following the 2013 elections:[31] the former outlawed not only direct business relationships with listed companies, but also the use of American currency to make any financial transactions. They were also applied equally to non-citizens and Americans. In Zimbabwe and beyond, ZANU-PF successfully created a political narrative that blamed all of the country's ills on these Western sanctions. Included in this narrative were arguments that sanctions had denied Zimbabwe the full market value for its diamonds. This may have been true, but as the late Edward Chindori-Chininga, a former ZANU-PF Member of Parliament and Chairman of the Parliamentary Portfolio Committee on Mines and Energy, told this author: 'Those who complain the most about sanctions, are also those that are benefiting the most.'[32]

Edward Chindori-Chininga, MP, Chairperson of Parliament Portfolio Committee on Mines & Energy

How was this possible? Simply, US sanctions did not stop the illicit trade, nor did they prevent some shadowy individuals from getting fabulously wealthy. Rather they served to push the diamond business into a

---

31   The EU dropped all sanctions on the ZMDC, other state entities and the majority of politically exposed officials, including Minister Mpofu. The travel ban on President Mugabe and his family was kept in place.

32   Private conversation, Kempton Park, South Africa, 1 June 2013.

dark corner where all deals were transacted in other currencies, such as Rands and Euros, often in cash and at discounted prices. Sanctions also saw international security companies, couriers and insurers declining to touch Marange stones for fear of prosecution in the US. As a result buyers were forced to take their chances with commercial carriers or private jets to fly their stones direct from Harare to Dubai. The UAE also lobbied within the KP to block efforts that would have required all transactions be undertaken through official banking institutions – a measure that almost certainly would have exposed individuals and companies in Dubai to possible legal liability.

Secretive, tax-free havens – primarily Mauritius and Hong Kong – have also played a key role in hiding ownership structures and providing banking mechanisms through which mining companies can hide profits. In the case of companies like Mbada, registered in Mauritius, the implication is that Zimbabwe has been deprived of significant tax revenues. Forcing companies listed and operating in Zimbabwe's extractive sector to publicly divulge the ownership structure and location of any offshore trust accounts could lessen the opportunity for public officials or their family members to hide pecuniary relationships to companies they may have oversight over. This, however, is premised on the ZANU-PF government championing legislative changes that would require the mandatory disclosure by companies operating in Zimbabwe of any offshore relationships, with stiff penalties for non-disclosure. South Africa implemented such legislation in the early 2000s, but the idea has gained no traction in Zimbabwe, given the symbiotic relationships between political elites and Marange's mining companies. The same applies at the regional level, where the Southern African Development Community has a weak record of passing conventions that could embarrass the politically connected.

International collusion with the shadowy Marange trade was not only the domain of ethically challenged governments or secretive banking jurisdictions. The December 2010 arrest of Israelis Gilad Halachmi and David Vardi shone a brief light on how even individuals with respected track records were tempted, and ultimately compromised, by the lure of Marange. Vardi, a veteran of the Israeli Diamond Exchange, was exposed after Halachmi was questioned in a random customs stop at Ben Gurion airport in Tel Aviv. Both admitted complicity in smuggling $140,000 in rough stones, and received stiff penalties – Vardi's diamond license was revoked and he was served with a lifetime ban from the IDE; Halachmi, who described himself variously as a water consultant or manager of a plastics company, was fined an undisclosed amount.

Vardi was not the only Israeli with a keen interest in Marange stones. Lev Leviev, the legendary diamond and real estate entrepreneur known for boasting that he 'only deals with Presidents', has been a frequent visitor to Zimbabwe in recent years and is known to have participated in an auction of Mbada diamonds in May 2010 – a full three months before the KP authorized two conditional sales as per the St. Petersburg Agreement.[33] In that instance 3.5 million carats, worth an estimated \$150 million, were tendered at an auction at the Harare airport that also included representatives of Zar Diam (Dubai), Samir Gems (Antwerp), Supergems (Belgium/Dubai) and Rosy Blue (Antwerp). One well-placed industry source claimed that these diamonds received KP certificates 'signed by the KP Monitor',[34] although another said they were not actually exported from Zimbabwe until August 2010, as allowed by the St. Petersburg Agreement. At the very least this incident showed that credible and respected diamond companies were prepared to do business with Marange mining companies prior to receiving the all-clear from the KP.[35]

Marange has also served to expose a cutthroat scramble for Zimbabwe's resources between China and India. While Chinese investment in Marange has been primarily through Anjin's mine-level access, Indian diamantaires have been content to profit further down the diamond supply chain. India's rising prominence – as with Dubai's tussle with Antwerp – shows how the diamond industry has been increasingly moving

---

33 The agreement was negotiated between the KP and the Government of Zimbabwe on the sidelines of the World Diamond Council's annual general meeting in St. Petersburg, Russia, in late July 2010.

34 Email, industry source, 30 June 2010.

35 A representative of Rosy Blue confirmed Vishal Mehta attended this auction on the company's behalf and made a bid, conditional on 'the seller [being] fully responsible for securing all required export documents' – something Zimbabwe failed to obtain a month later when the KP meeting in Tel Aviv ended in deadlock over lifting export restrictions for Mbada and Canadile. Rosy Blue subsequently withdrew its offer. Rosy Blue admits it may have purchased legal Marange goods following the KP's lifting of restrictions on Mbada and Marange Resources in November 2011, but says it never did so at any time before then, including prior to the 2009 embargo. Source: email communication with Chikashi Miyamoto, 29 August 2012.

eastward and breaking down once entrenched monopolies, not the least that of De Beers, which has seen its global market share shrink by over 40% in the last decade.

Surat, outside Mumbai, has become the biggest diamond manufacturing centre in the world – responsible for cutting or polishing 92% of the world's stones. Although Chinese manufacturing centres remained small – lagging behind Tel Aviv, Antwerp, London and New York – growing investments in key mining countries like Zimbabwe have caused concern to the Indian industry. Ashit Mehta, CEO of Blue Star Diamonds and one of Surat's biggest players, has repeatedly encouraged his government to follow Beijing's lead in developing African mines, arguing that China's ability to secure rough supplies from Africa would leave Surat dependent on Beijing.[36]

Mehta was also the driving force behind the Surat Rough Diamond Sourcing India Limited (SRSDIL), a consortium of companies[37] which signed a $1.2 billion deal with the Government of Zimbabwe in October 2010 to obtain exclusive access to Marange diamonds. The deal signalled Surat's willingness to court Marange diamonds, despite the KP ban and associated reputational risks. Mehta is known to have visited Obert Mpofu in Zimbabwe at least six times between September 2010 and April 2011, and personally chaperoned the Minister around Surat on several of his trade missions there. Mehta's embrace of Mpofu was a win-win situation. Surat got guaranteed access to a rough supply and loosened De Beers' iron grip on Indian DTC sightholders in the process;[38] Zimbabwe

---

36 'Help us by investing in African mines: Diamantaires to govt', *Times of India*, 13 June 2010.

37 SRSDIL members buy stakes – ranging from $110,000 to $1.1 million – which gives them the right to share in its supply. Half the supply would be offered to members, while the remainder would be sold on the open market. By doing so they cut out middlemen like De Beers, from whom many Surat companies buy their diamonds. The founding directors of the SRSDIL are: Ashit Mehta (Blue Star and Arjav Diamonds Group), Kishorbhai Shah (K. Girdharlal), Chandrakantbhai Sanghavi (Sanghavi Exports), Bububhai Sanghvi (KP Sanghvi), Kishorbhai Virani (Karp) and Govindbhai Dholakia (Shreee Ram Krishna Exports).

38 De Beers' marketing and distribution system is based on approving certain dealers and manufacturers with which to do business. While this system has changed over time, it continues to essentially enforce a 'closed shop' featuring an elite group which gets privileged access to De Beers' supply, on De Beers' terms and prices.

got access to a big market.[39] More crucially for Zimbabwe, it won a key political ally within the Kimberley Process, with the Gem and Jewellery Export Promotion Council, the Indian industry lobby that makes up part of the Indian delegation to the KP, blocking any efforts to improve the management of Marange.

While Mehta and the SRSDIL have always been careful to act above-board, the Indian Directorate of Revenue Intelligence (DRI) has had its suspicions. In November 2011 it seized a $70 million shipment belonging to Mehta's company, Arjav Diamonds India. The seizure was related to a series of trades worth $160 million that occurred a year previously, in breach of the KP embargo on Marange goods. At the time, Israel, the then KP Chair, issued a notice invalidating the shipments. The goods were seized in UAE, where they sat for over 200 days until UAE officials appealed to the KP to release them due to concerns they would be sued for breaching WTO rules.[40] It was a questionable request, and one that did not receive consensus at a June 2011 meeting of the KP in Kinshasa. Nevertheless, the KP silently granted UAE's request, and the diamonds proceeded to India.

But the DRI took exception with one of Mehta's shipments. Its certificate (number ZW000114) was out of sequence with the others and appeared to have been backdated to legalize an otherwise illicit consignment, according to DRI sources. Moreover there was no mention of the certificate number in Zimbabwe's 2010 annual report to the KP.[41] It was a serious allegation for Mehta to face. In addition to being a De Beers sightholder, Arjav's Belgian operations made it one of the biggest rough distributors in Antwerp. DRI had a problem, however. The only way the shipment could be confiscated and charges laid was if either Zimbabwe, the KP Monitor or the Indian company complained or admitted something was amiss – none of which happened. In December 2011 the DRI

---

39 Most Antwerp and New York based manufacturers are hamstrung because of US and EU economic measures that forbid them to buy diamonds from listed entities like the ZMDC. While the purchase of diamonds in American dollars can technically subject anyone to the legal wrath of the US Treasury Department, the Indian industry has nevertheless courted Zimbabwe with great diligence.

40 Presentation of Peter Meeus, diamond expert, Dubai Multi Commodities Centre, to KP participants, Kinshasa, DRC, 20 June 2011.

41 Zimbabwe 2010 Annual Report to Kimberley Process Certification Scheme.

released the goods without pursuing any legal action.[42]

The early interest in Marange of other establishment figures like Beny Steinmetz, whose company the Antwerp-based Steinmetz Diamond Group supplied De Beers with rough diamonds, was confirmed in the course of the 2012 trial of former Canadile CEO Lovemore Kurotwi. According to court testimony by both state and defence witnesses, Steinmetz is alleged to have been involved in unsuccessful negotiations with Canadile in early 2009 to provide operational capital. This would have been months after the infamous October 2008 gunship incident that first brought state-sponsored human rights violations in Marange to international attention. In that instance the Zimbabwean military surrounded hundreds of illegal panners and opened fire, including from a helicopter gunship, killing as many as 200 miners.[43]

Tichaona Muhonde, a former ZMDC legal adviser and prosecution witness, testified that Steinmetz sought to form a partnership with Core Mining (the private sector half of the joint-venture) in 2009 but withdrew his offer of financial support after he could not win assurances from the government on human rights concerns.[44] In 2010, the Steinmetz Group issued a statement asserting 'unequivocally that it has no connections whatsoever to either Core Mining and Minerals, Canadile Miners, or any of their shareholders'.[45] The denial may have been technically correct, but it would not win Steinmetz any awards for corporate social responsibility. On at least one occasion in 2007 his company, BSG Resources, bought diamonds directly from the MMCZ – including one shipment of $620,000 that came directly from police 'mop-up' efforts.[46] As the MMCZ was listed on the US Treasury Department's Office of Foreign Assets Control's registry of individuals or state agencies with whom not to do business, Steinmetz placed himself in uncertain legal territory by purchasing these diamonds.

Steinmetz was not the only entrepreneur who tempted the possible

42   'DRI releases 120 crore roughs seized from Surat diamond firm', *Times of India*, 21 December 2011.

43   For more detail see: Human Rights Watch (2009: 30-34).

44   'Muhonde testifies in Kurotwi trial', *The Herald*, 31 May 2012.

45   As quoted in 'International Diamond Figures head to Zim', *SWRadioAfrica*, 15 November 2010.

46   *Forensic Report to the Office of the Comptroller and Auditor General in Respect of the Marange Diamond Reconciliation*, Ernst & Young, (2010, pp. 31-32, 68).

wrath of American lawmakers. In August 2013, two American business-men, Prince Ben Israel and Gregory Turner, were charged with illegally lobbying to have US sanctions against the Mugabe regime lifted. Their indictment listed the involvement of a South African – identified only as 'Individual C', and a member of the 2008 KP Review Visit to Zimbabwe – and their efforts to set up a company to exploit Marange diamonds. While no formal charges were laid against the individual in question, and the business plans never came to fruition, the biographical and factual details point to that person being Ernie Blom – the current President of the World Federation of Diamond Bourses. The revelation was a bomb-shell and underscored the extent to which reputable members of the di-amond industry, outside the context of the KP embargo, were happy to consider doing business with some of the most questionable people in the diamond supply chain who maintained deep links into Marange.

Conclusions: Winners, losers and shining a light on paths forward

After eight years of continuous, growing and often chaotic exploitation of Marange's diamonds, the primary beneficiaries of Southern Africa's biggest modern diamond rush have emerged in sharp contrast to its 'losers'.

Undoubtedly, the biggest winners have been elements of ZANU-PF's political and military elite; to a more limited extent, local businesses, traders and sections of the local economy have benefitted as well. Al-though this aspect of the Marange boom has not been investigated in much depth, it is hard not to notice the domestic impact the diamond wealth has had on the struggling formal economy. Communities across Zimbabwe, but primarily those in and around Mutare, Harare and Bula-wayo, have benefited from the influx of diamond money as people have sought to legitimize black market gains. This is evidenced in many ways, but primarily in the purchase of private taxis, and investment in small and medium sized businesses and the tourism sector.

One of the most ostentatious examples of such spending has been Ob-ert Mpofu himself, who spent tens of millions of dollars buying several commercial buildings in Bulawayo, and undertaking substantial reno-vations to his farms, homes, and tourist operations in the Victoria Falls area.[47] Mpofu has often boasted that he is the biggest cattle farmer in the country and he operates many hotels, safari lodges and resorts in the Victoria Falls area. In recent years, however, he has expanded his business empire beyond farming and tourism into the transportation (and possibly extraction) of coal in the Hwange area. All these expenditures exceed his modest cabinet salary and his known business dealings.

Real estate and construction are other sectors that have benefitted disproportionately from ill-gotten wealth from Marange. In Harare's upscale neighbourhoods there has been a noticeable construction boom led primarily by military elites building private mansions. Robert Mhlanga, the reclusive and titular head of Mbada, has also made multi-million dollar purchases of properties in Johannesburg's wealthy northern suburbs and along the KwaZulu-Natal coast. Many of these were at prices far above market rate, raising suspicions that the transactions were consistent with a commonly used money-laundering technique.

Other winners include members of the international diamond industry (particularly those in Dubai and Surat) who took an early interest in compromised Marange goods. During difficult KP negotiations between 2009 and 2011, they lobbied for the lifting of the embargo, which helped them win access to important flows of Marange stones. During the embargo period, international and regional traders and smugglers made a good profit from the illicit trade. The risks, as the case of David Vardi shows, can be high, but the payoffs more than adequately compensated for them.

The biggest losers from Marange are clearly the Zimbabwean treasury and, by extension, the wider economy and government social and development programmes. This is primarily seen in lost revenues to the fiscus, theft and various forms of corruption at the institutional, business, private sector and individual level.

Local residents in Marange and surrounding areas who have suffered from rights abuses, and community dislocation and relocation due to mining operations, have similarly realized little sustained economic benefit. Informal miners and traders, who have been harshly treated and enjoy no legal standing, have been marginalised from the benefits of the diamond exploitation in favour of powerful political, economic and business interests.

---

47   The unexplained wealth accumulation and spending of Obert Mpofu is examined in greater detail in Martin and Taylor (2012).

Government transparency, accountability and openness – particularly during the Government of National Unity period (2009-2013), when management and benefits of Marange's exploitation were deliberately and systematically obscured by ZANU-PF mining and security ministries and officials – was critically undermined, as were wider aspects of co-operation within government, and the financial stability of the country.

In some ways, then, the benefits of Marange's exploitation reflect the broader balance of political and economic power and interests in Zimbabwe in the 2000s. This, of course, raises the question of how to address both the causes and consequences of the 'Marange problem' within the context of an environment in which those who have benefited the most remain in control of the political and economic order.

It is clear that the illicit activity of Marange remains first and foremost a Zimbabwean problem. In this respect, most attention should be placed on the activities of the all-powerful Zimbabwe Defence Industries, which controls directly, or through association, all of the illicit trade. Its partnership with Anjin, and the role its former CEO has at the head of Marange Resources, suggests that they play a similar role in the 'legal' trade as well; it also underscores the reality that it is the ZDI who calls the shots, leaving senior public servants and elected ministers only nominally in charge of Marange.

That said, there are several steps the Zimbabwean government could take were it sincere in its efforts to remedy the taint that continues to undermine Marange's promise. Two aspects in particular are worthy of attention.

First, the unaccounted accumulation of wealth by political and military elites has only added to suspicions that Zimbabwe's diamond revenues are not being properly accounted for or managed in the public's interest. Senior ZANU-PF officials have dismissed calls for revenue transparency claiming that it would only expose Zimbabweans and those who purchase their diamonds to legal liability from US economic measures. Another way to approach this matter would be to see the adoption of transparency measures as a way to assuage Western, and domestic, fears of how diamond revenues are being mismanaged.

In this context, a commitment to revenue transparency might actually benefit Zimbabwe in its calls for economic measures to be lifted, particularly on the ZMDC, MMCZ and the diamond companies. Doing so would raise prices for Marange goods and it could also help to attract legitimate mining companies – something that has so far eluded Zimbabwe. While established international mining giants have had a contested and uneven record in many parts of Africa – particularly in the area of fair wages and labour rights – there is a valid argument to be made that their presence in Marange could result in more efficient mining, better prospects of receiving tax revenues, and almost certainly fewer rights violations. The main reason is that they are vulnerable, and accountable, to public and shareholder pressure in a way that the current group of Marange mining houses – private, opaque and inexperienced – can never be.

Secondly, with the KP's failure to respond appropriately to Marange's challenges, not least its tainting of the entire diamond supply chain, pressure is growing on the industry to prove its commitment to the ethical and legal sourcing of diamonds. The record has shown that both the Kimberley Process Certification Scheme and the World Diamond Council's unregulated System of Warranties have proven themselves both unwilling and unable to track and respond to the illegal flow of Marange diamonds, both during the embargo period and afterwards. Smuggled diamonds continue to reach cutting and polishing centres accompanied by KP certificates fraudulently obtained in second countries, or without any at all. The extent of this illicit trade may have declined substantially since 2009-2011, but it remains an important obstacle to realising the full value and fiscal benefits of Marange. Meanwhile, the irregular discounted trading of other stones that move through legal KP channels continues to deprive the public treasury of Marange's full economic potential.

All segments of world diamond supply – not just a few ethical, boutique diamond retailers – need to differentiate themselves from those who are happy to look the other way when it comes to matters of poor governance in producing countries like Zimbabwe. One way this could happen would be for the World Diamond Council to commit itself to nascent efforts to create due diligence practices, similar to those that the OECD has done for other high-value and conflict-prone minerals. In the case of diamonds, this would mean clearer expectations of acceptable corporate behavior that would underpin more responsible sourcing practices. It would also result in private sector actors taking on a greater share of responsibility for their actions than is currently the case with the KP, which judges 'compliance' to minimum standards by governments only.

Such recommendations are not a panacea to Zimbabwe's challenges, but they could go a long way in returning legitimacy to Marange diamonds, the authorities who have supervised their exploitation, and the battered reputation of the international diamond industry as a whole.

4

Enforcer or Enabler? Rethinking the Kimberley Process in the Shadow of Marange

Shamiso Mtisi

Introduction

The Kimberley Process (KP) Certification Scheme, an international agreement established in 2003 to regulate the rough diamond trade, is sometimes held up as a leading example of how diverse interests can co-operate globally for the common goal of development and peace. However, ten years after its founding, the KP's uneven record underscores its complex, ambiguous character as an international organisation increasingly influenced by powerful interests that stand against its founding objectives of transparency, fairness and the upholding of rights in the diamond trade. Nowhere is this seen more clearly than in the case of the KP's handling of Marange diamonds after 2006. Rather than enforcing global standards of best practice in the extraction and marketing of Marange's stones, the KP often served as an enabler of practices that violated its own core principles and practices.

How was the KP knocked off track in its engagement with Zimbabwe – and which forces within it have fought to ensure that justice and development are consolidated in Marange's diamond fields? How has a small number of actors come to manipulate the organisation for self-interested ends – and what can be done to democratise and bring greater transparency to the KP and its practices? This chapter provides an insider's perspective on the KP in addressing these and related questions. It is grounded in the author's experience as a member of the KP civil society coalition, including five years of participating in KP meetings, deliberations, country monitoring and other activities in Zimbabwe, and around the world. From this standpoint, the KP displays both important strengths and potential, and worrying weaknesses and possible pitfalls. The Marange story brings both sets of characteristics into stark relief, and raises critical questions within and outside the KP about its viability and pathways to reform. It demonstrates how an embattled government and certain powerful politicians within it can work successfully to fan conflict among KP members, deliberately trampling upon the tripartite and consensual nature of the organisation and undermining its core monitoring functions, to ensure the trade in tainted diamonds proceeds undeterred. At the same time, Marange also reveals the limitations of the KP more broadly, and provides a context for the growing calls for the organisation's reform and revision in order to meet the challenges of the rough diamond trade in the twenty-first century.

The discussion begins with an account of the KP's basic structure, rules and processes, and Zimbabwe's first engagement with the scheme. It then focuses on the emergence of Marange as a point of contention among the organisation's key tripartite forces, including the Zimbabwean government, other government signatories to the scheme, industry and civil society. The ebbs and flows and distorting effects of conflicts among these actors is charted through an account of the difficult and controversial meetings, missions and negotiations involving the prohibition of rough diamond exports from Marange – and the conditions for its lifting. The concluding section reflects on the KP's strengths and weaknesses, and identifies lessons learnt from the Marange debacle that perhaps point to a new way forward for the KP. Throughout, the challenges, advances and opportunities for civil society's contribution to the renewal of the KP remain an important point of concern.

PM Tsvangirai, Minister Mpofu and senior government officials touring Anjin in 2012

Mechanised mining at Anjin in 2012

The Kimberley Process Certification Scheme and Zimbabwe: Institutions and interests

The KP Certification Scheme is the main global governance institution for regulating the trade of rough diamonds. It is a tripartite organisation which brings together diamond producing and consuming country governments, the diamond industry and civil society organisations working on rights and minerals, and was founded in line with several United Nations Security Council and General Assembly Resolutions.[1] Its primary objective was to eliminate the trade of 'conflict diamonds'. For the KP, which was partly inspired by the key financing role of diamonds in the violent civil conflicts of Sierra Leone and Angola, the definition of conflict diamonds focused on stones exploited by rebel movements and their allies to finance their fights against legitimate governments.

Under the KP, a certification scheme was set up to exclude conflict diamonds from the legitimate trade. This works via internal systems of controls enacted through national laws which ensure that national standards of diamond extraction, handling and export meet minimum standards set by the KP. KP Working Groups comprised of both KP members and expert observers focus on specific thematic issues. These include the Working Group on Monitoring (WGM), responsible for monitoring national compliance with KP requirements; the Working Group on Statistics, which looks at diamond production and export statistics submitted by participants; and the Working Group on Diamond Experts, which focuses on 'foot printing' diamonds, or determining the geological origins of different rough diamond material.[2] Country members are monitored and assessed for compliance through occasional WGM team visits, and KP Certificates are issued for the export of rough diamonds once it is determined through a monitoring process that minimum standards had been met. Stones exported without valid KP Certificates are deemed illegal, not to be handled by KP member countries or enterprises, and subject to seizure and impoundment pending investigation.[3]

---

1 United Nations Security Council Resolutions 1173 (1998), 1295 (2000), 1306 (2000), and 1343 (2001) and United Nations General Assembly Resolution 55/56 (2000).

2 Kimberley Process Certification Scheme, 'Working Groups and Committees' (2013-2014), available at http://www.kimberleyprocess.com/en/working-groups-and-committees

3 In Zimbabwe, this is in terms of Section 7A (1a) of the Precious Stones

The KP members gather twice a year in intersessional and plenary meetings to consider and act on the work of the Working Groups and to debate emerging KP related issues. According to its Core Document, all of the KP's decisions must be reached by consensus, a condition which has often made decision-making processes complex and difficult, particularly as membership in the KP has grown to include a wide variety of interests and member agendas. The KP is a truly global body: by the end of December 2012, the scheme had a total of 49 participants representing 75 diamond producing, processing and trading countries. For each country member, it is expected that representatives of government, industry and civil society observer groups will be included in KP country deliberations and delegations. Industry groups include representative bodies such as the World Diamond Council (WDC), and also an array of diamond exchanges, producers, retailers and other businesses from diamond cutting, polishing and trading countries.

At the international level, the KP Civil Society Coalition was made up of Global Witness, Partnership Africa Canada (PAC), the Bonn International Centre for Conversion (BICC), Green Advocates, Zimbabwe Environmental Law Association (ZELA), Centre for Research and Development (CRD) and other organisations from West Africa.[4] Like industry observers in the KP, the coalition has contributed to debate in all matters, and provided delegates for various KP Working Groups and Review Missions. Due to its ability to pool resources and carry out independent research, the Civil Society Coalition became a key source of information for KP monitoring in many instances.[5] However, as the experience of Marange would demonstrate, the production of critical monitoring and assessment reports by civil society organisations – and especially those based in Zimbabwe – often provoked harsh responses from government 'partners' in the KP, tensions with national and international diamond industry KP representatives and, ultimately, questions about the equitable status accorded civil society organisations within the KP.

Trade Regulations as amended by the Precious Stones Trade (Amendment) Regulations (SI 282 of 2002).

4   A number of African countries are represented in the Civil Society Coalition, including, in addition to Zimbabwe, the Democratic Republic of the Congo, Guinea, Ivory Coast, Sierra Leone and South Africa.

5   For example Global Witness and PAC research on human rights abuses and the smuggling of diamonds from Marange. Key reports include Global Witness (2012); Martin and Taylor (2012); Human Rights Watch (2009).

Government of Zimbabwe: Key institutions

The KP's Core Document requires country participants to enact or amend appropriate national laws, policies or regulations to implement and enforce the KP.[6] As a KP founding member, Zimbabwe amended its national laws in 2002 to comply with the KP requirements. The Precious Stones Trade (Amendment) Regulations[7] was the key legal instrument in this regard, formally binding Zimbabwe to the legal requirements and conditions of the KP.[8] Subsequently, the Minerals Marketing Corporation of Zimbabwe (MMCZ), a parastatal established under the mining ministry in the early 1980s to market most minerals in the country,[9] was designated as the unique exporting authority for all rough diamonds from Zimbabwe. However, the main government institution representing Zimbabwe in the KP was the Ministry of Mines and Mining Development, which under Minister Obert Mpofu spearheaded government's and the local diamond mining houses' often difficult and conflicting relations with the KP in the 2000s. In keeping with KP standards, the Ministry established a KP office and focal point person, tasked with the implementation of the KP, co-ordinating government participation in KP meetings and assisting with logistical issues during KP Review country visits.

In practice, Minister Mpofu became the singularly prominent player on Zimbabwe's KP team, which attended KP meetings in numbers as Marange diamonds emerged as a flashpoint of debate within the KP after 2008. Inside the country, the Minister wielded considerable power and influence. Zimbabwe's mining ministry administers all mining laws and regulations, and is also an active, direct and indirect participant in the industry. In addition to overseeing marketing through its MMCZ, the Ministry engages in diamond mining directly through the parastatal Zimbabwe Mining Development Corporation (ZMDC).[10] It also plays a key role in the Minerals Unit, a body established by the Mines and Minerals (Minerals Unit) Regulations of 2008 (SI 82 of 2008), whose main

---

6   KPCS (2003), Section IV (d).

7   Statutory Instrument 282 of 2002.

8   Dhliwayo and Mtisi (2012).

9   With the exception of gold, the export of which is overseen by the Reserve Bank of Zimbabwe.

10   Its mandate is derived from the Mines and Minerals Act (Chapter 21:05), which is the principle legislation on mining.

objective is to prevent the theft of minerals and their smuggling outside Zimbabwe.[11]

In the Marange context, each of these main institutions under Minister Mpofu would play critical roles in shaping the trajectory of development – and crisis. In the case of the ZMDC, the mining parastatal emerged as the key vehicle by which government contested and then controversially acquired the diamond claims staked by African Consolidated Resources, a private company which had started working the Marange fields in 2006. By means of four Special Grants,[12] the ZMDC was established by government as the key holder of mining rights in the diamondiferous fields, even though it was publicly acknowledged by government officials at the time that the corporation had little capacity and no experience in diamond mining. Later, in 2010, the ZMDC entered into four joint venture partnerships with different investors to form Mbada Diamonds, Anjin, Canadile and Diamond Mining Corporation (DMC), taking a 50 per cent stake in each. The number of joint venture companies has since increased. For each joint venture the ZMDC selected the investment partner, negotiated the confidential terms of incorporation and appointed ZMDC representatives to company boards. It was later determined that the processes by which these companies were set up was highly irregular and violated government and industry best practices for procurement, management and revenue sharing.[13]

The MMCZ also occupied an important position in the state's management of diamonds. It was responsible not only for marketing and collecting sales receipts and royalties for diamonds, but also for issuing KP Certificates. This meant that all diamonds designated for export needed first to be certified as conflict-free and in compliance with the KP requirements by the MMCZ before being sent for sale.[14] Without the MMCZ's approval and subsequent issuance of KP Certificates, diamond exports would be illegal under both Zimbabwean law and KP require-

---

11   The Minerals Unit also includes officials from, in addition to the Ministry, the Zimbabwe Republic Police and Reserve Bank of Zimbabwe.

12   Namely, SG 4718, SG 4719, SG 4720 and SG 4765. See Chikane (2010).

13   Parliament of Zimbabwe (2013). Canadile was later taken over by Marange Resources after allegations of corruption and misrepresentation of facts and financing by Canadile officers during the initial negotiations for the acquisition of mining rights.

14   See generally, Precious Stones Trade Regulations, 1978 as amended by the Precious Stones Trade (Amendment) Regulations, SI 282 of 2002.

ments. Indeed, when Mbada Diamonds unilaterally attempted to auction a total of 300,000 carats of rough diamonds without the knowledge of the MMCZ in 2010, government stopped the sale after advising Mbada of the illegality of the transaction.[15] During the course of the embargo on Zimbabwean diamonds, MMCZ officials regularly attended KP meetings in numbers as well.

The Minerals Unit was also accorded important jurisdiction in an industry fraught with informal mining, smuggling and transfer pricing problems. In terms of the law it had authority to enter any mining location, inspect mining operations and examine books or records.[16] Theoretically, this law was perhaps a good attempt by government to create internal control and security measures to prevent smuggling as contemplated in Section IV of the KP Core Document.[17] However, in practice the Unit did very little to curb illegality and smuggling of diamonds in Marange in terms of the KP minimum requirements. It would prove especially difficult for the Unit to effectively curb theft and smuggling when other state agencies, notably the police force and military, were deeply involved in facilitating the illegal digging and smuggling of diamonds through syndicates established with the security forces' connivance.

Zimbabwe Diamond Industry and Civil Society Observers

In addition to the Ministry of Mines and its sub-institutions, Zimbabwe's KP representatives included designated officials from the local diamond industry and civil society observers. Their key role was to implement and monitor the KP standards, respectively. Industry was represented at national and international level within the KP, with some of the staunchest defenders of Marange's mining companies being elements in the WDC, the Dubai Diamond Exchange and dealers and other businesses from a variety of diamond cutting and polishing countries, notably Israel, Belgium and India. Within Zimbabwe, the key diamond mining companies from Marange were prominent and relentless in their

---

15   Revelations were made by MMCZ officials during a hearing of the Parliamentary Portfolio Committee on Mines and Energy on the operations of ZMDC and its partners in the Marange diamond mining area. The hearings were held on 1 and 8 February 2010.

16   Section 4 of the Mines and Minerals (Minerals Unit) Regulations of 2008 (SI 82 of 2008).

17   Dhliwayo and Mtsi (2012).

lobbying at KP meetings. This effort included a significant amount of campaigning to disparage the reports, complaints and recommendations of independent Zimbabwean and international civil society voices in the KP. They actively resisted access of civil society groups to mining areas, working closely with government to lift the KP's embargo on rough diamonds from Marange.

Zimbabwe civil society groups operated as KP official observers at three strategic levels. Firstly, at the international level as part of the KP civil society coalition. Secondly, at the national level, in what is now called the KP Civil Society Coalition Representatives in Zimbabwe (formerly Local Focal Point). And thirdly, at the community level where community-based monitoring was promoted to enhance the gathering of information by those who were affected by diamond mining operations in Marange.

At the national level, Zimbabwean based civil society organisations formed a coalition in response to the 2009 KP Zimbabwe Country Review Mission. Before that, several organisations worked independently, but without co-ordination, in different projects in Marange focused on human rights, environmental justice, legal advice and medical support.[18] But in the wake of gross human rights abuses in late 2008 and with a critical KP Review Mission looming, the groups began to co-ordinate and compile their research for a joint report to the KP Review team. This loose coalition was transformed into the Local Focal Point (LFP) through the KP-negotiated St Petersburg Agreement of 15 July, 2010. The establishment of the LFP broke new ground in the context of the KP: it officially recognised and created space for civil society research and contributions, and specifically provided civil society with a role in the implementation of Zimbabwe's KP Joint Work Plan (JWP) and the work of the KP Monitor for the country. From civil society's perspective, the primary purpose of the LFP was to support the KP Monitor in assessing the implementation of the JWP by providing independent research, contacts and expert information.

In this context, the LFP monitored the situation in Marange, visiting some of the mining sites. It also produced quarterly reports that were presented to the KP. However, the coalition's work was tainted by the fact that many LFP members were frequently threatened by government

18   These included Zimbabwe Lawyers for Human Rights, ZELA, CRD and Counselling Services Unit.

officials and mining companies operating in Marange. One of its members, Farai Maguwu of CRD, was arrested and detained for more than a month, while others were threatened with physical abuse and legal prosecution. Government alleged that LFP members were working against the economic interests of the country by campaigning for an embargo on Marange exports; and moreover, that the group was being used by international NGOs such as PAC and Global Witness and some western governments to pursue an anti-ZANU-PF political agenda.

In order to provide credible information to the KP, the LFP also worked closely with community monitors in Marange, training them to enable the gathering of information on smuggling, diamond leakages and the human rights situation in the diamond fields and surrounding areas. This proved an innovative way of ensuring a constant flow of information from Marange, and overcame the problem of poor LFP access to Marange because of its status as a designated 'protected area' for which government and security forces permission was required to enter legally. The community monitors were mainly drawn from the Chiadzwa Community Development Trust (CCDT), which became prominent in public education surrounding community rights in Marange and, specifically, by organising local resistance to the forced removals which made way for the new mining companies.

One response of the Zimbabwean government to the emergence of a strong LFP was to form a parallel structure of government-aligned NGOs, labelled the Civil Society Coalition. Some sources alleged the group was financially supported by Mbada Diamonds, one of the main mining companies.[19] The 'Coalition' included organisations with nice names but dubious origins and no evidence of previous on-the-ground work in civil society; for example, Resource Exploitation Watch, whose point man, Tafadzwa Musarara, was named as part of a group demanding bribes from prospective Ghanaian investors. Other members of the government-backed coalition included ZANU-PF supporters such as Joshua Marufu, Supa Mandiwanzira (since 2013 a ZANU-PF MP and Media and Information Deputy Minister), Paddington Japajapa and Goodson Nguni. It appears that the main brief of this previously unknown coalition was to paint a rosy picture of the situation in Marange for the international community and the KP. The group also seems to have been tasked with

---

19 'Chiyangwa takes over AAG', *The Herald*, 17 October 2011.

tailing, disturbing and otherwise harassing the genuine and independent civil society activists from Zimbabwe at various KP meetings. However, many non-Zimbabwean KP participants were informed of the coalition's origins, and appeared to dismiss its weak claims to credibility.

Truth, Justice, Power and Politics: The KP's bitter struggles over Marange

At the launch of the KP in 2003, Zimbabwe's diamond mining operations included only two significant installations: River Ranch, an old and low-producing mine in Beitbridge, and Murowa, a recently established and modest kimberlite pipe mine in Zvishavane.[20] The latter was the main producer of diamonds, and easily met the KP's minimum criteria for rough diamond exports. However, with the discovery of alluvial diamonds in Marange in 2006, Zimbabwe's relations with the KP would shift dramatically. Like all other sources of 'conflict diamonds' in Africa, Marange's alluvial deposit presented considerable regulatory challenges: the stones were found on or near the surface, across a large terrestrial area, were easily accessed without mechanised mining, and were difficult to secure. Moreover, they were found in a very poor, rural area of the country, which itself was in the midst of a serious economic crisis which had thrown countless numbers of people into deep poverty and economic desperation.

Under circumstances that were complex and involved encouragement by government of informal mining on ground contested by private mining claims, an extraordinary 'diamond rush' ensued in late 2006. Very quickly it appeared that the state had lost control of the diamond fields – not only over the influx of miners, traders, dealers and criminal elements, but also the flow of diamonds, which the state had expected to monopolise via onsite purchases by the MMCZ. The response by government after the diamond rush had spun out of its control, and possibly after realising they were contravening the KP requirements, was to launch clean-up and control operations using the security forces aimed at containing informal mining, smuggling and other illicit activity. The most sustained operation was a combined police and military one, 'Operation Hakudzokwi' ('You Will Not Return'), in October-November 2008. This was aimed at instilling fear in the minds of all those who were involved in the digging,

---

20   Government of Zimbabwe (2012).

illegal trading and smuggling of diamonds. The result was a cascade of serious human rights abuses, including the deaths of over 200 informal miners who were massacred by ground troops on foot and on horseback, as well as by helicopter gunships.[21] The area was subsequently declared a protected area in terms of the Protected Areas and Places Act. Marange's designation as a security-protected zone provided the state with a cover of secrecy and enabled continuing rights violations, including seizure of property, restrictions on freedom of movement, bans on public transport, disruption of sources of livelihoods and widespread beatings.[22]

When reports of the calamity in Marange started to filter out, civil society organisations began to document the multiple serious abuses. The first published reports of the human rights crisis emerged in early 2009; by March the Civil Society Coalition was demanding investigation of the Marange situation and a pre-emptive ban on its export of conflict-tainted stones. In response to the unfolding emergency in Marange, and after many delays and considerable indecision, the KP deployed a Review Mission to Zimbabwe from 30 June to 4 July 2009.[23] The mandate of the team was to assess concerns regarding the implementation of KP internal controls and related reports of violence and smuggling in Marange and to provide the KP with complete and objective information on all aspects of the Zimbabwean system of internal controls and compliance with KP requirements. The timing was meant to ensure that the KP would discuss the issue as a matter of urgency at its June 2009 Intersessional meeting.[24] At last, it seemed, the KP was willing to take action.

The Review Mission was led by Liberian Deputy Minister of Mines, Kpandel Fayia, who himself had witnessed atrocities committed by rebel groups in his own country during the diamond-fueled conflicts of the 1990s. For Fayia and one of the civil society representatives, Alfred Brownell, the fact-finding mission to Zimbabwe proved to be an emotionally difficult experience.[25] The KP group met with government officials, civil society and communities. They heard moving first-hand tes-

---

21 Martin and Taylor (2012).

22 Chiadzwa Community Development Trust (2010).

23 Personal communication with KP participants and observers who attended KP meetings where the issue of Marange was raised.

24 Personal communication with KP participants.

25 'Civilians abused at Zimbabwe diamond mines', *Agence France-Presse*, 8 July 2009.

timonies from members of the local community of serious human rights abuses committed by state security forces. Video and physical evidence of graves, and the remains of miners and traders killed by security forces, was provided by the people of Chiadzwa and civil society groups. The team also met civil society activists in Harare who had prepared a dossier chronicling abuses in Marange.[26] Together, the compelling evidence plainly weighed upon and disturbed some members of the Review Mission.[27] The team leader made it clear that the atrocities in Marange reminded him of earlier violations in Liberia during the reign of Charles Taylor, who had since been indicted and tried for war crimes and crimes against humanity in the Special Court on Sierra Leone in The Hague.

The Review Mission's report concluded that Marange's diamonds were not compliant with the KP's minimum requirements due to widespread smuggling and illegal mining, the failure to secure the diamond fields and stop cross-border trade.[28] At the November 2009 KP Plenary meeting in Namibia, the report was debated and despite intense lobbying by the Zimbabwe government and its KP allies an export embargo was imposed on Marange diamonds on the basis of the Review Mission's findings. This marked a big victory for the Civil Society Coalition, which had campaigned heavily for action in the wake of the Marange rights debacle of 2008. At the same time, the path to KP compliance for Marange was clearly spelled out in an agreed JWP. The JWP called for an immediate cessation of rough diamond exports and the creation of a Supervised Export Mechanism by which all future exports were to be assessed and monitored by a KP-appointed Monitor, a position soon filled by Abbey Chikane of South Africa.[29] The JWP also provided for the KP's engagement of investors, and the installation of security systems,[30]

---

26 Zimbabwe Lawyers for Human Rights et al. (2009).

27 'Civilians abused at Zimbabwe diamond mines', ibid.

28 Martin and Taylor (2010).

29 Abbey Chikane was a former Chairman of the KP and a partner at Ernst & Young in South Africa, whose Zimbabwe-based subsidiary was also given the contract by government in September 2010 to conduct a Reconciliation Audit of production and sales records for Marange diamonds from 2007 to 2009. The coincidence and results of the audit raised a lot of questions. Some speculated that Chikane took his brief from the ANC and some powerful politicians and business people in South Africa.

30 It was the responsibility of mining companies to install adequate security measures, including modern hands-free processing equipment, surveillance

phased withdrawal of the military and tightening of border security between Zimbabwe and Mozambique to curb smuggling.

Zimbabwe started to implement some of the actions recommended in the JWP, albeit in a piecemeal way. In order to assess progress, a KP meeting was held in Tel Aviv in June 2010. During that meeting evidence was presented by civil society members to show that Zimbabwe had done very little to comply with the JWP.[31] There were credible reports of human rights abuses and smuggling of diamonds by syndicates of the military, police, and illegal miners and dealers.[32] These reports contrasted sharply with those of the KP Monitor, Abbey Chikane, who claimed that the country had made significant progress in implementing the JWP recommendations. The focus of the dispute between the KP Monitor and the civil society evidence became the issue of human rights violations, which Chikane appeared to ignore or discount. For civil society, these violations were real, documented and ongoing – and constituted a violation of the KP's minimal conditions on conflict diamonds. The dispute was exacerbated by Chikane's seeming involvement in the arrest and detention of Farai Maguwu, a civil society activist and director of the CRD in Mutare, who had supplied Chikane with evidence of human rights abuses by state security forces and was subsequently arrested when Chikane handed this confidential information to Zimbabwe state security agents.[33] As a result, Chikane lost the trust and confidence of civil society members, who argued that he appeared to be partisan in advancing the Zimbabwean government's campaign for a lifting of the KP embargo on Marange stones. The meeting and negotiations in Tel Aviv ended in deadlock.

In trying to resolve the dispute and encourage Zimbabwe to improve the implementation of the JWP, the KP met in St Petersburg in July 2010. This resulted in a negotiated deal that allowed Zimbabwe to make two export shipments of Marange diamonds, auctions which were certified by Chikane in August and September 2010. At the same time, because of concerns raised by civil society groups about Chikane's conduct, especially regarding Maguwu's arrest, the St Petersburg Agreement also included provision for the establishment of an LFP person appointed by civil socie-

equipment and fencing, and the contracting of private security.

31 See for example, Martin and Taylor (2010); Global Witness (2010).

32 Kimberley Process Civil Society Representatives in Zimbabwe (2010).

33 See the chapter by Farai Maguwu in this volume.

ty organisations to assist the KP Monitor in assessing the implementation of the JWP. The original idea was to appoint one civil society individual with technical expertise and knowledge of the issues in Marange, and Farai Maguwu was initially appointed. But based on recent experience with Maguwu's detention, which highlighted the vulnerability of one individual to intimidation and interference, civil society subsequently resolved that a better option would be to form a technical committee consisting of six organisations, with a representative delegated to attend all KP meetings.[34] I was appointed to be the LFP representative, given my position as a lawyer working with ZELA on KP issues.

With mistrust hanging heavily in the air, yet another Review Mission was sent to Zimbabwe in August 2010 to assess progress made in implementing the JWP. This time the mission found that Zimbabwe had managed to implement some of the elements of the JWP: companies like Mbada and Canadile (now Marange Resources) had secured mining claims and invested in security systems and infrastructure. However, the mission's report crucially identified areas where significant progress was still required. These included the shutting down of digging and smuggling by military and informal miner syndicates, the phased withdrawal from Marange of the military which had been responsible for human rights abuses, the suppression of the cross-border trade into Mozambique and the engagement of small-scale miners on their legal regularisation by statute.

The Review Mission's report was presented at the next KP Plenary in Jerusalem in November 2010. It resulted in intense debate, and a failure to reach an agreement on the lifting of the embargo. Zimbabwe argued that it had satisfied the KP's minimum requirements and must be allowed to trade without any conditions or supervision. The dispute between Zimbabwe and the KP escalated. Subsequent meetings and consultations in Belgium and Dubai resulted in a deadlock. Due to the deadlock, the existing supervised export mechanism remained in place and no exports were to be made by Zimbabwe without the authority of the KP. But changes in the leadership of the KP following the November 2010 Plenary soon altered the situation on the ground and further escalated the tensions into a crisis within the KP.

---

34   The LFP/KP civil society representatives included NANGO, Crisis Coalition, Zimbabwe Environmental Law Association, Counselling Services Unit, Zimbabwe Lawyers for Human Rights, Centre for Research and Development and the Women's Coalition.

In 2011 the DRC assumed the rotating KP Chair for one year under Mathieu Yamba. Almost immediately there were dramatic and ultimately unprocedural developments. With limited prospects for an agreement for further exports from Marange, Abbey Chikane visited Zimbabwe and unilaterally certified some Marange diamond parcels for export. He was backed by Mathieu Yamba, who issued a notice in March 2011 confirming stones from Mbada and Marange Resources as KP-compliant. All of this was done without warning and without attempting to reach consensus through consultation, as required by the KP. Civil society suspected that both individuals were acting under political influence, owing to the historic ties between ZANU-PF and South Africa's ANC (with whom Chikane was close) on the one hand, and the DRC government on the other (on whose side ZANU-PF intervened militarily in the DRC's civil war). The KP and Marange's diamonds, it seemed, were caught up in complex geopolitical forces that threatened to undo the principles of the KP and undermine human rights.

Matters came to head as governments and civil society disagreed openly at the KP Intersessional in Kinshasa in June 2011. Tensions escalated when Minister Obert Mpofu launched a dismissive and condescending attack on the Civil Society Coalition, breaching fundamental KP principles concerning equity of the KP's tripartite nature. Civil society representatives walked out of the meeting. At the November Plenary in the DRC, the Zimbabwean members boycotted in protest at their treatment and the failure of the KP to act meaningfully on a range of issues raised in the last Review Mission report – the first time in the 10-year history of the KP that such an action had been taken.[35] Despite this protest, the Plenary approved the lifting of export restrictions on Mbada and Marange Resources. Moreover, a KP monitoring team composed of a renowned diamond expert Mark Van Bockstael and Abbey Chikane was mandated to continue monitoring the situation in Marange in terms of the JWP. Shortly afterwards, in January and February 2012, Anjin and the DMC were granted export rights following approvals by the monitoring team. By November 2012 all restrictions on Marange exports were lifted when the KP met in Washington and declared that Zimbabwe had satisfied all JWP requirements.[36] Thereafter the country fell off the KP supervised export mechanism.

35 Martin and Taylor (2010).
36 Kimberley Process Certification Scheme (2012).

The Civil Society Coalition's long fight for justice in Marange provided some hard lessons about the opportunities and obstacles for pursuing human rights and fairness within the KP. Our experience revealed foremost the importance of alliances and co-ordination among political interests within participating governments, and their capacity to use KP rules, structures and processes to undermine what we felt were key principles of the KP, particularly with regard to human rights. Indeed, the KP's commitment to upholding the latter, as specified in the first pages of its Core Document, seemed to be actively under attack from many senior government delegates in the KP. The Marange saga also underscored the considerable power of government players, the sway of economic interests in the position of some in the diamond industry and the special vulnerability of civil society to both.

To some extent, the lifting of restrictions on Zimbabwe's diamond trade, in spite of the continuing smuggling and shadow dealings in the country, spoke to the notion that the KP operated as a club for politicians from diamond producing countries. It seemed increasingly clear that governments used the organisation for legitimation and to enable their counterparts to accumulate wealth through trade, rather than policing and enforcing minimum standards to protect ordinary citizens and ensure that they also benefit. Here the roles played by Abbey Chikane and some of his colleagues were especially illuminating, and testified to an abiding regional solidarity among nationalist politicians in the KP. In a sense, the solidarity displayed among Zimbabwe, DRC, Namibia and South Africa, among other African countries, seemed to be rooted in parallel experiences as governments in direct contest with civil societies demanding transparency, rights and development. While the KP's performance around Marange offered some reason for hope, notably in the use of KP Monitors and the provision for civil society groups to support their work, in practice the performance of Abbey Chikane as the KP's Monitor in Zimbabwe seemed part of the problem, not the solution. However, Mark Van Bockstael fared very well in consulting civil society during his tenure as KP Monitor.

The formidable capacity of governments to deploy resources and arm-twisting to get their way was also evident. The former Minister of Mines and Mining Development, Obert Mpofu, was a very powerful player during Zimbabwe's pursuit of the lifting of trading restrictions.

He attended every KP meeting from 2009 to 2012 as the point man and chief player for the Zimbabwean delegation, and always seemed more intent on demolishing critical reports by civil society organisations than engaging in dialogue around human rights violations, diamond smuggling or the security forces' use of violence against artisanal miners and local people in Chiadzwa. Rather than engage with and fix these issues, he focused on what he claimed were the negative impacts of the export embargo on Zimbabwe's economy, and portrayed the embargo as an attempt to inflict economic damage and impose regime change in the country. Minister Mpofu was supported at KP meetings by an often vocal team composed of state security agents, military and police officers, legal consultants, mining company officials, pseudo civil society activists and other officials from state entities.[37]

The Zimbabwe government also nurtured foreign and local supporters in the KP. These included Peter Meeus, the Dubai Diamond Exchange Chairman, and Chaim Evan Zohar, President of Tacy in Israel. They relentlessly criticised civil society reports on illegality, human rights violations and corruption in Marange, and went further to question the integrity and agendas of organisations and individuals producing these materials. For example, during a Diamond Conference meeting in Victoria Falls in December 2012, Chaim Evan Zohar, chairing a session, accused local civil society organisations, and me personally, of fabricating reports in cahoots with international organisations like Partnership Africa Canada with the aim of undermining Marange's legitimate trade. Chaim's tone incited the crowd, largely made up of state security agents, to demand my arrest as the KP's LFP person. It was another reminder of civil society's vulnerability to intimidation, harassment and legal censure by a state that controlled the security agencies and most national media, and exercised heavy influence in the justice system. Even the then KP Chair, Ambassador Gillian Milovanovic of the USA, was not spared abuse: her motives were questioned and she was heckled.[38]

Marange and the KP: Looking back, thinking ahead

The lifting of the embargo and supervised exports from Marange in

---

37   Among Mpofu's delegation to plenary sessions were a lawyer, Farai Mutamangira, and the Attorney-General of Zimbabwe, Johannes Tomana.

38   Milovanovic was accused of failing to balance the interests of the KP and those of the US Government, which had imposed sanctions on the export of Marange diamonds.

2012 brought to an end one chapter in the parallel stories of the KP and Marange diamonds, and pointed the way towards new debates, policies and activism in the future. On the one hand the Marange crisis exposed shortcomings within the KP system at international and national levels; on the other it led to innovations, advancements and discussions about new ways forward in regulating the world diamond business to enhance its transparency, fairness and developmental impact.

Shortcomings

Several of the KP's weaknesses stemmed from inbuilt design flaws. It was hamstrung by the necessity of membership consensus on all key issues, a weak interpretation of its founding document's commitment to protecting human rights as an integral part of its mission, and important technical and managerial shortcomings. In the first instance, Marange exposed divisive faultlines among the tripartite membership within the KP, and demonstrated that a decision making process based on consensus can make it very difficult to reach decisions. The Zimbabwe issue dragged on for almost three years without resolution, taking up considerable time and resources, and inflaming polarised positions. With regard to giving greater weight to human rights issues as a defining element of 'conflict diamonds', the KP failed to move beyond its narrow original definition, which was limited to cases where diamonds were used to fund rebel militias – for example, in Sierra Leone and Angola, which had prompted the formation of the KP. Civil society provided an opportunity to widen the definition of 'conflict' to include situations like Marange, where governments themselves were the perpetrators of violence and rights abuses in the extractive process. Some in the Civil Society Coalition argued that contemporary government and military cliques bore the hallmarks of abuse and violence for which the rebel movements of days past had been targeted by the KP; Zimbabwe's Joint Operations Command, for example, was portrayed as acting like a secretive rebel movement in asserting its control over informal mining in Marange.[39] On this key issue, however, the KP retreated under pressure from government and some industry members. As a result, provisions embedded in the KP Core Document's Preamble for a more expansive, rights-based definition of conflict diamonds were left to languish, even though they appeared to be far more relevant to many contemporary cases of dia-

39   Martin and Taylor (2010). See also Towriss (2013).

mond-fuelled conflict than the KP's standard accepted definition.[40]

Other KP weaknesses related to the auditing, analysis and supervision of extraction and trading data from governments and companies. In the case of Marange, some of the statistics did not tally and stockpiles of diamonds that were mined before the embargo were not properly accounted for. A forensic audit by Ernst & Young revealed significant problems. However, the KP was not forceful in demanding convincing answers from government, notably when it conducted a reconciliation and audit of production and sales records for 2007-9; nor was the KP insistent on the government accounting for rough diamond stockpiles recovered by the police from illegal miners and dealers.[41] The KP ignored these troubling facts and proceeded to pretend that such things were normal; in the end, although the diamonds were never accounted for, the KP removed them from the embargo. This lack of complete or reliable information on diamond production and trading was underscored by the KP's own secretive handling of data.

Access to the KP's own diamond statistics and monitoring reports was made difficult by their location on the private, password-protected part of the KP's website. Public policy debates were therefore disadvantaged. At the same time, the Civil Society Coalition could not access mine level data on diamond production from the mining companies, except for the aggregated numbers on the KP website and materials included in the sometimes incomplete reports by the KP Monitors on DMC and Anjin.[42] The management of mining companies declined to disclose the production figures or information related to the export of rough diamonds. These are issues that should have been addressed by the KP: without such information, there was little possibility of determining the likelihood of illegal transactions, including smuggling from production sites.

It seemed clear in the case of Marange that some KP participants were attracted and dazzled by the infrastructure set up by the mining compa-

---

40   The KP's founding document recognises the importance of preventing 'systematic and gross human rights violations' related to diamond extraction.

41   A September 2010 audit by Ernst & Young revealed that they had not physically audited and verified the existence of a total of 357,118.12 carats of rough diamonds that were confiscated by the Zimbabwe Republic Police. Moreover, another unchecked stockpile at Canadile apparently totaled 56,867 carats, which also had not been fully accounted for.

42   Kimberley Process Civil Society Coalition Representatives in Zimbabwe (2012a). The KPCS visit to Marange took place on 7 and 8 March, 2012.

nies, so much so that they failed to take note of the serious leakages and weak internal controls on the ground, many of which were revealed by a Zimbabwe parliamentary committee investigation published in June 2013.[43] Moreover, the KP failed to act to censure government for foregoing the use of official banking channels – a KP-recommended best practice[44] – and instead relying on courier services and men with briefcases for handling cash payments. While the Zimbabwe government and mining companies argued these cash payment methods were necessary to evade the threat of financial seizures and other obstacles under US and EU sanctions against the ZMDC, the negative consequences for transparency and accountability were enormous.

Finally, the KP fell short of its nominal commitment to ensuring that diamonds are a tool for development in poorer countries. The preamble of the KP Core Document recognised that conflict diamonds negatively affect trade in 'legitimate diamonds which make a critical contribution to the economies of many of the producing, processing, exporting and importing states, especially developing states.'[45] Evidence compiled by civil society in Zimbabwe and presented to the KP strongly supported the view that these kinds of negative consequences were manifest with Marange diamonds: neither the country nor the communities were benefiting – only a few secretive institutions and political elites, including the Minister of Mines and Mining Development. Yet the KP ignored these arguments and refused to act to correct the problems identified.

Steps Forward

Civil society's long dispute with the Zimbabwe government in the KP focused on the former's attempts to ensure that the KP enforce its standards to curb illegal mining, the smuggling of diamonds and human rights abuses in Marange by both state and non-state actors. While many in civil society were disappointed with the KP's failures in this regard, several changes in the way KP structures worked, and the impact of some decisions taken, demonstrated that the KP did have the capacity to act as an enforcer of its minimum requirements, even if this capacity was sometimes weak.

The decision by the KP to send the first Review Mission in 2009 ex-

---

43 Parliament of Zimbabwe, (2013).
44 Kimberley Process Certification Scheme (2003), Annex II.
45 Kimberley Process Certification Scheme (2003), p. 1.

posed the situation in Marange to the international community, helping to highlight human rights violations, smuggling and illegality. Further, the adoption of the JWP in 2010 encouraged Zimbabwe to adopt sound measures towards compliance with the KP which it might not otherwise have undertaken. By December 2012, the Civil Society Coalition noted that significant progress had been made by Marange's producers in the implementation of KP minimum requirements and issues identified in the JWP.[46] By that time the situation in Marange had largely stabilised, companies had put in place security systems and infrastructure, investors had been engaged, cases of human rights violations had declined and phased withdrawal of the military had started. There was evidence of reduced smuggling, illegal digging and illicit trade among the informal miners, and the flourishing diamond trade centers in Mutare and Vila de Manica had largely dried up.[47] To that extent, the KP actions resulted in some positive changes in Marange. However, the persistence of officially recognised smuggling rings has remained a problem. International airports and other points of entry in Zimbabwe continue to be used by some ZANU-PF politicians and mining companies; this highly irregular cross-border traffic is justified by government under the pretext that it is necessary to evade sanctions imposed by the USA and other western countries on the ZMDC and affiliated government entities.

One of the most innovative and positive changes in the KP due to Marange was the decision to establish a civil society LFP to improve local level monitoring. It resulted in civil society working with the KP monitoring team and producing reports that directly informed debates and decisions at the KP's plenary and intersessional meetings. More broadly, the Zimbabwe innovation came to serve as a model: the KP's Washington Communique of 2012 called for the setting up of national level tripartite arrangements by all KP participants to enhance local level monitoring and the implementation of minimum requirements.[48]

While some observers have questioned the impact of civil society monitoring in addressing government's human rights abuses in 2008 and

---

46 Kimberley Process Civil Society Representatives in Zimbabwe (2012b).
47 For an assessment of the trajectory of informal activity and the trajectory and impact of its exclusion, see chapter by Nyamunda in this volume.
48 Kimberley Process Certification Scheme (2012).

beyond, it can be argued that the simple act of noting and including such abuses in review mission reports acted, to some extent, to deter the government from committing further atrocities after 2010. In Zimbabwe this seemed clear: whenever a KP Review Mission or monitoring team visited, government was prompted to create an impression of peace and order in the diamond fields. Some have argued that this demonstrated that the KP's global regulatory authority and influence could, in some cases, act as a checking mechanism against states violating its standards.

Finally, another mostly positive outcome of KP involvement in Zimbabwe was Zimbabwe's Diamond Policy, developed by government to address the policy gaps and weaknesses related to diamond exploration and licensing, value adding and beneficiation, marketing and export, and protection from smuggling and theft. The Policy, approved by Cabinet in May 2012, represented an attempt to comply with the KP's minimum requirements concerning the elaboration of clear legal frameworks for national diamond industries. However, three years later, at time of writing, the policy has not resulted in the passage of legislation to regulate the diamond sector, amid new unilateral moves by government to force changes in the structure of existing mining companies in Marange in the wake of fresh allegations of corruption and maladministration.

Marange, the KP and Beyond

In important ways, the struggles over Marange within the KP were a prism through which to read the alignment of power and interests in both the KP, and the murky world of the global diamond industry more broadly. On the one hand, both claimed to be committed to the consolidation of a transparent, fair, pro-rights and development-friendly global diamond industry; on the other, key players in government and industry worked hard to undermine, bend, dilute or evade the rules of fair play put in place through the KP, and to disparage those who fought to uphold them. For many participants and observers Marange came to represent a key test case for the KP: if in the face of a great deal of evidence of non-compliance with KP criteria Zimbabwe's diamonds could be declared 'clean', then what value was the KP as a regulator of the global illicit trade?

Much of the KP's debate over Zimbabwe turned on the question of human rights and their inclusion as a criterion for conflict and non-compliance. In this sense, Marange became a defining moment for the KP on the issue of human rights and, indeed, the future direction of the organisation. The failure by the KP to seize the opportunity to deal with new forms of conflicts associated with diamond mining and trade deeply frustrated many actors and civil society groups, and ultimately led to the departure of several widely respected KP founding members. Among them was Ian Smillie, who publicly resigned from the organisation and explained that its repeated violation of its own principles in decisions on Marange – and the 'pretence of the KP members that failure is success'[49] – had eviscerated the body of its integrity and its practical utility. Others who left included the UK-based NGO Global Witness, and New York-based diamond trader Martin Rappaport, both of them also prominent founding KP members.

In light of the heightened tensions around the issue of rights, the departure of key players and the resulting questions over the KP's continued relevance and credibility, the organisation undertook to entertain efforts to redefine the concept 'conflict diamonds'. To date this has generated little in the way of actual progress. The KP did establish a Committee on KP Review to work on various reform issues, including assessing whether there is need to redefine what constitutes conflict diamonds. Under South Africa's KP Chairmanship in 2013 the Committee made attempts to put in place a new set of definitions for conflict, but no agreement was reached and the Committee's mandate expired at the end of 2013.[50] The KP recommended the establishment of an 'innovations committee' to drive reforms, but most civil society participants see little evidence that this will be any more successful than recent efforts to push a rights-based redefinition process. Where progress has been made, it has involved administrative reforms, including the establishment of an Administrative Mechanism to provide permanent offices and secretariats for the body.

Despite recent disappointments, the demands and need for reform of global diamond industry practices are unlikely to fade, either inside or outside the KP, or its individual country members. For some in civil society, the Marange crisis represents an opportunity for the rebirth of the KP, not its end. New ideas for developing and enforcing effective criteria for both the diamond industry and government regulators are fuelling cur-

---

49   Smillie (2010 a).
50   Key opponents of the reform of definitions included the Zimbabwe government, and other countries including China, Russia and South Africa; and the business grouping, the African Diamond Producers Association.

rent discussions, with the aim of creating parallel structures alongside the KP to tackle human rights issues in the extractives sector. In these consultations, Marange's diamonds will continue to help illuminate the way forward to a fairer, more transparent, and sustainable diamond industry.

5

MARANGE DIAMONDS AND THE KIMBERLEY PROCESS: AN ACTIVIST'S ACCOUNT

Farai Maguwu

In late 2008, without warning and with terrible ruthlessness, the Zimbabwe National Army (ZNA) was deployed to Marange District in Zimbabwe's eastern province of Manicaland, where the government aimed to reclaim control over recently discovered alluvial diamond fields. Since 2006, when the existence of diamonds in Marange was made public, more than 30,000 people had moved into the area to earn a living from artisanal mining. Government and the political-military elite came to see these informal miners and local residents as an obstacle to their own prospects for accumulating wealth. Sporadic and growing conflict between state security agencies and 'illegal' miners mounted as the richness of the diamond fields became apparent. These conflicts culminated in the deployment of the ZNA and its massacre of hundreds of miners in the space of five weeks in October-November 2008. By December, the state-controlled *Manica Post* newspaper reported that mortuaries in the provincial capital of Mutare were filled to capacity with bodies brought in from Marange. Moreover, the military atrocities reached beyond Marange to include Mutare, where the ZNA intercepted Harare-bound buses and commandeered drivers to take passengers to Marange where they were assaulted, robbed of cash and valuables, and forced to fill the gullies left by artisanal miners.

The cruelty and disregard of government to the plight of those it was attacking was proudly put on display by a columnist in *The Herald*, Nathaniel Manheru, widely believed to be President Mugabe's spokesperson George Charamba:

> *The Untouchables of Chiadzwa are either slaving, wounded or dead. Gullied Chiadzwa needs to be reclaimed, declared the authorities. Reclaimed by those who wounded it in the first place. Those accused of damaging it may not use shovels, hoes or some such implements. They shall use their fingers, and accomplish the job in record time, these* gwejas *and* gwejesses. *It is a season of tears as man becomes beast to get beastly men and women to repair the heinous damage they have wrought on innocence. It is painful payback time. The deep gullies are being refilled with bare hands. Fingers are sore and finishing, well before a quarter of the job is done. Chiadzwa, once a place for dashing fortune-seekers, has become Chiadzwa the place of unrelieved pain.*[1]

While few details were publicly known about the unfolding tragedy in Zimbabwe at that time, evidence was becoming clear for those of us working in, or with other connections to, the rural areas of Manicaland. In my own case, these connections were mainly through my role as a civil society activist. In 2006 I founded the Centre for Research and Development (CRD) as a civil society organisation (CSO) based in Mutare and focused mostly on promoting human rights and democracy in rural areas through civic education. We had established strong networks with, and a passion for, rural communities in Manicaland. Through our local connections we learned of the growing number of citizens who were being forced to go to Marange by the military where they were subjected to inhuman and degrading treatment. I personally encountered people who had been abducted from Mutare and taken to Marange, and discovered that most of them did not even have links to Marange. They were clearly traumatised by the terror they had endured, as were many more thousands of people in Marange itself.

Something terrible was happening in Marange, yet there was silence

---

1   'Reasserting authority in the wild, wild East', *The Herald*, 24 November 2008.

in the national media – and in civil society – possibly due to fear of the military. At CRD we felt an urgent need to address the events in Marange as part of our broader strategic objective of promoting human rights and democracy in rural Zimbabwe, even if we were also wary of the repercussions involving the security forces. We had no notion at the time that this work would so suddenly and deeply change our organisation, our work and in fact our own lives.

Uncovering and Reporting the Killings: The first steps, and hostile responses

We began the difficult task of investigating how it all started, identifying the actors involved and tracing victims of military abuse to their homes and hospitals. This meant visiting hospitals to talk to victims, taking photographs of their wounds where possible and using this opportunity to get a clear picture of what was happening in the diamond fields. Sometimes we went to hospital mortuaries posing as relatives of missing persons who had been last seen in Marange, as this enabled us to access the records of those 'Brought in Dead' from Marange.

In January 2009, CRD released its initial report.[2] It was the first comprehensive report to cast light on the bloody events of late 2008. The first recipients were diplomats, who expressed great appreciation and interest in our work. The report would soon be used as an important source of information by the Kimberley Process (KP) Certification Scheme's Review Mission to Zimbabwe of 30 June - 4 July 2009, which cited it as a key document.

Due to the leading role I had personally taken in exposing human rights abuses in Marange, I was invited to attend the KP plenary in Namibia in November 2009, where the situation in Marange featured prominently on the agenda. With donor backing, CRD – which had a small budget and limited funds – managed to send two officials to the Namibian meeting. On the other hand, the Zimbabwe government, knowing how damning the review mission report was, and aiming to avoid censure and penalties at the hands of the KP, deployed a large delegation. With as many as 40 delegates in attendance, the Zimbabwe government was clearly trying to create an intimidating atmosphere for their critics from civil society. Members of that delegation followed me everywhere I went; they mon-

---

2   Centre for Research and Development, (2009).

itored every conversation I had, and possibly even recorded some. I felt insecure and highly vulnerable, but refused to be cowed. I was determined to speak for the victims of violence in Marange at whatever cost to my personal security.

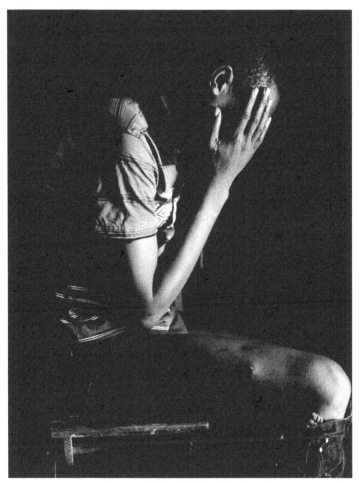

'Tendai Moyo', victim of torture and beatings at the hands of a diamond syndicate led by military personnel

During the meeting I was invited to the podium to speak about what CRD had observed in Marange. I confirmed the contents of the KP Review Mission's report as a true reflection of events, adding some specific cases that I had personally come across. Predictably, the Zimbabwean delegation did not take my contributions lightly. However, the first to attack me was the Namibian Chair, Bernard Esau, who accused me of speaking without his mandate despite the fact that I spoke during the session allotted to the Review Mission, which had invited me to the podium to confirm their report. This open and unusual rebuke was likely meant to appease the Zimbabwean delegation, due to the historical political ties that exist between the ruling parties of Zimbabwe and Namibia. But the attack did not stop there. Subsequently, Obert Mpofu, then Minister of Mines for Zimbabwe, dedicated a significant amount of time during his KP presentation to attacking me, claiming I was Western sponsored and paid to tarnish the image of Zimbabwe's gems. Later, during a reception hosted by the Namibian Chair, Zimbabwe's Ambassador to Namibia confronted me, personally attacking me for being a 'sell out'. Her public rage was witnessed by – and shocked – many delegates.

But evidence spoke louder than threats. At the conclusion of the meeting, and on the basis of the overwhelming evidence of non-compliance with the KP's criteria for 'clean' diamonds, the KP plenary suspended diamond exports from Marange. At the same time, following negotiations involving the tripartite members at the KP meeting, a year-long Joint Work Plan (JWP) was agreed between Zimbabwe and the KP, which stipulated the conditions and processes Zimbabwe would have to put in place in order to bring Marange diamonds into compliance with the KP's criteria.[3] The JWP provided for a KP Monitor for Zimbabwe, and South African Abbey Chikane was appointed to the position.

At the conclusion of the Namibian meeting a number of diplomats advised me not to return to Zimbabwe, offering me the safety of their countries. But I turned down the offers, preferring to return to Zimbabwe to continue with my work. On my arrival in Zimbabwe, some representatives of diplomatic missions escorted me from the airport. One diplomat drove me all the way to Mutare.

Monitoring with a Mission?

Back in Mutare, it was not long before the limits of the KP's commitment to monitoring and improving the situation in Marange became apparent. On his first visit to Zimbabwe, in March 2010, Abbey Chikane refused to meet with CRD to discuss the current situation in Marange. We wrote him emails requesting a meeting but he did not respond. His silence

3   Kimberley Process Certification Scheme (2009b).

sparked a crisis within the KP, as Western KP members threatened to discredit his first monitoring report, arguing that he needed to reflect the tripartite nature of the KP by including evidence provided by industry and civil society, as well as the government in Zimbabwe.

This pressure seemed to have an impact. In May 2010 I received an email from Chikane, requesting a meeting with me on his second visit to Marange. He asked me to prepare reports and documents that would help him appreciate the situation in Marange better. He told me the dates he would be in Manicaland and asked me to choose a day to meet from two options he proposed. I responded with my choice, and in the run-up to the agreed date I received numerous emails and calls from diplomats and other stakeholders who wanted to make sure I met with him. In the end that proved difficult, due to circumstances that appeared contrived by Chikane to prevent my meeting him: the time for our meeting was changed without warning, then changed again at such short notice that it was nearly impossible for me to attend.

My suspicions were further raised when I arrived at Chikane's hotel. There were several people there who appeared to be state security agents, leading me to deposit in safekeeping at another location my printed dossier of new evidence from Marange, before returning to meet the KP Monitor. When I did find him in a public space he was surrounded by a number of people, and I expressed my discomfort in speaking with him about such sensitive issues in a hotel lobby. He told me he had diplomatic immunity and nothing would happen to me since Zimbabwe had given him assurances that his informants would not be victimised.

I gave him a lot of information pertaining to the events that were unfolding in Marange. I gave him information on artisanal mining, local and international illicit dealers both in Mutare and Mozambique, and human rights abuses by state security agents, in particular by the army. Because of my discomfort with the presence of suspected state security agents nearby in the hotel lobby, I told him I would email him my reports. But he persuaded me to have them printed in the hotel business section. I told him this was not safe for me but he insisted on having hard copies printed so that he could read them on his way to Marange. I complied.

The following day, 26 May, President Mugabe appeared on television saying that some local NGOs were sponsored by the West to block the sale of Marange diamonds. He warned that government was going to take action against them. The next day I did not go to work, fearing arrest. I was planning to leave Mutare for a week or two, till the dust settled. However, before I had a chance to leave home state security agents encircled my home. They were accompanied by my CRD programmes officer, whose brother happened to be a member of the ZANU-PF Central Committee. As state security agents ransacked my home he was sitting in their truck in the street in front of my house.

I was lucky. I managed to evade the agents and hid in the neighbourhood until dark, when I escaped and arranged to meet with my colleague – who claimed he'd been 'abducted' and forced to point out my home – before going into hiding. A week later, on the advice of my lawyers, I handed myself in to the police and was arrested on sight. I was charged with publishing or communicating falsehoods prejudicial to the economic interests of Zimbabwe. In all I spent five weeks in prison as the courts kept denying me bail. My release from custody on 12 July 2010 was the culmination of two different challenges to government. The first involved the fierce battle waged in the courts by my excellent legal team. The second, perhaps more decisive challenge, came from the KP, which had no legal jurisdiction in my case, but used political suasion effectively. While I was being held in prison, the KP Intersessional meeting in Tel Aviv directly addressed my plight. Several senior KP officials including the 2010 KP Chair Boaz Hirsch of Israel condemned my detention, with Mr Hirsch saying, 'Harassment or mistreatment of the civil society members of the Kimberley Process is intolerable … The Kimberley Process was founded on the basis of respect for the rights of all its members, governments, the diamond industry and civil society. The KP cannot and will not accept injurious actions taken against any of its members, all the more if they are carried out by a participating government.'[4]

Negotiations for my release continued beyond Tel Aviv. I was finally released ahead of the annual meeting of the World Diamond Council in July 2010 in St Petersburg where my continued incarceration had threatened to dominate discussion. Effectively, in exchange for my release Zimbabwe was allowed to hold two KP supervised exports in August and September 2010. Former WDC President Eli Izhakoff, who played a leading role in negotiating my release from custody, demanded that the charges against me be dropped altogether. Izhakoff stated categorically

---

4   'Release Maguwu or else, Zimbabwe told', *ZimEye*, 20 June 2010.

that my continued detention had virtually blocked debate on Zimbabwe's rough diamond exports, and that my release was needed as part of measures to break the wider impasse over exports from Marange.[5]

Another important aspect of the agreement struck at the St Petersburg meeting was the appointment of a civil society 'Local Focal Point' (LFP) for the KP in Zimbabwe. The rationale behind the LFP was to protect organisations like CRD and persons like myself who had helped the KP in its efforts to bring Zimbabwe to its minimum standards. My arrest and detention had revealed the vulnerabilities of activists who risked their lives to expose diamonds-related human rights abuses. With the establishment of the LFP, the KP and the Zimbabwe government jointly recognised and undertook to protect the CSOs which were monitoring the Marange diamond fields. The LFP, which would be appointed by the civil society coalition of organisations in Zimbabwe in consultation with the government of Zimbabwe and the KP's Working Group on Monitoring, was explicitly accorded the right to 'present facts in full independence and support the KP Monitor in the performance of his duties pertaining to his function to report on the overall implementation of the JWP … [and] have free and unfettered access in Zimbabwe to perform his/her duties, in accordance with the JWP and the terms of reference on the KP Monitor.'[6] However, while my own release from custody and the establishment of the LFP marked positive milestones for the CRD and its work, it also represented a difficult turning point in CRD's relations with civil society and donors, and ultimately the KP itself.

Changing Relations with Civil Society

When CRD started its investigations of killings and rights abuses in Marange we had few resources and were little known, hence we did not receive much solidarity or recognition from other more established organisations in civil society. However, as we continued to circulate weekly updates on Marange, we drew the attention of two Harare-based organisations, Zimbabwe Lawyers for Human Rights and Counselling Services Unit, who soon provided support. They complemented our efforts by training us in organisational and personal security and human rights monitoring. Through these and other contacts, relations with civil

---

5 'WFDB Presidents welcome the release of Farai Maguwu', http://www.diamondintelligence.com/magazine/magazine.aspx?id=8830
6 Kimberley Process Certification Scheme (2010).

society organisations began to develop as CRD became more visible.

We received solidarity when I was arrested in 2010. The Crisis in Zimbabwe Coalition,[7] Zimbabwe Lawyers for Human Rights[8] and Zimrights issued several statements and updates throughout my detention. There are many others too who contributed secretly during the struggle to free me from detention. Some of them I will never know. However, another group of civil society organisations remained silent. I was not certain why, but I think that two issues could have contributed to their silence. The first was the fear factor. Due to the sensitivity of the matter many organisations feared being dragged into it and preferred to stay out of trouble by being silent. As well, a number of CSOs started to distance themselves from me and my actions, with some reportedly saying that I was too careless with information, and deserved what I was getting from the state. Upon release from custody, I received many congratulatory messages from both the organisations that were vocal and the silent ones. It was hard to distinguish between foe and friend.

The second factor pertains to those who saw in my arrest an opportunity to attack and marginalise CRD with regard to human rights monitoring in Marange. It was after I was released and tried to resume CRD operations that I realised a lot had changed. I approached a colleague at another CSO working on the extractive sector, and proposed that we develop a broader strategy where we would collaborate, combining our organisational energies and competencies as the two leading organisations working on the sector. We arranged a meeting with a potential embassy donor. But during our meeting, revelations were made by a senior embassy official which stunned me. During a meeting of donors while I had been in detention, it was suggested by an unnamed informant that some of CRD's published information had been obtained from another organisation working in the Chiadzwa community. The implication was that others were doing the on-the-ground work for which CRD and myself were taking credit. The allegations were false and yet very serious. I rejected them, and noted my belief that they were raised by opportunistic organisations which wanted to elbow CRD out of Marange by discrediting our work.

---

7   Crisis in Zimbabwe Coalition, 'Zimbabwe: End Persecution & Harassment of Civil Society Activists', http://www.actsa.org/newsroom/2010/06/zimbabwe-end-persecution-harassment-of-civil-society-activists/
8   'Police feast in Maguwu's house', *The Legal Monitor*, Issue 52, 5 July 2010.

The onslaught against CRD continued in various forums in Harare where we were attacked in absentia. These attacks by civil society dovetailed with certain donors attached to embassies in Harare who now wanted a different approach to the Marange discourse. Some key donors wanted to manage the information which civil society was reporting on Marange. They began sponsoring Harare-based organisations to do 'monitoring' work in Marange, showering them with praise for being 'professional and balanced' and at the same time dismissing CRD reports as not credible. One of the civil society organisations which had been a CRD partner between 2009 and the time of my arrest in May 2010 suddenly turned against us, with a senior management figure accusing CRD of exaggerating facts.

The extent of the tensions and the challenge to CRD were made plain when it came time to setting up the LFP. In August, the KP's country review mission met with four Harare-based CSOs to discuss the situation in Marange and, more pointedly, the issue of relations between civil society and the Ministry of Mines, which were clearly very strained. According to the review mission's report, the four CSOs all expressed a strong interest in developing their relationship with the Ministry and this encouraged the review mission team to propose to the Permanent Secretary the idea of a joint meeting to establish greater dialogue.

After the visit, the National Association of NGOs (NANGO) began consultations with local civil society for the appointment of an individual as the LFP. At this point CRD was the only civil society organisation active in the KP and I was the CRD representative there. According to the St Petersburg Agreement, the qualifications of the LFP included 'technical and KP related expertise'. There was no one with better knowledge of the KP than myself. I was therefore nominated to be the LFP through an announcement made by NANGO. At the same time, a technical support committee of the LFP was set up comprising representatives from key CSOs, namely the CRD, Counselling Services Unit, Crisis in Zimbabwe Coalition, NANGO, Women's Coalition, Zimbabwe Environmental Law Association and Zimbabwe Lawyers for Human Rights.

Government immediately dismissed my nomination, arguing that I was in principle against the sale of Marange diamonds. I was not bothered, since I consider it dangerous for civil society work to be acceptable to government, especially in countries where human rights abuses are rife and where democracy is in short supply. But when government rejected my nomination, donors and Western diplomatic missions in Harare then demanded that I step down. For a while I refused to step down since I thought civil society was united behind me. Certain donors and diplomatic missions started lobbying local CSOs to dump me and find a candidate for the LFP who was acceptable to government – the implementation of the St. Petersburg agreement was at risk. Some donors also promised to support the work of the LFP if a government approved candidate was found. All of this seemed to intensify fighting within civil society, and a serious impasse was reached. I felt increasingly vulnerable given that donors, a section of civil society, and the government seemed to be uniting against my nomination.

In November 2010, organisations that were part of the LFP were asked to attend a donor-hosted meeting at a local embassy to discuss the situation. At the meeting, which I also attended, one civil society activist favoured by some diplomats for the LFP role suggested I step back from the LFP as a way of moving things forward. While some vowed to continue to fight to keep me in place, in the interests of the LFP and KP monitoring processes I withdrew and successfully helped put in my place a CSO activist who was acceptable to the diplomatic and donor community. In my view, this move helped fulfil a long term wish of those who wanted CRD to stop reporting on Marange, as our reports were said to be fuelling the Marange impasse within the KP. Looking back, this was the culmination of a long process of sidelining CRD from the work it had started in Marange in 2009. One result of this was that the CRD was subsequently excluded from some key meetings on Marange, and Harare-based organisations came to dominate opinion and debates.

Apart from the controversy around my appointment, the LFP created new challenges for CSOs in terms of working as a group. Harmonising the expertise and interests of the seven organisations proved difficult. The voice of CRD was drowned out, as one influential organisation imposed on CRD certain stringent reporting conditions whilst campaigning for donors to stop funding. My feeling was that some CSOs sought to take over the CRD's leadership on Marange. It was a difficult period, and many wild accusations against CRD and myself, some by well respected civil society leaders, were flying in all directions – creating space for some CSOs working around Marange. While this seemed to please certain diplomats and donors, it had a very negative impact on civil society interventions in Marange. Work on the ground slowed down, despite continuing need. At the same time, some CSOs focused more intently on clamouring for donor attention and funding.

Changing Relations with Donors

CRD's engagement with donors began in 2009 after we had started research and documentation on the human rights situation in Marange. Because certain Western diplomats were keen to gain an understanding of what was happening there, they recommended that CRD's work be funded. Apparently no organisation was willing to take the same risks as CRD at that time. We received small grants for fieldwork, which excluded institutional support, in grants that were typically of three to six months' duration. Although we produced credible reports, with detailed content and unchallenged records of events as they unfolded, their written quality was often poor due to our inexperience and limited resources. We were forced to rely on interns since it was difficult to recruit experienced and qualified researchers.

Despite these constraints, the CRD remained the main source of information on Marange, and our interactions with donors and diplomatic missions increased. Beginning in January 2010 we held monthly briefing meetings with Western ambassadors in Harare, among whom the level of interest was very high. A single meeting would attract 15-20 such ambassadors and their senior officials and a few African diplomats. Their interest was matched by their principled political support for us as an organisation: when the KP monitor refused to meet CRD on his first visit to Zimbabwe in March 2010 there was an outcry from diplomats who threatened that his report would not be considered credible without civil society input. Diplomats wanted Chikane to meet CRD because they had confidence in the information we had been supplying. Similarly, when I was arrested on June 3, 2010, Western diplomats raised the international alarm and offered support. As a result of their interventions the European Parliament passed a Resolution in July 2010 demanding my unconditional release from custody.[9] The government of Canada also issued a strong statement denouncing my arrest and the conditions in which I was being held.[10]

9   http://www.marietjeschaake.eu/2010/07/resolution-on-zimbabwe-notably-the-case-of-farai-maguwu

10   http://news.gc.ca/web/article-en.do?m=/index&nid=542179

I had every reason to believe this relationship and solidarity would continue and be even stronger going forward. Nevertheless, with revelations that Zimbabwe had stockpiled millions of carats, the feeling towards Zimbabwe among certain Western governments changed. Within Europe there was growing pressure from Belgium to lift sanctions on the Zimbabwe Mining Development Corporation (ZMDC) so that Zimbabwe's gems could be accepted in Europe, and notably in the diamond cutting and polishing centre of Antwerp. Consequently my work became a major obstruction to countries that were exploring possibilities of doing business with Zimbabwe. There was a campaign to suppress the truth about the real situation in Marange, and seemingly more interest in engaging the government than in exposing it for continued human rights abuses, and questioning it about disappearing diamond revenues. A high-ranking European Union diplomat informed me personally that the EU aimed to fund CSOs which sought solutions to the Marange problem, and claimed that CRD was failing to offer positive alternatives for a way forward. The diplomat indicated that CRD was being blacklisted by donors because of the problems it was creating for those who were seeking to 'normalise' KP-Zimbabwe relations and lift the KP's export embargo on Marange stones.

Changing Relations with the KP Certification Scheme

CRD's relations with the KP changed as the Marange story changed. In 2009 CRD had been the only organisation reporting on human rights in Marange, and we were seen as trusted and reliable informants concerning human rights abuses and informal mining in the area. Our credibility was also reflected in the number of donors, diplomats and international CSOs which stayed in frequent contact with us to gather information and advice. Respect for my work was underlined by the immediate and important international and local support during the time of my detention in 2010.

But as the Zimbabwe crisis in the KP dragged on, becoming increasingly difficult – perhaps the most difficult case the KP had handled since its formation in 2003 – there was growing exhaustion and frustration within the KP. There was consensus that a balance had to be struck between the business interests within the KP and the concerns of civil society. As a result, an increasing number of countries came to disown the KP's albeit weak mandate to protect human rights. A good number of KP participants expressed their desire to see the Zimbabwe impasse resolved through negotiation, but the Zimbabwe government showed no interest in undertaking meaningful reforms. As the chorus within the KP to move beyond human rights abuses in Marange grew, the role of Zimbabwean CSOs in the KP was diminished. Most efforts within the KP were channelled towards lifting the ban on Marange diamonds. Talk of addressing the continuing problems of human rights abuses, human security concerns, lack of transparency in revenues and fiscal benefits and so forth, fell on deaf ears. Those who persisted in pursuing such themes were increasingly marginalised within KP discussions.

CRD: Crisis and restructuring

The same interests and pressures which subverted CRD's work in the KP and in Zimbabwean civil society gradually came to play out within the CRD itself, leading to a crisis and the departure of myself and several others from the organisation in 2012. The seeds of this problem had been planted at the inception of the CRD, when I had attempted to establish some political balance during a hotly polarised period in Zimbabwe by bringing into the organisation a colleague with links to the ZANU-PF Central Committee. At the time, I was perceived as being sympathetic to the opposition Movement for Democratic Change. In my view, this openness created opportunities for manipulation of CRD from the inside by surveillance and meddling on behalf of government, and particularly at critical times, such as when I was being sought for arrest by state security agents. Infiltration of CSOs critical of government is common practice in Zimbabwe, and at CRD there seemed to be lots of evidence – which accumulated over time – pointing to it.

While ZANU-PF contacts could sometimes be useful for us, for example in getting access to information in the first phase of our Marange research, such benefits came at a high price. It proved very difficult to contain and control people I believed to be ZANU-PF sympathisers or willing informants and agents, and limit their damage to our organisation. Working with senior colleagues and giving them even modest amounts of responsibility also means being vulnerable to them. At CRD, both the organisation and myself were doubly vulnerable due to our critical stance and the fact that we had to produce much of our own confidential evidence as part of our work in the KP and in public education. Important means for undermining the CRD's work included subverting the authority of CRD management, leaking or passing confidential information to state security agencies, and disrupting our relationships with donors and CSO partners in Zimbabwe. All of these actions helped push CRD into crisis by 2010. I was therefore not surprised that a senior CRD officer was the person who led the police and CIO operatives to my residence, claiming he had been abducted. Whilst he occupied a very senior position in the organisation, he did not spend a single night in police cells. This raised serious concerns and led many observers to conclude that CRD had been compromised. I tried to conceal the difficulties I was facing in order to keep the organisation running while a solution was being sought by the CRD board. However, the pressure was intensified. Government media were part of the strategy. For example, in early 2012 a ZANU-PF-aligned newspaper published project proposals that CRD had sent to donors, as well as the responses we received. The article was clearly authored or at least heavily informed by someone from within CRD. In another case, following an LFP training workshop in March 2012, participants were shocked to see a front page article in the fiercely pro-ZANU-PF *Sunday Mail* covering the workshop. The article gave some accurate details of what had been discussed, but also attributed words and positions to me which I never spoke and did not believe. This was clearly a ploy to undermine the LFP and its relations with government. It was evident that within the workshop, attended by only twelve people, there was a CIO operative working against civil society's monitoring of Marange and indeed against my own role in that work.

The emerging problems with surveillance and duplicity within CRD also exposed the organisation's governance weaknesses. No employee was on contract, which made it difficult to retrench problematic staff. We were advised that all employees be put on contracts pending CRD's management restructuring, and an administrator was appointed to assist in this process. But this new challenge to those infiltrating our organisation was met with resistance and open threats against not only me but other senior staff pushing for management reform. Threats of death and personal violence against us by a colleague brought the conflict to boiling point. CRD became ungovernable. Our internal detractors appeared determined to facilitate the demise of CRD from within. I fought hard to give the organisation an image of stability and remained determined to protect the CRD brand. I had hoped for an amicable separation from our compromised staff. But this was not to be; instead of agreeing to leave, CRD's problem staff engaged in ever more malicious and destructive behaviour, making wild and undocumented allegations and even attacking me from a distance while I was attending the KP Intersessional Meeting in Washington in June 2012. In my absence many CRD assets were stripped – including a projector, cameras, scanners and other materials – in what appeared to be an attempt to cripple our operational capacity.

In August 2012 I was directly threatened with death by those responsible for this chaos in CRD. I was advised to report the threats to the Zimbabwe Republic Police by the CRD Board. A docket was opened and a case number (CR315/08/12) established. The individual in question was later arrested, but as often happens in Zimbabwe in the matter of politically-charged cases, the police officer who arrested the individual was persecuted instead. The docket was later said to be missing or destroyed. Meanwhile, surveillance by state security agents at my home intensified while conditions at work became extremely difficult.

It was at this point that a decision was reached to register a new organisation, as the CRD brand and organisational structures were beyond fixing. All five CRD Board members resigned and three of them moved along with me to register a new CSO, the Centre for Natural Resources Governance (CNRG), to carry on and expand the work we had started at CRD. CNRG is growing very fast, with on-going projects in five mining locations in Zimbabwe: Penhalonga, Hwange, Bikita, Mutoko and ARDA Transau, where families displaced from Marange's diamond fields were resettled. We remain vigilant – we've been told that threats are still being made against us – but we are also moving forward with our work. We have learned from the hard experience of CRD's past destruction at the hands of a sustained attack made by forces aligned to ZANU-PF, and through the party's evolving relations with powerful donors and diplomats. But we are strong in our belief that our struggle for rights and justice in Marange continues with new energy.

Conclusions: Unresolved rights, uncertain allies and shifting terrains

Between 2008 and 2010, human rights monitoring in Marange was considered dangerous, and many NGOs stayed away from the area. This changed in July 2010 when the KP formally acknowledged the role of civil society in monitoring the situation, leading to the formation of the LFP. Suddenly there was an opportunity for Zimbabwean civil society to be visible on the international stage; the LFP opened up new space for local civil society to engage on diamonds, and provided a new degree of protection for civil society in the face of the high risks associated with human rights monitoring in Marange. It also gave civil society an important platform for reporting directly to the KP Working Group on Monitoring.

But the expanded role of civil society also brought new challenges, particularly from within. There was much jostling for recognition as some CSOs presented themselves as the most suitable candidates to carry out the LFP work. More broadly, there was intensified in-fighting within local civil society as organisations competed for recognition and resources. From CRD's perspective, there was much fault-finding and underhand manoeuvring aimed at discrediting us, and creating space for Harare-based organisations to do the monitoring in Marange.

Donors contributed to the problem by funding certain organisations whose information and reports they had control over, and by actively criticising civil society reports which highlighted the continued occurrence of human rights abuses. Organisations with no monitoring activities on the ground in Marange were funded to carry out desk research which noted 'progress', whilst CRD reports were rubbished for allegedly exaggerating facts. One donor pledged to fund the activities of an organisation on KP related matters, including the LFP, but would not fund activities of the LFP as a consortium. This organisation was given money to carry out workshops aimed at educating the public about the mandate of the KP and its success in Marange. Consequently the LFP mandate was diluted, as donors used money to divide the coalition by sponsoring an individual organisation to do work that was supposed to be done collaboratively by seven organisations.

The 'opening' for civil society was also restricted by the way in which some structures at the KP continued to operate, and by the deepening politicisation of KP debates on Zimbabwe by the Zimbabwe Government. The LFP was required to present its reports to the Working Group on Monitoring where the government was represented by a strong delegation which included the Minister of Mines, the Permanent Secretary in the Ministry of Mines, the Attorney General, the Zimbabwe Broadcasting Corporation and many suspected CIO operatives and organisations sympathetic to ZANU-PF. This created an intimidating environment for civil society. The situation required strong characters who could withstand intimidation and who were ready to take on the risk associated with crossing ZANU-PF's path.

At the same time, ZANU-PF intensified its political attacks on opponents within the KP. Western governments were accused of using the KP to pursue their 'regime change agenda' aimed at toppling President Robert Mugabe from power, and local civil society groups were portrayed as their puppets. This put pressure on certain members of the LFP, who tried hard to please both ZANU-PF (for security reasons) and Western donors (for financial reasons) by giving Marange diamonds a clean bill of health whilst ignoring horrific human rights abuses, disappearing revenues and the plight of the relocated Marange villagers. Meetings with donors were conducted by certain members of the LFP in the absence of others. The briefings which CRD had carried out with diplomats in 2009 and 2010 were now being conducted by a Harare-based organisation whose mandate in the LFP was greatly influenced by Western donors. As a result Western diplomats started convincing the world that the situation in Marange had vastly improved, as evidenced by LFP reports whose contents they influenced.

By November 2011 it was apparent that the KP would lift the embargo on Marange diamonds. Several donors indicated that they were going to compromise on Zimbabwe so as to reach consensus and to save the KP from collapse, because Zimbabwe and many African countries were threatening to withdraw their KP membership. They also argued that lifting the ban and allowing Western countries to buy Marange diamonds would improve transparency since they would declare what they had paid to Zimbabwe. When it became clear that the KP was going to lift its ban on rough diamond exports in spite of the continuing rights abuses and lack of transparency, a founding civil society member of the KP, Global Witness, quit the grouping in November 2011. Another key figure in the formation of the KP, Ian Smillie, had resigned earlier in protest, citing the failure of the KP to reform and protect human rights.

In Zimbabwe, the silence of the main opposition party, the Movement for Democratic Change (MDC), and later its contradictory statements – which included occasional calls for the KP embargo to be lifted – further weakened the position of local CSOs within the KP. For instance, during the KP Intersessional Meeting in Kinshasa in 2011, where the Zimbabwe impasse took centre stage, the MDC issued a statement calling on the KP to lift the ban on Marange diamonds. It argued that doing so would help the country generate revenue and improve its record on diamond trading transparency. While ZANU-PF would send delegations of up to 30 people to KP meetings, no MDC official attended, with the exception of then Deputy Minister of Mines, Murisi Zvizvai, who went to the June 2009 Intersessional in Namibia – only to deny that artisanal miners and villagers had been killed by the army in Marange. On the other hand, Morgan Tsvangirai, Prime Minister during the life of the Government of National Unity (GNU) and President of the MDC, only demanded accountability from government on Marange diamonds when his party was at loggerheads with ZANU-PF.

During the life of the GNU and Prime Minister Tsvangirai's tenure in office, the MDC as a party never spoke out strongly about issues of transparency, accountability and human rights in Marange. Despite the country having an MDC Deputy Minister in the Ministry of Mines throughout the lifespan of the GNU, the MDC never published research on how the diamond revenues were disappearing. Neither, to my knowledge, did the MDC request a single meeting with local CSOs working on Marange diamonds in order to gain a deeper understanding of how diamond revenues were disappearing. Despite widespread evidence provided by both official sources like the MDC's Finance Minister Tendai Biti and CSOs that diamond revenues were missing and rights abuses were continuing in Marange, the Prime Minister never attended KP meetings. There were unsubstantiated rumours that some MDC officials in government had been bribed by ZANU-PF to not criticise operations in Marange.

The MDC's crushing defeat by ZANU-PF in the July 2013 election can be partly attributed to the latter's total control of Marange diamonds, which were used to help ZANU-PF regroup after the 2008 electoral humiliation at the hands of the MDC. The regaining of total control of government by ZANU-PF marked a new twist to the Marange saga. Donors started hinting that support would be given to CSOs working with the government. The European Union announced that it was removing the ZMDC from its sanctions list in order to pave the way for Marange diamonds to be sold in European markets. Some donors categorically stated that they would no longer fund any civil society activities on Marange; some local CSOs likewise began engaging with the ZANU-PF government in order to attract donor funding. Reports on Marange became lukewarm as civil society feared crossing the path of donors. Prominent civil society organisations working on Marange dealt in highly technical terms on KP related issues, while avoiding pertinent issues concerning human rights abuses, the forced and uncompensated displacement of families and the lack of transparency around diamond revenues.

Since 2011 there has been further fragmentation of civil society working on Marange, with CSOs putting their survival ahead of the interests of the community. Some have held private meetings with Ministry of Mines officials in an attempt to gain greater legitimacy with donors, thereby compromising their role in Marange itself. Recent years have also seen unfortunate efforts by some prominent Harare-based civil society interests to undermine and destabilise CSOs considered to be rivals. However, there have also been positive moves by some CSOs working on Marange to collaborate on research and advocacy. Joint research and lobbying activities have been undertaken to highlight the plight of the Marange community. In the period ahead, these efforts need to be cultivated to ensure that the civil society work on Marange is protected from compromise by donor interests and government pressure.

A rare find: sources of riches and ruin.

6

'FREE-FOR-ALL'?
ARTISANAL DIAMOND MINING AND
ECONOMIC REDISTRIBUTION ON THE EDGES OF
THE STATE, 2006-2008

Tinashe Nyamunda

Introduction

This chapter focuses on accumulation networks and redistribution effects among the artisanal diamond mining communities around Chiadzwa during what is commonly known as a 'free-for-all' phase of 2006-2008.[1] It argues that artisanal mining and trading activities, which emerged as an unintended consequence of government's efforts to remove and

---

1   This study is based on 28 structured interviews conducted between 2007 and 2012 with *magweja*, diamond buyers, community members, shopkeepers and wholesale firm employees, as well as lower ranking police and army officers and officials from the mining company African Consolidated Resources (ACR). Half of the interviews were held during the 'free-for-all' period and half afterwards. The range of respondents reflects the diversity of experiences of those within and on the margins of Marange's informal diamond economy. It was difficult to gain the trust of and speak with many in the illegal trade, including not only *magwejas* and dealers but also police; there was pervasive wariness of exposure, and as a result real names have not been used.

control artisanal mining in Marange beginning in 2006, established a thriving informal economy which directly benefited the rural and urban poor, particularly in Manicaland province but also more broadly in other parts of Zimbabwe; and that this economy was severely undermined by government's commercialisation of diamond mining in Marange after 2008. It explores the extent to which diamond mining's 'multiplier effects' spread beyond those individuals directly involved in the illicit diamond trade to wider communities in Manicaland and further afield, and charts the resilience and inventive strategies of artisanal miners in response to the state's efforts to contain or remove them from Marange. The discussion considers how, under the umbrella of state interventions – both legal and illegal – artisanal miners developed mining and trading structures which constituted a hidden diamond value chain that reached from the *magweja*[2] through local buying agents to international traders and diamond dealers.[3]

Benefits of the diamond economy have often been measured by the material acquisitions and improvement in the quality of life made possible by new income from mining – and by the erosion of material well-being in the absence of continued access to minerals. The Chiadzwa story before 2008 is dominated by narratives of wealth, redistributed earnings and a rising tide of activity in the rural economy; and after, by stories of how poor communities' incomes dried up following regularisation of mining activities. Contrasted with the national formal economy, the artisanal diamond trade demonstrates the power of local, informal forms of commercial organisation and the economic influence they wielded in the local communities of Mutare and surrounding districts. While it played a critical role in alleviating poverty and enabling new investment and entrepreneurial activity, artisanal mining's local developmental effects stood in sharp contrast to the post-2009 anti-developmental, state-managed commercial exploitation of Marange diamonds which evolved in response to a ban on Marange rough diamond exports by the Kimberley Process (KP) Certification Scheme.[4] Finally, and in contrast, the discus-

---

2   Colloquially, artisanal diamond miners were referred to as *magweja* (male) and *gwejeleen* (female), but *magweja* will be used to loosely refer to both. Chi*gweja* referred to the practice of actually digging for the mineral. See Nyota and Sibanda (2012).

3   Human Rights Watch (2009: 15).

4   Mukwakwami (2013).

sion explores the extent to which the informal diamond economy was 'developmental', and juxtaposes the 'free-for-all' phase period with the state-led commercialisation phase that began in 2009.

The chapter begins with the origins of the artisanal diamond rush and government's responses to it. It then explores the organisation of artisanal diamond digging and trading, and goes on to examine how the informal economy which emerged during this period produced multiplier effects for both formal and informal commerce in Marange and surrounding districts. It concludes by considering the aftermath of the artisanal period, and the developmental impact of the two main contrasting forms of diamond extraction in Marange.

The State, Artisanal Miners and the 'Free-for-All' Diamond Rush in Marange

Diverse economic and political factors provided the key motivating factors for the diamond rush experienced in Marange in 2006. These included the state's move to confront and control new commercial mining capital in Marange, the politics and rhetoric of 'indigenisation and empowerment', and a deepening economic and social crisis in Zimbabwe which saw household incomes and formal employment's viability plummet sharply. In the latter case, the decline of household income in poorer communities in rural and urban areas was compounded by disruption of the commercial farming sector by the Fast Track land resettlement programme, and turmoil associated with Operation Murambatsvina in several urban areas in 2005.[5] With the decline of the rural economy, the pressures for obtaining 'off-farm' income increased, and informal sector diamond mining soon represented an alluring prospect for income support. It was not long before government and senior state officials, recognising the inherent economic value of Marange, moved to challenge the role of the burgeoning informal diamond mining sector. By 2008 it had been effectively displaced by means of state-sanctioned violence, legal intervention and other forms of regulation.

An initial challenge to government was the dislodging of African

---

5 See, for example, Vambe (2008).

Consolidated Resources (ACR),[6] the mining house which acquired an Exclusive Prospecting Order (EPO) for an important part of the diamond fields following the exit of De Beers in 2006. When the existence of artisanal diamonds became publicly known in that year, government aimed to displace ACR both legally and by resorting to political means through the invocation of indigenisation and empowerment principles. At a rally attended by Manicaland Governor Tinaye Chigudu, Minerals Marketing Corporation of Zimbabwe (MMCZ) Director Onesimo Moyo and Minister of Mines and Minerals Amos Midzi, officials argued that ACR was a British company with no right to exploit the indigenous resources of the country.[7] On 25 September 2006, the Deputy Minister of Mines, Tinos Rusere, encouraged artisanal miners to continue mining and selling their diamonds to government.[8] Communicating through the local media, Rusere encouraged local villagers to start mining in place of 'foreign' mining capital 'as long as it benefited the local inhabitants' families'.[9]

Some saw the state's actions in the context of populist politics: 'as it had done with white owned farms in 2000, in 2006 it did with white owned mines – ZANU PF played the race card'.[10] For others, government's cancellation of ACR's EPO undermined conventional property rights within the context of discourses of land ownership in the post 2000 period, and deployed a parallel rhetoric of 'indigenisation' to justify seemingly extra-legal interventions.[11] In the process, land patronage networks were reorganised in the Communal Areas affected by artisanal diamond claims: where local inhabitants claimed traditional tenure, the state principally weakened it, assuming the role of guardian of the land and its resources. In the uncertainty of tenure rights which resulted, Chi-

---

6 African Consolidated Resources was an AIM-listed multi-commodity resource development company focused on Zimbabwe since 2004. ACR claimed to develop projects in gold, nickel, platinum, copper and phosphate in Zimbabwe, and billed itself as utilising its 'first mover advantage' to acquire assets at various stages of development. See http://minesite.com/company/african-consolidated-resources-plc.

7 'Diamond Rush', *The Post*, 6 October 2006.

8 Human Rights Watch (2009: 14).

9 'Diamond Rush', *The Post*, 6 October 2006.

10 R. Bates (2012).

11 Nyamunda and Mukwambo (2012: 156). For a summary of the secretive nature of the state's involvement in Chiadzwa, see, 'Chiadzwa mining: A tale of shady deals and characters', *Zimbabwe Independent,* 19 March 2010.

adzwa was laid open for thousands of *magweja* who soon descended on the diamond fields with government's tacit blessing.

The term 'free-for-all' denoted the organisation of production and trade, in which people could get involved in diamond digging, buying, smuggling or become part of the commerce that exploited the operators. The networks of extraction and trade soon came to involve the agencies meant to supervise and uproot 'illegal' diggers: the police and other state security agencies, including the army and intelligence personnel. Direct participation in syndicates and indirect earnings through bribery became a feature of the accumulation matrix in Marange. State security deployed to Marange was porous, and this made the diamond fields accessible to a broad community of *magweja*.

Artisanal mining in the 'free-for-all' period, 2006

While the state had initially hoped to use the MMCZ to regulate the selling of diamonds produced by informal diggers it soon found itself contesting for control of the diamond trade with an emerging illicit network and an economy on the margins.[12] Many *magweja* were suspicious of the intentions of the state and the role of the MMCZ. Some argued that the state wanted to acquire diamonds on the cheap without heavily

---

12   Although the exact wealth of Chiadzwa or what was accrued from artisanal activity is not known, Gideon Gono, former Reserve Bank Governor and member of the Joint Operations Command (JOC), once estimated the value of smuggled diamonds to be $400 million in 2007 alone. See Martin and Taylor (2010: 17). See also 'Zim loses $400 m in diamonds', *News24.com*, 5 April, 2007.

investing in production, leaving *magweja* to assume a high burden of the risk. Disenchantment and uncertainty over the MMCZ's capacity to pay good prices in cash for stones quickly opened a space for illegal buyers and dealers who could offer better prices and pay immediately in foreign currency.[13] Many *magweja* were also skeptical given the experience in other informal mining activity, notably gold, where state engagement and regulation had been seen as oscillating between tolerance and intolerance, at the unpredictable political and economic expediency of the state.[14] As a result, the MMCZ was soon pushed to the edges of the market, and state-*magweja* relations became increasingly characterised by violence – a recognition as well of failure on the state's part to contain the informal trade using its institutional and regulatory powers of political suasion and financial incentives.

The state shifted from supporting 'indigenisation' in diamond mining to emphasising the criminality of artisanal activity. A key initiative which underscored the change in approach was 'Operation Chikorokoza Chapera' ('End to Illegal Panning') in 2007. For *magweja*, Chiadzwa increasingly became an 'enter at your own risk' area.[15] By 2008, it was reported that the head of the Zimbabwe Republic Police in Mutare, Chief Superintended O.C. Govo, had issued instructions to 'shoot on sight' illegal miners found in the diamond fields.[16] The arbitrary arrest of local community members suspected of mining became commonplace,[17] a practice which continued to the time of writing.[18] Elsewhere in Zimbabwe, informal activity and economy irregularly operated on the edges of the state, not least artisanal mining in such minerals as gold.[19] In practice, the state shifted between tolerance and intolerance, underscored by chronic unemployment and the broader context of a rising social and

---

13 Interview with Dombo.

14 See, for example, Jones (2010); see also Mawowa (2014).

15 Interview with Dombo.

16 Human Rights Watch (2009: 24-25).

17 Ibid, p. 25.

18 'Spirits Angry at Government over Diamonds says Chief', *Zimbabwe Situation*, 22 June 2014, available at http://www.zimbabwesituation.com/news/ zimsit_w_bulawayo24-news-spirits-angry-at-govt-over-diamonds-says-chief/ Accessed 24 June 2014.

19 See, for example, Jones (2010); see also Mawowa (2014).

economic crisis.[20]

'Push' factors also contributed to the rush of people into Chiadzwa. These included the prevailing economic crisis at that time characterised by record inflation, unprecedented unemployment which peaked at over 90 per cent, worsening food insecurity, displacement in many areas including commercial farms, as well as political intolerance by the state.[21] Chimonyo et. al suggest that the government's 2005 Operation Murambatsvina, displacing more than 700,000 families, was an important factor for many who went to the diamond fields.[22] More broadly, the increasing importance of 'off-farm income' for rural livelihoods since independence was reflected in the rising significance of gold panning by rural dwellers; Marange represented vital new opportunities in this regard.[23]

Informants in this study insisted on the importance of the crisis of household livelihoods in motivating their involvement in 'free-for-all' mining.[24] One *gweja* said those days were good and the risk involved was worth it, given the alternative; 'Kusiri kufa ndekupi kana usina basa', ('if you are unemployed, you are as good as dead anyway'). He argued that 'if only those in charge created formal employment and offered us jobs paying enough to sustain our families', there would be no need for artisanal mining. He argued further that the way things were, 'a person is prepared to die, be bitten by dogs, be shot by mossback or guns or even have tunnels collapsing on him'.[25] Another argued that he was prepared to deal with the consequences of getting into Chiadzwa because it was the only livelihood alternative that could help him sustain his family.[26]

20   For an example of this shift in informal gold mining, see Mabhena (2102: 221).

21   Raftopoulos (2009: 219).

22   Chimonyo, et al. (2012: 8). Operation Murambatsvina was deployed by the ZANU PF state to destroy illegal structures in the country's cities. These included market stalls, informal roadside sheds for furniture making or other activities, tuck shops, unplanned and unapproved houses and backyard rooms.

23   Mabhena (2012: 230). Citing the case of southern Matabeleland, Mabhena suggests that the phenomenon of 'off-farm income' had been growing for more than thirty years, fuelled by the cyclical and uncertain nature of crop farming in poorer areas, and the demonstrated wealth effects of those who worked in gold panning.

24   Interview with David, Chakohwa shopping centre, 18 August 2009.

25   Ibid.

26   Ibid.

Although it is difficult to estimate the precise number of informal diggers who descended on Chiadzwa, the Zimbabwe Mining Development Corporation (ZMDC) found during an exploration exercise in December 2006 that up to 25,000 were already in the fields.[27] At the peak of artisanal mining in 2008, some reported, there were up to 35,000 miners and traders in the area.[28] The diggers were drawn from both Zimbabwe's urban areas and the surrounding districts of Chimanimani, Chipinge and Buhera,[29] and comprised both the unemployed and those employed in the formal sector, where real incomes were increasingly fragile and in decline. An important number of *magweja* were veterans of informal gold mining – the so called *makorokoza* – from various far-flung districts of the country. In the early days especially, these numbers sometimes included whole families. In others, it involved school teachers and many of their students, severely eroding time spent in the classroom – an alarming development which illustrated the sudden and deep impact of the diamond rush on local communities, as well as their growing desperation in a time of crisis.[30]

While Operation Chikorokoza Chapera and successive state interventions contributed to increasing tensions between *magweja* and government, *magweja* devised strategies to manage their volatile interactions with the state. Many were effective and adaptive and, as a result, various government-led eviction operations largely failed to produce their desired results until late 2008.

Inventive Organising for Flexible Accumulation

The Marange situation illustrates not only the ambiguities that can exist between formal and informal economies, but also how strategies and imperatives can shift through time. In the context of informal mining, many illicit arrangements proved to be effective avenues of local accumulation. For Duffy, while informal and illegal gem mining 'might look anarchic and chaotic … it clearly has a logic and organisational form of its own that roams outside the formal structures of governance through the networks of states, international NGOs and donors'.[31] While poten-

---

27 Chimonyo, et.al. (2012: 8).
28 Human Rights Watch (2009: 14).
29 Katsaura (2010: 109).
30 See the chapter by Ruguwa in this volume.
31 Duffy (2005: 289).

119

tially highly productive in their extraction, artisanal miners nonetheless have often been the most visible and vulnerable in the chain of production and marketing.[32] Zimbabwe's *magweja*, located at the bottom of the rough diamond value chain, proved to be the foundations for wider illicit networks as part of their survival strategies. Following Kaplinsky and Morris, a 'value chain' refers to 'a full range of activities which are required to bring a product or service from conception, through the different phases of production (involving a combination of physical transformation and the input of various producer services), to delivery to final consumers...'.[33] Value chain analysis is a critical tool 'to ask important questions about the distribution of power and value along the chain and is therefore eminently capable of addressing the agency of workers and small producers'.[34] As in the case of Chiadzwa, analysis of local value chains 'acknowledges the political and competitive nature of relationships involved'.[35] Diamond digging and trading was illicit, with diggers at the bottom of the chain vulnerable and at the greatest risk, whereas some of the buyers who realised higher returns went to great pains, usually with little success, to remain unknown because of the illicit nature of their activities. The Mutare buyers tended to sell their stones to foreign buyers, typically in Mozambique and sometimes also in South Africa, where they would then ascend along the global value chains.[36]

A highly nuanced process of class formation emerged around informal rough diamond trading structures, wherein trading chains were sometimes facilitated by political connections. Influential 'strong men', particularly politicians or those connected to them, emerged as important dealers, their survival of state harassment and trading success often coming at the expense of the state's own formal revenue channels. Successful traders not only required skills, but also state and ruling party contacts,

---

32   Machonachie (2008: 9). As Machonachie observed in the case of Sierra Leone, it was the diggers who were the most vulnerable, often working 'at the bottom of the supply chain... endur[ing] dangerous conditions ... liv[ing] on less than a dollar a day'.

33   Kaplinsky and Morris (2001: 4).

34   Mitchell et al. (2011: 10). For a broader analysis positioning African with the global value chains, see Gibbon and Ponte (2005).

35   Ibid.

36   Interview with Mati; see also Martin and Taylor (2010: 45).

and had to be strategically positioned along the chain.[37]

For the *magweja* who arrived in Marange in 2006-7, the diamond fields appeared to be a source of salvation. They were inspired by the promise of improvements in the quality of life, of formal and informal commercial opportunities that emerged and the wealth accumulated, especially by the diamond buyers as reflected in the lavish lifestyles they had. Yet the practice of informal mining and the conditions surrounding it were far less appealing.[38] The reality was characterised by difficult conditions and violence perpetrated by the law enforcement and military arms of the state, which secured Chiadzwa and limited access by *magweja*. Those who managed to gain access evaded state authorities, bribed or worked in syndicates with them. The relationships between security personnel and *magweja* were highly unpredictable, volatile and frequently characterised by violence.[39]

The state's shift towards intolerance of artisanal mining reflected the view that the commodity started and ended with the wrong hands: from informal miners to foreign-linked international buyers, Marange's rough diamonds were falling almost entirely beyond the formal reach – and benefit – of the state. Ironically, the state, through the MMCZ, initially encouraged artisanal mining in Marange in 2006, at a time when government was aiming to marginalise ACR and its legal claim in the diamond fields; moreover, MMCZ had actively traded with *magweja* when it had sufficient resources to buy on the informal market. Once the MMCZ had itself been marginalised from the heart of the trade by its uncompetitive prices and insufficient liquidity and purchasing resources, it lobbied for the securing of Chiadzwa by state security agencies and later, commercial mining operations nominated by the state.

Magweja new to the fields faced two sets of challenges: on the one hand, finding and mining available ground and linking into illegal trading networks; on the other, evading violence in the form of both sporadic raids by mostly hostile state security agencies, and attacks and intimidation carried out by *magombiro*, diggers turned gangs of thieves of

---

37   Interview with Bothwell, Romeo's Braai Spot just outside Mutare Urban on the Mutare Harare Highway, 10 August 2009.

38   See for example, 'Is Marange the Biblical Canaan?', *The Manica Post*, 9 November 2007.

39   Interview with Musweweshiri, Chakohwa shopping centre, 10 August 2008.

which the most notorious were the *maShurugwi*.[40] In addition, there were considerable challenges associated with living in the bush for extended periods without formal housing, water, food and other supportive infrastructure. For one digger, 'the whole process was like being in jail'.[41]

A key strategy for meeting these layered challenges was the formation of alliances known as 'syndicates'. Syndicates' membership ranged from three or four, to fifteen or more. Solo diggers were rare. The first syndicates in early 2006 consisted primarily of kin members; many became known by and were consolidated through the geographical origins of most of their members, and their own relations of trust, kinship and culture.[42] However, while familiarity remained a major factor in syndicate formation, increasingly the latter cut across kin linkages and areas of origin, as mining activities became more extensive and dangerous.[43] Mining was normally conducted at night, under cover of darkness. Depending on the syndicate, the division of labour typically involved two or three syndicate members to dig, collect and transport the ore to safe areas, where it would be sifted for diamonds.[44] Some members were placed on watch for security personnel. In other instances, female members were sometimes forced into sexual transactions with police or military officers in exchange for access, and for the release of captured syndicate members.[45] In most cases, the women provided these sexual services under duress, to avoid capture or gain access to the fields.[46]

While defence against violence, theft and the harsh living environment were important contributing factors, the major motivating feature in developing syndicates was their proven efficiency in mining and trading.[47] Although some *magweja* informants reported that relations within syndicates were usually cordial, others reiterated that tensions were born of cheating and lack of trust. This was a result of different power

---

40 That is, people from Shurugwi district in the Midlands Province, an area associated with a history of gold panning. See Nyota and Sibanda (2012: 140).

41 Interview with Musweweshiri. See also Nyamunda et al. (2012).

42 Ruguwa (2013).

43 Interview with Musweweshiri.

44 Partnership Africa Canada (2010: 15); See also Nyota and Sibanda (2012: 141).

45 Interview with Aggripa, Chakohwa shopping centre, 10 August 2007.

46 Katsaura (2010: 118).

47 Nyamunda et al. (2012: 124).

relations within the syndicates, especially during the penultimate phase of the 'free-for-all'. Where *magweja* worked alone with little state interference, especially in the earlier days, relations were relatively egalitarian. But as the state officials got increasingly involved in these illicit activities, soldiers and police were empowered by their status as weapon holders and by having access to legal channels or authority, to enforce the will of the state. This explains why some *magweja* syndicates were more comfortable with paying once-off bribes to gain access instead of working as part of soldier and police syndicates.[48] However, towards the end, with increasing militarisation and policing of the fields, working within police and military syndicates increasingly became an inevitable option for many who sought protection from the state law enforcement authority. Some reported that the excessive demands of police and soldiers involved in syndicates were a frequent cause of tension and disturbance within the groupings, typically around issues of dividing the spoils of a syndicate's production.[49]

Law enforcement and security personnel syndicates' relations with *magweja* were very fluid. *Magweja* acknowledged the prevailing unequal and disadvantageous power relations with state security personnel. These relationships were fraught with seeming contradictions, and yet a clear logic of power hierarchies lay within what appeared to be a disorderly arrangement. While one *gweja* expressed that he was 'used to the police, they are suffering like us so we must grease their palms for them to also survive',[50] a police officer noted that 'given our meagre salaries, which are worth less than five US dollars, we have to exploit this opportunity through bribes and working with *magweja* because if we don't, we will suffer – but when called upon to act in police operations, we will effectively perform our duty'.[51]

Yet the arbitrary and often brutal nature of state security forces' interactions with *magweja* remained the most common experience. The military, especially, were implicated in cases of forced labour, notably after

---

48   Interview with Gringo, Chakohwa shopping centre, 10 August 2008.

49   Interview with Mapaso, Chakohwa, shopping centre, 10 August 2008.

50   Ibid.

51   Interview with Gringo; see also, Human Rights Watch (2009: 21). The claim that the police officers' salary was less than US$5 was made during the period of hyperinflation when the Zimbabwe dollar was still in use before its official demonetisation in 2009.

2008, involving former syndicate members lured by the prospect of sharing proceeds with security personnel guarding the fields.[52] In the process they perpetrated many human rights abuses, including the forced labour of an estimated 300 children forced to carry ore for 11 hours a day, and the killing of over 214 diggers from 27 October to 16 November 2008.[53] Officials at the Zimbabwe-Mozambique border were also implicated as they facilitated the passage of traders to smuggle and sell their gems to dealers in Mozambique en route to international markets.[54] Others accumulated bribes they demanded at checkpoints and roadblocks along the Mutare-Masvingo highway that led to and from Chiadzwa.[55] During 'Operation Wakachiwana Kupi' ('Where did you get this?'), some uniformed forces raided rural shops and seized stock and cash from shopkeepers.[56] In other police actions the property of suspected diamond dealers was seized, ranging from small household possessions and cellphones, to motor vehicles.[57] Violent assaults were not uncommon. One notable case was that of Mutare businessman Maxwell Mandebvu-Mabota, whose vehicle was siezed along with other valuables and US$11,000 in cash; he would die after being beaten by soldiers.[58] Among *magweja*, reports were widespread of seized property and detentions by police in the pursuit of bribes.[59]

Despite these negative widespread experiences, the *magwejas*' trading of stones involved an intricate collusion with police and military personnel. Covert diamond sales, commonly made in the fields, local rural shopping centres or in Mutare, involved members of the security forces in different ways. Police were crucial not just in facilitating access for *magweja*, but also for buyers who required information on police operations and investigations, and who sometimes sought to instrumentalise the police in turf wars between buyers.[60] Some police engaged directly

---

52 Interview with Gunman, Chakohwa shopping centre, 10 August 2008.
53 See Human Rights Watch (2009: 4, 28).
54 Towriss (2013: 100).
55 Interview with Gringo.
56 Interview with Twoboy, Chakohwa shopping centre, 20 August, 2009.
57 Interview with Ngonjo, Chakohwa shopping centre, 10 August 2008; see also Katsaura (2010: 114).
58 Human Rights Watch (2009: 34).
59 Interview with Mati, Greenside, Mutare, 14 September 2010.
60 Interview with Gringo.

with foreign buyers, becoming important contacts for links between foreign buyers and middlemen in Mutare.[61] Reports by NGOs indicate that the state was implicated in these illicit arrangements, but to what degree is not clear.[62]

From the fields, diamond trading ascended into global value chains through local diamond barons in Mutare, and into Mozambique, specifically through the hotel Vila de Manica, among other places, en route to international diamond markets.[63] Those traders closer to the international export gateways generally fared better in earning power from the illicit trade. In and around Marange, prices for rough diamonds were relatively low compared, for instance, to the higher ends of the market in Mozambique. Industrial diamonds tended to attract a specific price, initially around $15, eventually rising to as much as $30.[64] Clearer stones were sold by the carat and this was visually determined by both the buyer and the seller. Senior members or those chosen as representatives within the syndicates negotiated prices with buyers. *Magweja* earnings from stones were outstripped by traders further up the distribution network. For example, it was reported that one syndicate of four Chakohwa residents struck three clear diamonds which were sold for $400 to a rural middle-level buyer, who then resold them for $1,200 to a Mutare-based trader with links to high-paying international buyers in Manica, Mozambique.[65] However, while traders reported that windfalls sometimes occurred, their profits were typically marginal and earnings depended mostly on pushing higher volumes of stones.[66]

Alongside the extraction and trade in diamonds grew an economy that indirectly promoted enlarged markets in Chiadzwa, rooted in the circulation of money among locals and benefiting far-flung families and communities. The focus now turns to this informal diamond economy.

61   Human Rights Watch (2009: 21).
62   Ibid, pp. 51-52; Partnership Africa Canada (2010: 15).
63   Partnership Africa Canada (2010: 17 and 19).
64   Interview with Mati's sister (also a buyer introduced to the trade by her brother), Greenside, Mutare, 14 September 2010.
65   Interview with Emmanuel, Mutare, 4 July 2011.
66   Ibid.

The 'Magweja Economy' and its Redistributive Effects

Diamond mining during the 'free-for-all' phase produced a thriving informal economy at the edges of state. 'Edges of the state' refers to the notion that the informal diamond economy was initially officially encouraged by the state but later tolerated unevenly under the terms of new legal interventions and the evolving activities of state security institutions. The concept of 'irregularity' is used to understand a situation in which the formal and informal intersect; for example, collusion between police and artisanal miners.[67] Whereas Sachikonye argues that there was 'no structure or mechanism to ensure that the local community bene-fit[ed] either directly or indirectly', concluding that there was need for formalisation of diamonds to 'benefit the whole country',[68] *magweja* and other villagers and rural business informants told a different story. For villagers and rural businesspeople in Manicaland, the artisanal diamond economy became a crucial livelihood alternative to local marginal agriculture in an ecological zone typified by poor soils and low rainfall.[69] In their view, the state's rationalisation of diamond mining in Marange after 2009 not only denied them the financial benefits they had enjoyed, but also failed to redirect diamond revenues to the national fiscus in meaningful, clear ways.

For most respondents, the 'free-for-all' period is fondly remembered for the largely unregulated wealth that revolved around diamond mining and related commerce, manifested in economic redistributive effects. In all economies there is a circular flow of income and spending. In Chiadzwa and surrounding districts, and more broadly in the rest of the country, artisanal diamond income was redistributed through both short-term consumption and longer-term investment and savings. *Magweja* consumed their earnings in basic necessities and services, and pursued multiple opportunities for income generating and household investment.[70] Other existing rural entrepreneurs also benefited from a rising tide of dia-

---

67   The concept was adapted from Roitman (2005); other forms of irregularity can be seen on cross-border trade and movements as demonstrated by Nyamunda (2014).

68   Sachikonye (2007: 15).

69   Poverty Reduction Forum Trust (2013: 25).

70   Interview with Gringo.

mond-generated consumption.[71] Some reported a wave of local investment in new commercial and private construction, along with renovation of existing business and household infrastructure.[72]

The economic benefits of the diamond economy were visible most immediately in Mutare urban and rural as well as the surrounding districts of Chimanimani, Chipinge and Buhera.[73] At Chakohwa shopping centre in Chimanimani, the improvement in community income was evident in increased consumption patterns. Formal and informal business expanded to meet the demand produced by the enhanced propensity to consume by large numbers of *magweja*. *Magweja* used their income in a variety of ways, ranging from buying foodstuffs and basics, something that was increasingly difficult to do given the harsh economic times produced by the Zimbabwe crisis especially after 2005[74] to the acquisition of motor vehicles. One informant noted that he first used his share of syndicate diamond money to pay *roora* (bridal price), subsequent sojourns provided funds which he used to improve his homestead and pay for siblings' school fees.[75] Eventually he invested in an up-market vehicle – though it was later lost in an accident.[76] Another *gweja* told how he and his family used diamond earnings to invest in a lorry, eventually expanding with transport earnings and new diamond funds to build a thriving transport business.[77] Yet others used their money to start small shops, or cross-border businesses, some of which collapsed with the passing of the diamond boom.[78] Although *magweja* were frequently maligned for conspicuous alcohol consumption, the extent to which their income improved their families' lives was a frequent point of reference

---

71   Interview with Murehwa, Bhadhela Wholesale employee, Mutare, 17 January 2009.

72   Chimonyo (2012: 10).

73   Due to resource constraints, most of the interviews conducted for this chapter took place in Chakowa, Chimanimani District and Mutare urban. However, the few interviews held in other growth points reflect similar characteristics.

74   Poverty Reduction Forum Trust (2013: 29).

75   Interview with Musweweshiri.

76   Ibid. The respondent referred to his 'VW Jetta 2 CLI, my powerful, beautiful machine'.

77   Interview with Bernard, Harare, February 2010.

78   The author lived at Chakohwa shopping centre for most of 2008.

for this study's informants.[79]

Income derived by security forces from bribes or involvement with digging syndicates was also evident. Respondents reported that some police and army personnel invested in new business ventures, including commuter taxis.[80] According to Gringo, police officers 'fell over each other' and in some cases bribed superior officers to be posted to Chiadzwa so they would have an opportunity to extract capital which could then be used to purchase otherwise inaccessibly expensive assets.[81] Cars, in particular, became a target and status symbol for those more successful in diamond digging and the low ranked police officers and soldiers who extracted value from *magweja*.

ZNA with detained informal miners: containment or collusion?

Local markets for goods and services expanded rapidly. The range of consumer goods and services provided was varied and extensive, and became the manifestation of a multiplier effect in the diamond economy. They included marijuana, spiritual cleansing and healing services, commercial sex work, drinking water, foodstuffs and accommodation.[82] Traders came from as far as Harare and Masvingo to take advantage

79   From interviews with shop owners, Chakohwa shopping centre, at different times in 2008.
80   Interview with Ngonjo.
81   Interview with Gringo.
82   Katsaura (2010: 116).

of the burgeoning market. One woman reported travelling more than 300 km to Chiadzwa to sell a 20 litre bucket of fish, earning a 100% profit for her efforts.[83] At most shopping centres close to Chiadzwa, new shops were built and informal markets thrived which in addition to food-stuffs, used clothing and electrical goods, included roadside currency exchanges and even a car sales outlet.[84] While there was competition with local businesspeople who pressured the municipality to remove the informal traders who did not pay rates, the manner in which the informal trade persisted suggest that trading was lucrative.[85] Some locals provided lodgings for both *magweja* and security and other government personnel stationed in the area.

'Twoboy', a local shop owner, recalled how he ended up failing to meet the demand for goods in his shop, forcing him to adjust his trips to wholesalers from less than twice a week to daily travel to Mutare, 72 km away.[86] Bread deliveries by established suppliers became a source of competition among business people, who sought advantage in expand-ed stocks: some shop owners bribed delivery personnel to accord them priority in the provision of supplies so that they could corner access to rising market demand. In one shop, demand rose from four dozen loaves per day to more than 30 dozen, even though prices had doubled.[87] Female food vendors provided a secondary local wholesale market for bread, margarine and other basic foodstuffs sold to diggers in the fields. Other traders dealt in alcoholic beverages purchased from local bottle stores and informal brewers, selling them at considerable profit to *magweja*.[88]

Individuals and companies in Mutare also cashed in on the secondary circulation of informal mining revenues. Some diamond dealers became famously wealthy through the diamond trade, for example, the late Both-

---

83   Interview with Chiedza, Norton, 12 February 2012.

84   Trade in cars was evidently brisk. Even a car wash business was estab-lished. Interview with Twoboy, Chakohwa, 20 August 2009.

85   These views were expressed at a meeting held between local author-ities and Chakohwa businesspeople in August 2008. There were also many security concerns as a result of the huge number of people who flocked to Chiadzwa via Chakohwa shopping centre.

86   Interview with Twoboy.

87   Interview with Mbuya Mukwada, Chakohwa shopping centre, 13 August 2008.

88   Trade in *Lawidzani*, a home-brewed Mozambiquan spirit, was particularly brisk. Interview with Mbuya Mukwada.

well Hlahla and Tarzin Machingura.[89] In an interview, Hlahla noted that the diamond trade had turned his fortunes around and that he had benefited from his connections with other foreign traders such as the Lebanese buyers stationed in Manica.[90] Another dealer explained how he acquired real estate and that he no longer considered cars to be an important asset as he had many.[91] Unlike the *magweja* who shared earnings within their syndicate, the dealers profited from economies of scale.

Even larger shops and wholesalers benefited from improved sales. Shops in districts surrounding Mutare reported rapid inventory turnover.[92] Other large entities such as DairyBoard, the milk products supplier, reportedly also exploited the lucrative captive market by supplying directly into Chiadzwa.[93] Improved business meant increased staff complements to help cope with demand. Bhadhela, a prominent local wholesaler whose full-time staff almost doubled due to Chiadzwa-based custom, was one such case.[94] Later, however, with the suppression of artisanal mining after 2008, the once booming Mutare branch of the wholesaler would close.

But not everyone benefited from the burgeoning local artisanal economy. Some locals interviewed complained that their lives were disrupted by the '*magweja* nuisance'.[95] The *magweja* culture was accused of undermining, and even replacing, local practices with a new social order. Although cordial relations prevailed when *magweja* managed to strike diamonds, they were accused of being thieves and cheats when the fields were not rewarding.[96] Their activities also led to the rise in the cost of living for the locals, some of whom did not directly benefit from diamond proceeds. Livestock and grain prices went up, including basic commodities. *Magweja* were also blamed for sexual misconduct, violation of sa-

89 Martin and Taylor (2010: 17).
90 Interview with Bothwell.
91 Interview with Mati.
92 Interview with Twoboy. Also indicated in an interview with Murehwa.
93 'Business Boom at Chiadzwa', *The Manica Post*, 10 November 2006.
94 In contrast, a Bhadhela employee in Harare indicated no comparable increase in business in the capital, suggesting that the diamond-fed demand was the key reason for business expansion in the Mutare branch of the company. Interview with Murewa.
95 Interview with Mbuya vekwaMukwada.
96 Chimonyo et al. (2012: 10). This was also frequently referred to in the interviews.

cred traditional and religious practices, use of foul language which was considered disrespectful of the rural customs of diction and etiquette, trespassing through villagers' fields, and prompting the breakdown of family structures and values.[97] Violence and the threat of violence by the police and army, but also by *magombiro*, manifested in occasional beatings and arrests of villagers, continued to cast a shadow over local communities as they were caught in the crossfire among state security, *magweja*, *magombiro* and traders.[98]

The closure of Chiadzwa to informal diamond digging in early November 2008 led to the drying up of commerce, not just in Chakohwa, but also in Mutare and the districts immediately surrounding Marange. Few locals benefited from the transition after 2008 to the commercialised management of diamond mining; most suffered distinct disadvantages. In addition to the loss of direct mining revenues and indirect commerce in local communities, the local informal economy was also bruised by the relatively weak flows of capital from the new mining companies into surrounding local areas. Multiplier effects of the informal diamond economy quickly disappeared. Under the post-2008 dispensation, a parliamentary investigation found, diamonds provided little benefit to Marange's local communities and businesses.[99]

Some informants noted that local *magweja* soon began selling recently acquired assets to supplement their falling income. One diamond dealer who had invested in haulage trucks reportedly had disposed of his entire fleet by late 2012.[100] Commuter transport businesses which had once thrived by plying the route to the shopping centres such as Chakohwa, from where *magweja* and other informal traders would walk to the diamond fields, plummeted. By March 2009 at least five businesses had collapsed at Chakohwa shopping centre; the thriving informal market also shrank, leaving only fruit and vegetable vendors.[101] Only a handful still benefited, for example Chief Newman Chiadzwa who made a windfall from 43,000 carats diamonds worth millions of dollars; however for most of the Chiadzwa community, the story was one of despair, featur-

---

97 Ibid.

98 Human Rights Watch (2009: 25). See also 'State Terror Continues in Marange', *Now Daily*, 24 January 2014.

99 Parliament of Zimbabwe (2013).

100 Interview with Mati.

101 Interview with Twoboy.

ing diamond-induced poverty and displacement from traditional lands by new commercial mining entities ushered into Marange by government. Although government had agreed in the KP's Joint Work Plan of 2009 to make space for supervised small-scale mining, this failed to materialise and the prohibition on artisanal extraction in Marange remained in place. While there was evidence of some continued artisanal activity, it was on a minor scale compared to the 'free-for-all' period.

In sum, after the commercialisation of mining in Chiadzwa in 2008, an artisanal-fuelled economic 'boom' was replaced by an enduring recession and heightened levels of local livelihood insecurity. While the broader economic crisis in Zimbabwe was temporarily eased with the introduction of the multi-currency system dominated by the US dollar and the subsequent containment of hyperinflation in 2009 during the period of the Government of National Unity, the respondents interviewed after these developments indicated that the local situation had become dire in comparison to the 'free-for-all' period. National economic stabilisation may have removed a key factor which motivated people to head to the diamond fields in 2006-08, but it did not contribute significantly to the rebuilding of a formal economy at the local level in Marange.[102] Instead, economic activity associated with the new commercial mining houses in Marange soon became the source of controversy, when it failed to generate the kind of local benefits residents had been told to expect. Rather than development, locals experienced deepening crisis, dislocation and decline. The displacement and forced removal of hundreds of families to a distant, poorly-served relocation camp underscored the emerging crisis in the social economy.[103] There were tales of woe from those who were taken into employment by the new mining firms; for example, reports of worker exploitation emerged at GyeNyame Resources, where 400 workers went ten months without pay while their managers commanded hefty salaries.[104] More broadly, revelations of low returns to the state treasury from joint venture mining firms in Marange scandalised government.

102   Pilossof (2009: 294-299).

103   See contributions by Madebwe and Madebwe, and Chiponda and Saunders, in this collection. See also 'Marange Voices', a video documentary produced in 2015 by the Zimbabwe Environmental Law Association see: https://www.youtube.com/watch?v=NKU3riWz6nI.

104   Elias Mambo, 'Diamond miners unpaid for ten months', *Zimbabwe Independent,* 13 December 2013.

The principles of government's indigenisation and economic empowerment policies seemed to go unheeded in Chiadzwa, where the state's involvement in joint ventures with foreign diamond miners produced few benefits to those dispossessed of their land and livelihoods.

Conclusion

The 'discovery' of diamonds in Marange in 2006 and the subsequent artisanal diamond rush in a period of 'free-for-all' mining resulted in an informal economy with important economic multiplier effects. Rationalisation of mining through the commercialisation of diamond extraction and trading effectively decimated the alternative mining-fed livelihoods of tens of thousands of Zimbabweans – including informal miners, retailers and vendors, and formal and informal businesses in Manicaland and beyond. Employment levels fell sharply and rapidly, and agricultural production in Chiadzwa itself was restricted. The direct economic benefits of Chiadzwa diamonds, once scattered unevenly but widely, now accrued to narrow commercial and politically connected elites and, notably, foreign commercial interests.

As the survey of respondents undertaken here demonstrated, locals saw the alternative informal economy which emerged in Chiadzwa in 2006-08 as one which had the capacity to provide new and expanded economic opportunities for many of the unemployed and under-employed in the communities of Marange district and beyond. In contrast, the rationalisation of diamond mining after 2009 became synonymous with spatial and economic displacement and impoverishment. In 2006, ZANU-PF had deployed the rhetoric of indigenisation to encourage informal mining to meet its short-term aims of shoring up political credibility and vanquishing legal claims to diamond fields by a title-holder. But soon the party shifted, using the vocabulary of criminality and law and order as a means to asserting control.

Shifting state strategies and developmental outcomes at the local level in Marange raise questions about the state as a custodian of national resources, and the developmental intent and impact of its minerals management. In contrast, left to itself, the informal diamond economy in Marange provided consumption value from local resources and produced some important economic multiplier effects better than did the state and formal mining companies after rationalisation. However, this is not to conclude that the informal economy was preferable to the formal. Irregular activities admittedly represented an enormous loss of national income through smuggled stones which attracted no taxation that could be used for national benefit; vastly undervalued stones sold at deep discounts; and largely had a consumption, rather than meaningful 'investment', outcome. The foregoing is therefore a commentary of how, instead of instituting the desired investment outcome and benefiting the national economy, the narrative is one of a predatory political party that used its statutory powers to exclude locals and the national economy from deriving benefit from the diamond resources. It uses the lens of 'Marange narratives' to observe that for the local people, informal activities produced better survival strategies and redistributive benefits beyond the Marange economy than did state-led strategies after the formalisation of mining.

7

THE SOCIAL IMPACT OF DIAMOND MINING ON SCHOOLS IN MARANGE, 2006-2013

Mathew Ruguwa

Introduction

This chapter examines the social impact of artisanal and formal diamond mining on primary and secondary schools in Marange during the period 2006-2013, with a particular focus on schools in the vicinity of the diamond fields.[1] It reveals the paradoxical and changing impact of mining during the bvupfuwe ('free-for-all') period (June - November 2006), the intensification of informal mining (March 2007 - October 2008) and the subsequent period of formal mining (2009-2013). The study challenges the notion that the decline in Marange educational standards from 2006 to 2013 can be solely explained by the 'Crisis in Zimbabwe',[2] and charts the decline of Marange's schools alongside the rise of diamond mining to make the case that mining had a profoundly disruptive impact on Marange's social and community institutions. Indeed, even with the rel-

---

1   This chapter draws on my BA Honours dissertation, 'A history of the social impact of diamond mining on schools in Marange, 2006-2013', University of Zimbabwe, 2013.
2   Raftopoulos (2009).

ative 'normalisation' of politics with the inception of the Government of National Unity (GNU)[3] in 2009, mining continued to have a corrosive impact on education in Marange.

The main argument is that while the extraction and trade of diamonds in Marange had both negative and positive impacts on the local social fabric, it had particularly devastating consequences for the important social institutions of primary and secondary schooling. There is a need, therefore, to move away from the grand or meta-narrative approach that some scholars have used to explain the declining educational standards associated with the period under study, and introduce greater analytical nuance in order to fully understand the implications of diamonds' differential impact on the Marange community. It seems increasingly clear that whereas some community members were 'blessed' by diamond mining, key social institutions such as schools were severely disrupted, if not 'cursed'. The consequences of this divide for Marange's future were worrying.

The chapter begins by examining the factors that led schoolchildren and teachers to join a vast array of people – young and old, unemployed and employed, local villagers and 'outsiders' – who descended on Marange in the diamond rush that ignited in 2006. The discussion then turns to consider the uneven impacts on the local schools of diamond extraction and trading during the free-for-all period. The formal mining period beginning in 2009 brought new forms of disruption. These are investigated through case studies of Gandauta Secondary and Chiadzwa Primary, the two schools which were fenced inside the premises of one of the mining companies, Diamond Mining Cooperation (DMC).

The main evidence for this study was gathered through unstructured interviews with school children, education officials, school-leavers, teachers, diamond panners, parents, police officers and shopkeepers. Most interviews were conducted between June 2012 and April 2013. The author was a diamond digger and cross-border trader, and during 2006-2013 taught at a secondary school close to the Marange fields.

The Rise and Fall of 'Free-for-All', 2006-2009

Informal mining and cross-border trading were not new phenomena in Marange District; they have long been part of the livelihood strategies devised by the local people to make a living in an environment character-

3   See Raftopoulos (2013).

ised by poor soils and erratic rainfall. However, these strategies became more important in the 2000s, as a growing economic crisis punctuated by unemployment, collapsing government services and hyperinflation forced people to scramble to survive.[4] It was under such circumstances that local people came to learn of the existence of diamonds in Ushonje mountain in 2006.[5] Thereafter, the government encouraged people to dig for diamonds and sell them to the state's buying agents, and the floodgates opened. As artisanal diamond mining suddenly exploded, warning signals of future trouble for the surrounding communities were noticed by astute observers. As the then Manicaland Mining Commissioner, Isaac Rusuwa, said:

> *If nothing is done immediately to put an end to these illegal activities while they are in their infancy, we are going to have a catastrophe ahead of us. Firstly, the country is losing billions of dollars on a daily basis. Secondly, there are other activities like robberies and other social ills that are accompanied by this illegal mining of diamonds ... in the end, like what is happening in Chimanimani, some schoolchildren will abandon the classroom and join the illegal miners in the mountains.*[6]

Local teachers were among the first people in the district to gain awareness of the existence of diamonds and the emerging trade, and along with schoolchildren were key players in spreading the news of diamond trade opportunities. From the start of the diamond rush, teachers were approached by children and parents seeking help in selling packets of stones dug near their homesteads. Teachers and schoolchildren were soon playing multiple roles of panners, diamond buyers and vendors, in the absence of other local agents who could be trusted by diggers. The chaotic impact on daily life in rural Marange was immediate, as one former teacher at Gandauta Secondary School recounted:

> *I was among the first people to get hold of the diamonds in April 2006. My greatest challenge was that I didn't know the*

4   Raftopoulos (2009).

5   Interview with N. Mukwada.

6   'Diamonds Galore in Marange', *The Manica Post*, 14-20 July 2006. At the time, there was an upsurge in informal gold mining in Chimanimani District in Manicaland Province, with reports of schoolchildren participating in panning under difficult conditions.

value of diamonds and where to sell them ... In September 2006, I sold about 1kg of both industrial and clear diamonds to a certain buyer who had a vehicle which indicated a South African plate. I sold the big parcel for only R1,000 at Chipindirwe shopping centre. I decided to sell the diamonds because I needed money to buy some exercise books for the schoolchildren at my school who came to me in large numbers on almost a daily basis, asking for exercise books and ball point pens in exchange for diamonds.[7]

Poor prices and delayed payment by the Minerals Marketing Corporation of Zimbabwe, the official government buying agent, pushed many diggers into dealing with local schoolchildren, who also represented less of a security threat in the illegal transactions.[8] Trading with and vending for diamond diggers in the district was a key point of engagement, and sometimes meant travelling long distances and arriving early, before the buying and vending competition. This meant skipping morning classes. One school-leaver encountered at Zengeni Business Centre revealed why this choice was made:

The secret behind fetching a huge amount of money after a good fortune at paMbada [a section of the diamond fields where industrial diamonds were frequently mined] was to hunt for good diamond buyers at the business centres or along the major roads ... At times I absconded from lessons and travelled all the way from Chiadzwa where I reside to as far as Mutsago, Bambazonke, Chakohwa business centres, Mutare-Masvingo Road or even Mutare, searching for well-paying buyers.[9]

Rural business centres in the area were suddenly awash with schoolgoers and teachers, and schools started reporting incidents of regular absenteeism. The problem worsened as demand surged for vending by lo-

---

7   Interview with Mr Petros (not his real name), former teacher, Gandauta Secondary School, held in Chikanga, Mutare, 7 July 2012.

8   Interview with a group of boys from the local village, Mukwada shopping centre, 30 June 2012.

9   Interview with Lucky Chikide, school-leaver, Zengeni business centre, 13 June 2012. Business centres such as Bambazonke, Chakohwa, Zengeni and Mupedzanyota and most major roads near Marange were rendezvous points for diamond transactions.

cals in service of migrant miners. Teachers who were not strong enough to dig for diamonds and those who wanted to maintain their social status in the community by not mixing with panners and schoolchildren at business centres and digging in the tunnels, travelled to South Africa, Botswana or Mozambique to buy goods for resale at exorbitant prices. Their profits were substantial – reportedly often double the original investment. Those who participated as vendors usually bought consumer commodities, clothes, radios and televisions sets.[10] One teacher reported that at his school three out of six colleagues were cross-border traders who travelled regularly to South Africa to replenish their stock. Even primary school pupils were part of the trade, selling light foodstuffs, cigarettes and water on the edges of the diamond fields.

The arrival of thousands of informal miners in Marange ushered in growing opportunities and threats for those engaged in the diamond economy. While vending and trading continued, significant numbers of students and teachers joined the brigades of diggers, often working together.[11] The intensification of violence and insecurity at the hands of both mining gangs and state security forces, who were deployed to the area in late 2006, helped to forge more formal engagement between students and teachers. Schoolchildren and teachers began to operate from the 'base camps' that had mushroomed close to the diamond fields. These were rendezvous points used as refuge by panners within the same digging 'syndicates', and were developed as a defensive reaction by panners to *magombiro* (thugs), as well as a strategy to evade police raids.[12] Teacher-student partnerships in mining syndicates were not uncommon, with several informants indicating they had been members of such groups. A form three student at Mukwada Secondary School recalled how she took part in the re-sieving of diamond ore residue in 2008:

> *My friends, my grade six teacher, myself and other males*
> *who feared to sneak into the diamond fields would usually*
> *go for mutsvare [diamond ore] very early in the morning ...*
> *We usually re-sieved the residue of the diamond ore during*
> *weekends, holidays and at times during school days when we*

---

10 Interview with Petros.

11 One informant indicated that there were twelve members in his syndicate including five local schoolchildren and two local teachers. Interview with Chikide.

12 Interview with W. Mangoma.

absconded from school.[13]

As the changing relationships of teachers and students suggested, diamonds were quickly reshaping daily life and the social fabric of Marange in important ways. Rising incomes would have positive but ultimately uneven impacts, particularly with regard to schooling and education; but there would be more negative social consequences as well.

The transformative effects of diamond wealth were widely seen. Teachers noted that diamond earnings were deployed to buy learning resources and uniforms and to pay school fees. [14] The wearing of complete school uniforms by students, previously the sign of a household's relative affluence, became commonplace. At Mukwada Secondary, for example, where only one-third of students in a class of 36 had complete school uniforms prior to the start of the rush in June 2006, more than two-thirds sported them just one year later.[15] Others noted the improved availability of exercise books and other learning materials supplied by both teachers and students through trading activities.[16] The benefits of greater financial liquidity from the diamond trade also flowed directly into the school system:

> *At some schools beyond Marange the payment of school fees was very poor due to the prevailing economic crises. Contrary, at our school, cash flow tremendously improved between 2007 and 2008. In certain cases, some children would instead of paying fees for the current term, pay for the whole year – yet never turn up to attend school!* [17]

The wider impact of diamonds on rural consumption was glimpsed in the new-found purchasing power of students and teachers. Bicycles and cars came to signal good fortune in local trading markets. At Gandauta Secondary School the majority of students bought bicycles during 2007-2008.[18] A local newspaper noted that, 'at Chiadzwa Secondary School, almost every

---

13   Interview with K. Mutsago.

14   Interview with Mr R. Chirombo, teacher, St John's Secondary School, St John's Secondary School, 31 December 2012. He indicated that he also used proceeds from diamonds to pay his college fees when he was enrolled at Mutare Teacher's College between 2006 and 2008.

15   Interview with Mr S. Kadzima.

16   'Train Children the proper way', *The Manica Post*, 9-15 February 2007.

17   Interview with Mr T. Chiwanza.

18   Interview with Mr Siduna, senior teacher, Gandauta Secondary School, 34 years, Gandauta Secondary School, 6 July 2012.

student rides a new bicycle, while the few less fortunate are working hard to fund-raise.'[19] The impact of this change was uneven: on the one hand, the use of bicycles dramatically reduced the time it took for students to get to school – 'we were now able to attend assemblies every morning', recalled one student mountain bike owner;[20] on the other hand, this did not necessarily lead to improved attendance in school lessons. As one teacher noted:

> *One Monday morning in April 2007 I decided to count all the bicycles at my school. The bicycles added up to 165 while the enrolment was 320. From that day, we designed a bicycle park and implemented a school rule that no student was supposed to be seen riding a bicycle during lesson time... This, however, fell on deaf ears as children preferred not to attend lessons and ride bicycles the whole day!*[21]

Many locals displayed their wealth in the form of new housing, with bricks and asbestos roof sheeting replacing pole and dagga thatched rondavels. Electrification by means of solar panels and diesel generators powering televisions, satellite dishes and other appliances – previously seen rarely in Marange – spread throughout the district. 'Those in rural Chiadzwa,' one newspaper report noted, 'managed to build modern houses that can compete neck-and-neck with those in urban set-ups.'[22] As one teacher reported, the benefits of instant wealth were potentially transformative:

> *I was very fortunate to pick a sixteen-carat clear diamond during a live show [a daylight mining spree] at Pamadhaka [one muddy section of the diamond field where clear diamonds were mined]. Now I am very proud to own a ten-roomed house in the rural area. Since I joined the teaching profession in 1997, I was unable to pay people who would mould bricks for the construction of even a two-roomed house.*[23]

Other changes in the community were less welcome. The growth of com-

19   'Diamond panner throws cop into shaft', *The Manica Post*, 2-8 February 2007.
20   Interview with T. Mujima, school-leaver, Mukwada shopping centre, 11 June 2012.
21   Interview with Mr T. Chiwanza.
22   'Chiadzwa diamond story', *The Manica Post*, 6-13 July 2010.
23   Interview with Tupac (not his real name name), local teacher, Marange, 18 June 2012.

mercial sex work and the rise in the number of relationships between miners and schoolgirls – so called 'child marriages' – was destabilising social life in the district. The influx of thousands of miners, the vast majority of them male, and the flush of cash in the local economy, provided enabling conditions for expansion of the commercial sex trade. Profits were considerable, so much so that some female informants indicated they had arrived in Marange as diggers only to delve into commercial sex work because the earnings were comparable and more reliable. The problem of child marriages and commercial sex work involving local schoolgirls – mostly secondary students, but in some cases primary school pupils as well – proved highly disruptive and became prevalent at the height of the free-for-all period. A senior teacher at Kurauone Secondary School reported that during 2007-2008, twelve girls dropped out due to marriages involving artisanal miners – a significant increase over previous years, when less than one-third that number left for similar reasons.[24] While such marriages are illegal in Zimbabwe, the problem in Marange was compounded by the unwillingness of local law enforcement personnel to pursue the offenders, lest they incur the wrath of the gangs working the fields, or be deprived of access to the trade themselves. It was only the violent removal of informal miners in 2008 which brought about an end to the practice – and to the short-lived 'marriages' fuelled by diamond cash. But the scars of abuse remained in the community for long after, some informants reported, in the form of turbulence within families, children born to adolescent girls and increasing instances of sexually transmitted diseases.[25]

Strains on social service centres also proved a source of growing tension. The dramatic increase in number of migrant miners into the district in 2006-2007 and the lack of adequate infrastructure and facilities significantly disrupted local communities. Insufficient and expensive housing, scarcity of protected water and sanitary systems, the high cost of food and the low capacity of local health infrastructure generated multiple strains. Locals reported rampant theft of household items, as well as crops and domestic animals.[26] Water wells were overused and many were contaminated. These and other side effects of the migrant incursion

---

24   Interview with Mr Saungweme, teacher, Kurauone Secondary, 18 June 2012.

25   Interview with a group of mothers, local villagers, Kurauone community borehole, 28 June 2012.

26   Interview with Mukwada.

led to the rapid deterioration of environmental living conditions. As one environmental health worker noted,

> *At Muchena, Chipindirwe and Zengeni Business Centres, and at the panning site, cooked food, together with fruits and groceries, were being sold in the open dusty environment. The refuse and human matter that littered everywhere were a fertile breeding ground for flies. This facilitated the outbreak of diarrhoea diseases and cholera, which would claim the lives of panners, local villagers and also some of the state security forces who were in control of the diamond fields.*[27]

Evidence indicates that there was an outbreak of diarrhoea and cholera in Marange during the period of informal diamond mining. A local environmental health officer indicated that between October 2008 and May 2009 multiple cases of cholera were reported from the diamond panners' 'base camps' and from at least five nearby villages in Marange Wards 29 and 30; at least four people perished from cholera in October-November 2008 alone.[28] Even state security forces were afflicted, with a ranking police officer reporting that a medic had been deployed to Marange to attend to officers posted to the district.[29] Local clinics were unable to cope with rising demand fuelled by migrant miners. For example, the clinics at Mukwada and Chiadzwa, designed to cater for approximately 8,000 people, were charged with looking after at least 15,000 by August 2007. Clinics in Marange Wards 29 and 30, which typically restocked their drug supplies from the Provincial Directorate every three months, were now running out in only two weeks. During 2007-2009 there were critical shortages due to high demand of a range of basic antibiotics and other supplies in the three clinics nearest to the main diamond fields, while reported cases of sexually transmitted diseases rose dramatically.

Marange's schools, amongst the only places with the basic services sought by diggers living in the bush, were particularly affected: they were inundated by miners searching for water, who often raided school gardens in

---

27   Interview with Mr Tembo (not his real name), Local Environmental Health Officer, Chiadzwa Clinic 19 June 2012.

28   Ibid.

29   'Diamond panner throws cop into shaft', *The Manica Post*, 2-8 February 2007.

their hunt for food.[30] Teachers complained that the miners were destructive and abusive, and could not easily be chased away:

> They were a nuisance, they frequently invaded our prem-
> ises both during the day and at night. During the day, they
> swarmed the school yard especially around the borehole area
> fetching water. Our borehole ceased to function in August
> 2008 because of them... We could not control them. They were
> very violent with their migwara [iron bars]. They even stole
> tomatoes and vegetables from our school garden. During the
> weekends, holidays and at night, they turned our classrooms
> into 'base camps'. They destroyed our furniture, benches and
> windows. In the classrooms, our charts and exercise books
> were torn and the papers were used as wrapping paper for
> smoking tobacco and dzemabhinya [marijuana]...[31]

If illegal miners were a problem for schools, the presence of police added to it. During police operations to stamp out illegal mining the areas around schools frequently became battlegrounds. At times, lessons were disrupted by nearby police gunfire and by miners taking shelter near schools while lessons were in progress.[32] Students and teachers were among those sought in the fields by the police. When schools began for the third term in September 2008, many teachers and students were missing – and later discovered to be in police custody. As one newspaper reported, at some schools in Marange 'hundreds of schoolchildren and teachers were still missing and were reported to have joined the great trek to Chiadzwa'.[33]

As the diamond trade flourished, student absenteeism became the norm, as many students became full-time traders. The rapid accumulation of wealth by those households where children worked the fields as traders, vendors and, increasingly, diggers, led to changes in parents' and school children's perception of education. Parents, one headmaster reported, seemed less interested in ensuring their children remained in school and helping them with their homework, than in auditing the gems they brought home from the diamond fields and locating the most lucrative venues for their onward sale up

---

30   Interview with Mrs. Chishingwi, teacher, Kurauone Primary School, Kurauone Primary School, 28 June 2012.

31   Ibid.

32   Interview with Mr Saungweme.

33   'Teachers, pupils fail to go back to school over diamonds', *The Manica Post*, 5-11 September 2008.

the rough diamond supply chain.[34] School attendance dropped markedly, and participation in year-end exams fell. At one school, more than 10 per cent of the students failed to show up for exams; in previous years the attendance rate had been a consistent 100 per cent.

Some schools reported working effective half-days, as students and teachers left for the fields in the afternoon.[35] Among the large numbers of informal miners were teachers and pupils from distant schools in Manicaland. By 2007, schools in Chimanimani, Buhera, Zimunya and Chipinge were reporting abseteeism due to the allure of diamonds.[36] One teacher at Muzokomba High (Buhera) recalled that he and three colleagues absconded from work for two weeks to travel to Marange to dig. Others, citing the period of hyperinflation which was dramatically eroding teachers' salaries, reported that a number of schools within reach of Marange effectively closed for an extended period in 2008.

Between 2007 and 2008 there were consistent and dramatic falls in school enrolment and attendance. Statistics provided by a secondary school teacher at Gandauta reflected a broader reported trend: at Gandauta, enrolment declined from 320 to 260 in less than a year, and the downward trend continued through 2008. By the second term of that year, 13 students out of a class of 43 had dropped out of school, 20 were frequently absent at least three days a week and only 10 were usually present every day. While dropping out and non-attendance did not begin with informal diamond mining, there is every indication that they became far worse after it started.[37] It is worth noting that the wider representativeness of this enrolment and attendance data was difficult to confirm due to the generally shambolic state of record keeping during 2007-2008 in many Marange schools, a telling research finding in itself which some teacher informants explained by the fact of rampant teacher absenteeism.

By late 2008, the crisis in school operations had become a national one due to the severe economic crisis. Whereas most schools had informally shut by November, most in Marange had closed by October, many of them since

34 Interview with Mr .T. Chiwanza, then Headmaster of Mukwada Secondary School, Mukwada Secondary School, 11 July 2012.
35 Interview with Mr Chihlangu, teacher, Kurauone Secondary School, Kurauone Secondary School, 28 June 2012.
36 Interview with Mr Brown.
37 2007 Gandauta Secondary School enrolment records, and interview with Siduna.

the previous month. With the early informal shutdown in Marange and the bleeding of teachers into the diamond fields, a critical problem emerged in advance of the year-end ZIMSEC examinations in 2008. One teacher at a satellite school in Marange recalled a parlous state of affairs, with only two teachers out of a full complement of fourteen being present during the writing of the 'O' level exams – the rest having absconded permanently between June and July. The profound double impact of the crashing formal economy and the ascendant parallel one of diamonds was evident:

> *I administered the 'O' level students who sat for the 2008 ZIMSEC examinations with my headmaster. The two of us would see to it that all papers were written and submitted to the ZIMSEC offices in Mutare. In some examinations, I was helped by the Village Head and the SDC Chairman to invigilate because the headmaster had attended a funeral for one week. Most of the teachers were away, involved in informal activities in a bid to supplement their incomes. Three of them were employed as shop assistants by a certain local diamond buyer at Harare 2 [Chipindirwe Business Centre]. The other four had become regular cross-border traders who frequently supplied goods to most shops at Bambazonke, Chipindirwe, Mukwada and Zengeni Shopping Centres. The other five had just disappeared from school sometime in June and they were never located up until sometime in February 2009.*[38]

The immediately measurable impact of these circumstances was the extremely poor exam performance of students in the worst-affected Marange schools. At Chipindirwe Primary School, located about 3km from the diamond fields, an unprecedented failure rate of 100 per cent of seventh graders was registered in 2008. More worrying perhaps was the repeat of this standard in the two subsequent years.[39] In addition to Chipindirwe Primary there were a number of schools in the vicinity of the diamond fields that recorded a zero per cent pass rate during 2006-2010. As Table 1 indicates, in 2010 – long after the initial period of disruptions due to artisanal mining had subsided – Marange District had the highest number of primary schools recording

---

38   Interview with Tupac.
39   Interview with Mr Nengome, headmaster, Chipindirwe Primary School, Chipindirwe Primary School, 9 July 2012.

the worst results at Grade Seven in Manicaland Province, accounting for 44 per cent of the 18 schools province-wide registering a 0 per cent pass rate.

Table 1. District Schools Recording 0% Pass Rate in Manicaland (2010)

Mutasa	Buhera	Nyanga	Marange	Chimanimani	Chipinge
Chavhanga	Mugwenhi Mavangwe Nechikova	Sanzvenga St Monica	Tonhorai Chibiya Masasi Mangatu Mutoonwa Kushinga Mafunde Chinya-muchese	Cambridge Hot Springs Demeni	Charuma

Source: 'Poor pass rate in Schools worrisome', *The Manica Post*, 21-27 January 2011.

Results from Marange District schools over a longer period underscore the negative consequences of the diamond boom for local education. Table 2 shows that most schools failed to recover from the initial shock delivered by the chaos of the free-for-all period. Interviews with teachers, school administrators, parents, students, and school-leavers consistently attributed the poor examination outcomes to the disruption of schools, households and communities by the evolving diamond mining rush.

Table 2. Year and Pass-Rate (%) in Marange District Schools

School	2006	2007	2008	2009	2010	2011	2012
Mukwada Secondary	3.3	3	12.5	0	2.9	9.4	16,7
Mukwada Primary	68	64	43	63	27	46	44
Kurauone. Primary	26	24	8	9	27	14	16
Kurauone Secondary	16	12	0	0	12.3	0	0
Chipindirwe Primary	8	3	0	3	6	9	12

Source: School records of ZIMSEC 'O' level and grade seven results

It is important to note in comparing the results during 2006-2012 that the negative impact of mining on school performance continued in several instances long after the formalisation of mining in 2009. This slow progress in the recuperation of educational standards in Marange pointed to a new set of factors disrupting learning and community life in the period of diamond mining's 'normalisation'.

Formal Mining and Educational Outcomes, 2009-2013

Government's forceful eviction of artisanal miners and the formalisation of diamond mining in Marange in 2009 brought some relief to local communities, but also introduced new challenges and forms of community disruption. A prevailing fear among parents and school officials was that the discovery of substantial deposits of diamonds meant that mining was to be a long-term activity, with chronically destabilising impacts on locals. Key elements in this regard were changes in local employment patterns, the ascendency of mining companies in managing social infrastructure, environmental destruction resulting from mechanised mining and the forced relocation of communities to a resettlement scheme at ARDA Transau. All would directly affect local schools and the standard of education delivered.

With the formation of the GNU in early 2009, the beginning of economic stabilisation and moves towards formalising mechanised mining in Marange, a degree of peace and stability returned to the district. Schools that had closed in late 2008 reopened in February. But while the conditions that had prompted the exodus of students and teachers to the diamond fields had changed, many – especially children – were not keen to go back to the classroom. Some missed the few remaining opportunities for quick money – one teacher noted that it was 'difficult for "young barons" to carry their satchels back into the classroom'; [40] others testified that digging for diamonds and living rough with teachers had fundamentally altered their relationships and made it difficult for students to respect their teachers as authority figures in the classroom. In Marange, students were slow to return to their classes; at three secondary schools near the fields most classes were only half full up to late-April, with some recording attendance of less than a third.[41] One teacher observed:

40   Interview with Mr Saungweme.
41   Interviews with Mr S. Kadzima and Mr Siduna.

> *Schoolchildren found it difficult to throw away their migwara [iron bars used for extracting diamonds by panners] and carry their books back to school after making real money in the Matonera [tunnels] in the diamond fields... Four weeks after the schools began, less than 15 pupils out of 32 had reported to school in my class.*[42]

However, the attendance of schoolchildren gradually improved as the year progressed, and by mid-year had returned to traditional levels. So too had the complement of teachers. One of the key economic changes introduced by the GNU was the transition to a multi-currency regime and the dropping of the Zimbabwe dollar. Teachers, now paid in US dollars, and without easy access to artisanal mining, returned in numbers to their classrooms. But the commencement of mechanised mining would soon unravel some of the progress made in retaining teachers in the schools. As Mbada Diamonds and then other companies established operations, demand for local labour rose and a key target of recruitment was local senior school students and teachers. One third of the 30 workers employed by the Diamond Mining Company in January 2012 were local school-leavers; other companies arriving later continued this practice. But local schools also lost some of their most experienced teachers, who were employed as supervisors and diamond sorters.[43]

If the loss of income from the diamond fields was a blow to some in sustaining access to education for local children, some of the new mining operators promised to fill the gap through various forms of Corporate Social Responsibility (CSR). These were much heralded by the companies, government and government media, but were looked on with increasing scepticism by locals. An important component of CSR involved local education. Companies including Mbada and Marange Resources initiated supplementary feeding programmes, fee coverage and disbursement of learning materials in some local schools, and eight Marange schools reported receiving assistance from two of the five companies then operating.[44] In addition, Mbada pledged US$286,000 towards the construction of an entirely new school, St Noah Primary School,[45] located nearly

---

42   Interview with Chihlangu.

43   Interview with Kadzima. He stated that eight teachers in wards 29 and 30 had abandoned teaching for the diamond industry by January 2012.

44   Interview with Mr Bhasopo.

45   Named after the high priest of Johanne Marange Church, Noah Taguta.

30km from the diamond fields, which was opened by President Mugabe in July 2012. Controversy swirled around the school, however, as many locals questioned the need to build a school in a distant location – unreachable by children most affected by diamond mining – before rehabilitating and expanding schools closer to the main mine sites. Some saw the Mbada investment as a political favour to the president and his party, attempting to bolster their support from an important religious community in advance of hotly contested national elections in 2013.

Overall, informants reported disappointment with the outcomes of CSR, particularly in terms of support given to education. One headmaster compared the large funding pledged by Mbada Diamonds to Premier Soccer to the much smaller sums made available to struggling local schools:

> *Whilst sponsoring Premier Soccer is good, one would pause and ask a question: why should Mbada pledge a lot of money to Premier Soccer whilst some poor schools just three kilometres or so away from its premises have soccer pitches full of anthills? Whilst it had not yet supported the construction of classroom blocks in the schools most affected by diamond mining? Again one would ask: why should this company pledge so much money to Premier Soccer while some poor families just about three kilometres away from its premises do not have a simple radio to listen to the Premier Soccer it sponsors?*[46]

Traditional leaders shared these sentiments. Headman Mukwada pointed out that villagers were expecting Mbada and Marange Resources to go beyond feeding schemes and provision of exercise books to construct infrastructure like classroom blocks, science laboratories and libraries at the local primary and secondary schools. He argued that the diamond companies had promised much to local schools and delivered very little.[47] A Village Head, Booker Chipindirwe, expressed similar frustrations:

> *Our children are still learning in dilapidated buildings, our roads are in a poor state ...These companies are just making*

---

46   Interview with Mr Todd (not his real name), local headmaster, Marange, 19 July 2012.

47   Interview with H. Mukwada, headman, ward 29, Mukwada, 10 January 2013.

a lot of noise for nothing, yet people here are wallowing in abject poverty. We want a change of fortune here at Chiadzwa, with a modern medical referral centre, better schools and better social amenities that will clearly show the world that we are sitting on one of the richest diamond deposits.[48]

One 'solution' enabling expanded social infrastructure involved the forced relocation of Marange villagers out of the diamond areas to ARDA Transau, a settlement on state land more than 70km from Marange. This involved the removal of nearly 1,400 families by 2014 (with an anticipated final total of more than 4,000 by the time mining has finished), and led to severe disruption in community and household life, with housing, animals, fields and grazing land, traditional burial plots and other property being forfeited. In exchange they received new, standardised housing and plots provided by government and the mining companies; but these were often far smaller, less substantial and less developed than what they had left behind. Social infrastructure was decimated, and many families and villages were divided and destabilised by the move. Among the casualties was Marange's educational institutions.

Two schools were demolished to make way for a mining complex, and others were severely disrupted by the presence of mining infrastructure. At ARDA Transau, two new schools were constructed to replace the two demolished. However, there were delays in removals, and resistance from some households, and many families and schoolchildren stayed behind in Chiadzwa, putting additional pressure on the remaining school infrastructure. Some students were now forced to walk long distances of up to10km to attend schools that were suddenly oversubscribed. In many instances, schoolchildren stayed behind in Marange when families were moved to ARDA Transau in 2011-2012, in light of the experience of families that had been moved early only to find inadequate schooling facilities there. The continuation of feeding schemes and the provision of learning materials was also an incentive for some students to stay on.[49] Mukwada Primary School was an example of the congestion that resulted in Marange, as its headmaster observed:

---

48 'Chiadzwa diamonds poised to transform economy', *The Manica Post*, 11-17 January 2011.
49 Interview with Tafadzwa Mukwada, form three student, Kurauone Secondary School, Kurauone Secondary School, 30 June 2012.

The relocation programme increased our enrolment and this eventually stretched our resources, and worsened the situation that was at our school. Prior to the relocation exercise, our furniture and classroom blocks already needed attention... In 2010 our school enrolment was 412. Currently, we have 502. There are three classes learning under the musasa trees at the present. [50]

Despite entreaties by the school and the local School Development Committee (SDC) to government and Mbada, the company in whose area the school operated, there was little effective response forthcoming:

We saw this problem when it was coming. The SDC wrote to Mbada Diamonds requesting for building material to construct a classroom block. The first letter was written in November 2011 and the second one in May 2012. Mukwada Secondary School also requested financial help for the construction of a classroom block. Up to this day we have not received any reply. The Company officials at the diamond fields are saying your letters are being processed at the Head Offices in Harare. [51]

In the case of Mukwada, parents were lobbied by the SDC to construct a classroom block in 2012 to relieve the growing pressure of student numbers. That too was a battle, as some parents hesitated to contribute, not knowing if they would soon be targeted by the relocation exercise – such was the lack of transparency around the programme. For school administrators, the degree of uncertainty about the future led to a paralysis of normal school development activity in the community:

It became clear that parents were no longer interested in long-term developmental projects because of the rumours circulating that sooner or later they will join their relatives at ARDA Transau. At one meeting, I asked parents to raise funds to build the school signpost which was knocked down

50 Mukwada Primary School 2013 enrolment records, and interview with Mr Nyakujara. Similar growth in student numbers at Mukwada Secondary School, where there was a 70 per cent increase between 2010 and 2013, when 346 were enrolled. Interview with Mr M. Sithole, headmaster, Mukwada Secondary School, Mukwada Secondary School, 30 June 2012.

51 Mukwada Primary School 2013 enrolment records, and interview with Mr Nyakujara.

by a heavy vehicle delivering food to the school. However, most parents were very bitter about it. The majority of them responded by saying that they didn't have the funds. I then suggested that the school should use the reserved school funds for the same project; but again the results were negative.[52]

Meanwhile, Marange's schools were bleeding teachers due to strengthening 'pull' and 'push' factors. On the one hand there were incentives for teachers to relocate to more hospitable, less contested spaces, where new investment in schools – by government or by local communities – was more likely. On the other hand, working and living conditions in Marange were becoming steadily more difficult. The enforcement of a 'No-Go' area securing the diamond fields from artisanal miners had direct implications for teachers. Public transport was difficult to obtain, there were frequent security checks and harassment from security personnel and the costs of consumables therefore rose. The banning of public transport on many routes forced villagers, teachers and visitors to walk or find their own transport for distances of up to 25km to reach public transport at Bambazonke business centre.[53]

Working conditions were also a push factor for teachers. They continued to deteriorate due to the increasingly close proximity of mining activities, and of security personnel protecting the diamondiferous areas. The new discovery of diamonds at *kwaDozva* marked the beginning of a more severe disruption of educational activities in schools like Chiadzwa Primary and Gandauta Secondary. These deposits were only about 100 metres from the schools, and noise, air and water pollution from mining became a severe disruption to teaching. In other schools in the district,[54] army and police camps on school grounds brought an atmosphere of intimidation and tension, particularly for former panners among the students and teachers. Many had been either previously disciplined by the police and soldiers, or had witnessed the abuse of others at the hands of security personnel during earlier artisanal clearing operations.

The impact of formal mining on Marange's schools was most clearly seen in the case of Chiadzwa, Gandauta and Chishingwi, the three

---

52   Interview with Nengome.

53   Besides the ban on public transport, travellers into the area had to prove that they were bona fide residents of the area with IDs ending with -75 or produce a police clearance.

54   Including Betera, Kurauone, Chipindirwe, and Gandauta.

schools inside the fenced perimeters of the diamond mining companies in Marange.[55] At Gandauta, a succession of problems developed alongside the expansion of DMC's mining activities. The school lost valuable parts of its property, including the school garden, soccer pitch and borehole, all of which were taken by DMC. Schoolchildren were only permitted by company security to drink water at their former borehole during break and lunch time. For the deputy headmaster of Gandauta, one immediate result of DMC's fencing of the grounds was that both teachers and schoolchildren lost freedom of movement at their own school.[56] In a bid to maintain tight security, the company ended up breaching the rights of teachers and schoolchildren. Instead of entering and departing the school using multiple entrances, the security fence erected by the company provided only two gates in inconvenient locations which caused significant delays, especially for students.

Declining staff numbers and poor learning conditions at Gandauta and Chiadzwa schools contributed to their attaining only very poor pass rates. At Gandauta Secondary, the pass rate dropped from 30 per cent in 2009 to 27 in 2010, and eventually to zero in 2011.[57] As a result, the school decided to freeze the 2011 form three class and block students from moving forward to 'O' level studies, to prevent a repeat of the disappointing 'O' level results of 2011. 'As it stands', the deputy headmaster observed, 'the only solution to save the investment in education by parents is to relocate the school as soon as possible ... education at this station is collapsing due to formal mining.'[58] At Chiadzwa Primary School the story was only slightly better. Just two pupils passed the 2012 grade seven ZIMSEC examinations amid reports that there were a lot of disturbances from mining activities. Melanie Chiponda, the co-ordinator of Chiadzwa Community Development Trust, laid the blame firmly at the feet of the mining operators: 'There has been destruction of the education system due to mining activities to the extent that Chiadzwa had the lowest pass rates in the province last year ... there is a lot of drilling, digging and noise from machines while children are in class.'[59]

---

55   The first two schools were under the DMC and the third was under Jinan Mining.

56   Interview with Bhasopo.

57   Ibid.

58   Ibid.

59   'Two pupils pass at Chiadzwa school', *NewsDay*, 2 April 2013.

Conclusion

Drawing on first-hand accounts from teachers, students, community members and public officials, this chapter demonstrates the impact of diamond mining on schools and the delivery of education in Marange. It argues that although the 'Zimbabwe Crisis' is used by some to explain the decline of education standards in Marange District, taking into account the specific impact of diamond mining provides a more compelling and nuanced explanation. During the periods of informal artisanal mining (2006-2009) and mechanised production (2009-2013) the evolving social and economic dynamics associated with diamond extraction had powerful effects on the delivery of education. These were more pronounced, the closer schools and communities were to diamondiferous land and mining operations: the nearer to diamonds, the more damaging the consequences for teachers, students and the learning process. At the same time, the most affected schools were sometimes the most powerless in attempts to ameliorate the educational challenges faced; government, commercial and criminal interests and forces proved dominant in the shaping of the conditions of education.

While mining arrangements changed from the informal to commercial, and from criminal to legal, the impact on education evolved as well, often in negative ways. Informal mining during 2006-2009 led to chaos in school attendance and learning, and ultimately to periods of state-sponsored violence in the eviction of informal miners that further traumatised communities, teachers and students. But mining's formalisation saw new kinds of disruption, including the forced relocation of some communities, the closure, overcrowding and under-resourcing of schools left behind, and the direct and hazardous impact of the mining process itself on schools in the proximity of mine sites. In the formalised mining period, especially, schools' control over their learning environment and relationships with surrounding communities were severely weakened. This was the result of the transfer of effective power over social investment and development from government into the hands of the diamond mining companies. Mining companies' CSR initiatives fell short of both community expectations and schools' rising needs, and generated rising frustration and tension. A tragic irony emerged: some of Zimbabwe's richest mineralised land became home to schools with some of the poorest educational results.

The Marange experience raises a number of compelling questions for future consideration. By which means might the benefits of mineral and other resources be shared with those communities and future generations of Zimbabweans whose lives are most directly affected by their extraction? In what ways might resource companies be guided and held to account by government and communities in the development of their extractive projects and, specifically, in their contributions to local economic, social and environmental livelihoods? How might communities amplify and render more effective their voices and interests around shared needs, including viable educational institutions? Marange's extreme contrasts – of vast wealth generated beside miserable poverty; of great developmental potential surrounded by collapsing livelihoods – suggests the need for further research and debate on the relationship between resources, development and local communities. Education, situated at the centre of these relationships, will remain a critical point of study and intervention.

8

FORCED REMOVALS AND HIDDEN POWER: INVOLUNTARY DISPLACEMENT AND RESETTLEMENT IN MARANGE[1]

Crescentia Madebwe and Victor Madebwe

In Marange, mining related displacement has exacted severe social, environmental and economic costs on vulnerable and marginalised communities, eroding fragile livelihoods and breaking many of the intra-community bonds and cohesions which in the past have helped communities to weather challenges to their economic and environmental sustainability.

This chapter examines one particularly disruptive form of displacement that took place in Marange with the development of mechanised mining: the involuntary forced removal and resettlement of Chiadzwa villagers in preparation for new mining installations. In the case studied here, a total of 600 families were moved during May-December 2011 and resettled at a government-owned farm, ARDA Transau, in Odzi, Manicaland Province. More displacements from the diamond mining concessions would follow in 2012 and 2013, but in important ways the

---

1 This chapter is an updated and extended version of a previously published piece, C. Madebwe, V. Madebwe and S. Mavusa, "Involuntary displacement and resettlement to make way for diamond mining: the case of Chiadzwa villagers in Marange, Zimbabwe', *Journal of Research in Peace, Gender and Development*, Vol. 1, No.10 (November 2011), pp. 292-301.

experience of the first large group of relocated families would set a precedent for how displacement was managed and confronted. Resettlement activity in Chiadzwa became characterised by a lack of consultation and information provision involving affected communities; by the relatively free hand allowed to mining companies by government in managing and compensating forced relocation; and by rising frustration in the wake of diminished livelihoods.

Uprooted and bulldozed: a new landscape emerges in Chiadzwa

This discussion is based on a study of fifty families displaced in the first wave of removals in 2011 undertaken by the Mbada Diamonds mining company, one of the larger mine operators in the Marange diamond fields. The average household size was five, and targeted respondents were adults aged 29 years and above; 80 per cent were aged 29-50 years, a group with significant productive potential and therefore taken as an important indicator of the impact of relocation on household economies. The vulnerability of displaced villagers was reflected in a challenge faced in conducting the survey: some were reluctant to talk about their experiences. They were concerned that negative comments about their experiences could compromise their chances of getting compensation in the future. In a politically polarized setting such as Zimbabwe's, villagers also feared that if they complained too much they might be branded 'opposition supporters' and meet an even worse fate. Consequently, many displaced people from Chiadzwa preferred invisibility; others, faced with difficult economic circumstances in the new resettlement area, dispersed in search of work or family support, making it a challenge to obtain a large comprehensive sample. To manage these research obstacles we adopted a purposive snowball sampling approach to identify respondents. The entry point to the community was through the village heads or their proxies, and through respondents who had already been interviewed. Semi-structured questionnaires were the primary data collection method used, and were supplemented by key informant interviews. Field observation was carried out for the purposes of ground truthing to ascertain living conditions, resources to support livelihoods and access to basic resources and amenities.

Displacements under Mbada Diamonds

The Chiadzwa area of Marange District, the primary location of Marange's diamondiferous fields, has a population of 20,000 spread across 18 villages, and comprises Ward 30. The diamond fields cover more than 66,000 hectares, extending into Ward 29 under Headman Mukwada and intersecting with a number of villages in Wards 29 and 30.[2] Chiadzwa is located in Agro-Ecological Region IV, characterised by high temperatures, and low and erratic rainfall, and has long been one of Manicaland Province's poorest, least developed areas. Until the exploitation of diamonds beginning in 2006, its main sources of livelihood involved subsistence crop and livestock production, both highly vulnerable to frequent drought and sub-optimal climate conditions. After 2006, Chiadzwa's fragile productive ecology and community livelihoods would be stressed further, inundated by waves of fortune-hunting artisanal diamond miners and traders whose unregulated and widespread digging and siphoning of water and livelihood resources rendered subsistence farming and animal husbandry, and normal com-

---

2   Tabulating the numbers of villages, people and hectares of land in Chiadzwa and its diamond fields is an imprecise science because administrative and traditional authorities use different boundaries for the area known as 'Chiadzwa'. The bulk of the land under Headman Chiadzwa's authority lies within Ward 30. But while traditional authorities acknowledge only 12 villages in Chiadzwa, the District Administrator recognises 18. The 'Chiadzwa' diamond fields include some parts of Ward 29, and villages located there. In total, 31 villages in Wards 29 and 30 were listed for relocation.

munal life, increasingly difficult.

Successive waves of large-scale human displacements starting in 2006 weighed heavily on the lives of Chiadzwa villagers. The first involved the influx of thousands of informal miners into Chiadzwa, as well as the absorption of many local residents into the diamond trade as diggers, traders and vendors. By late 2006 there were likely more than 20,000 diggers working the scattered diamondiferous fields of Chiadzwa. This inward migration led to a series of counter-measures by government to remove or contain informal mining by means of brute force and security operations led by state security agencies. Resulting tides of inflows and outflows of artisanal miners operating in Chiadzwa in 2007-2008 culmi-nated in government's violent expulsion of most miners in 'Operation Hakudzokwi' in late 2008.

A third wave of displacement, involving far fewer people but com-prising more structured, permanent and in some ways more devastating forms of disruption, emerged as part of the extension and intensification of mechanised mining with government's concessioning of new mining companies beginning in 2009. One of the first of several concessions was awarded to Mbada Diamonds (Private) Limited, a 50/50 joint venture between government's Marange Resources and Grandwell Holdings, a subsidiary of the South Africa-based Reclam Group. Mbada was initially awarded an area of about 1,000 hectares; this was later vastly expanded to cover a total of more than 7,700 hectares, with Grandwell negotiating the right to manage the day-to-day production and marketing operations of the operation, including planning and overseeing villager relocation and resettlement.[3] The first phase of forced removals and resettlement by Mbada of 700 households began in May 2011, when 50 families were displaced and relocated to two new villages, Chiadzwa and Betera, con-structed on land at ARDA Transau, a government farm 25 km from Mu-tare. By December 2011 an additional 550 families had been resettled. Subsequent displacements and resettlement would be spread over the following two years.

Organising Displacement: Problematic beginnings

From the outset of the relocation process, respondents noted, villag-ers felt vulnerable and became increasingly fearful due to the lack of

3 'About Mbada Diamonds', http://www.reclam.co.za/zim_mbada_dia-monds.php accessed 2 November 2015.

consultation by government and mining companies, poor provision of information and lack of adequate notice for what was planned. They were not fully informed of the processes by which their household assets would be appraised and compensated, how and when they would be replaced, when they would be moved and how the arrangements in the new resettlement area would be made.

Villagers reported they were not consulted in the selection of the resettlement area, or in planning the physical arrangements and order of the area, and were given little choice but to accept the decision. Just prior to the first relocations Mbada had arranged a reconnaissance tour of the resettlement area for community leaders, but invited little input from the community. Evidence collected in this survey indicated that the large majority of respondents would have preferred resettlement in other locations, for the most part other ARDA farms where resettlement on unused land might have been possible, but that the mining company and government had been unresponsive to such suggestions when they were made. On the other hand, sharp disincentives for questioning the relocation to ARDA Transau were made clear: according to villagers, opting out of moving to the designated location would result in the forfeiture of all forms of compensation for land and household assets surrendered in Chiadzwa, as well as coverage of the costs of transport and removal undertaken by Mbada. With no other realistic option and under threat of imminent loss of their households in Chiadzwa, villagers grudgingly accepted the move to ARDA Transau. The presence of soldiers in their home area, and veiled threats from local government officials to obey the command to move so that diamond mining could proceed for the benefit of government, provided further negative incentives.

The first relocations in May 2011 came with little warning and in the middle of the crop harvesting period, with immediate and negative impacts on household food security for those who had not finished harvesting. Only 10 per cent of those surveyed reported they had been given more than one month's notice. Rumours swirled among villagers before formal relocation notification, considerably raising tension in the community. As one informant reported that:

> *People talked about what they had heard from other people*
> *that we would be moved. Nobody knew for certain who had*
> *started the rumour. It made us feel anxious. We did not know*

who to ask. At the mine they would not say anything. Government officials also did not want to talk to us. There were soldiers everywhere. We lived in fear.

Respondents argued that under these conditions their displacement was involuntary. Displeasure with the planned relocation was expressed during community gatherings and discussions with community leaders and, occasionally, government officials. But this had little impact – some suspected the complicity of local leaders to be a factor – and while villagers were keen to contest the company's instructions they lacked the organisational capacity to bring together a critical mass to mount an effective challenge, while safeguarding themselves against the perceived threat from state security personnel.

The situation that the first newly-settled households found at ARDA Transau caused further anxiety: social infrastructure was undeveloped, with poor access to health services, transport, adequate housing, water supply and grazing land. Villagers decried the false promises made by the mining company. For example, Mbada had promised to build a clinic and drill six boreholes in each phase of family displacement, but the clinic project was slow to get started, and the borehole yields were low, with boreholes not easily accessible to many households. Soon after the first relocations, 30 per cent of families reported they were reluctant to stay on given the unsatisfactory conditions in the resettlement area, and planned to move out once full compensation for their relocation and assets was paid. Meanwhile, the first wave of relocations continued.

Faded Expectations: Entitlements and compensation

A critical element in the organised displacement of villagers from Chiadzwa was the assessment and payment of compensation for their move and for the loss of livelihoods, social and other assets incurred in the process. Like the initial planning for resettlement, key decision making processes around the identification and compensation levels of entitlements were held firmly in the hands of the company and government, developed with little transparency, accountability or participation of those who were most directly affected. The mechanisms for the valuation of villagers' assets were opaque; Mbada and the government unilaterally established compensation rates to cover short-term costs, and the specification of 'economic' and 'non-economic' assets – and compensation for them – was similarly established by unilateral means. The confusion, exclusion and uncertainty that resulted fuelled tension and hostility in the community, amidst allegations of unfairness and inadequate compensation. Furthermore, the 'levelling' impact of similarly structured compensation at household level raised a challenge to established community social structures, and disrupted possible channels of communication between villagers, leaders, the government and the mining company. More broadly, reports of conflict over compensation shortfalls would inform discussions back in Chiadzwa concerning plans for future relocation project.

Compensation was of two kinds: for immediate disturbance and associated costs, and for longer-term loss of assets and livelihoods. In the short term, each relocated household, irrespective of size, was promised a one-off payment of US$1,000 as a disturbance allowance; one house; one hectare of land for each household, one hectare for dry land cultivation and one-half hectare for irrigated cultivation, as well as agricultural implements; and four-months' supply of foodstuff valued at US$400-480 (mine officials undertook to distribute food to each family once every four months until the next harvest). Government also undertook to provide 500 hectares of grazing land and set aside 1,000 hectares for potential investors. But while the basics of short-term compensation seemed clear they nonetheless proved problematic.

Under the house replacement scheme each family which had a kitchen in their Chiadzwa home was allocated a house, including adult sons who had built houses within the precincts of their parents' homestead. Having a kitchen was used as a measure of independence of a family unit. Families meeting this criterion were allocated a pre-built three-roomed house, a stand-alone kitchen and a toilet on a one-hectare piece of land. Village Heads received bigger houses of up to five rooms, and personal vehicles, with Chief Chiadzwa receiving an eight-roomed house, a Toyota Hilux double-cab and monthly fuel allocations and allowances from Mbada. This raised suspicion that some traditional leaders had either negotiated a better deal for themselves or had been corrupted by mining companies or government officials. On account of such preferential treatment, displaced villagers lost trust in some of their traditional leaders whom they accused of betraying them for personal gain. But more broadly, replacing houses lost to mining activities in like manner for the majority of households was fraught with problems. It created a sense of social sameness among a highly differentiated group of people. Many displaced people who had several houses or cumulatively more room space than the houses they were allocated in the resettlement area felt aggrieved and wanted to be compensated additionally for their loss: villagers who had worked hard and had found success in improving their lives and investing in their household economies and property felt cheated. While the provision of new houses at ARDA Transau averted homelessness, in many instances it significantly reduced the actual housing space of larger households, creating conditions of overcrowding and severe tension.

There were also problems with the provision of land and agricultural support. Two months before the start of the agriculture season, Mbada had not yet cleared the land for the first displaced families; four years later, the land allocated for dry cultivation remained uncleared and inaccessible to families. Moreover, disputes arose with villagers under Chief Zimunya, who arrived to occupy and claim land that had been set aside for the resettled Chiadzwa households at ARDA Transau.

Meanwhile, land for irrigation was not sufficiently demarcated and the irrigation canal system was dysfunctional, and would remain inaccessible to households and their half-hectare plots. While the company had promised to provide families with basic agricultural inputs, including seeds and fertilisers, to kick-start their first agricultural season in ARDA Transau, the absence of timely land preparation cast doubt over the chances of a good first harvest. Livelihood support also fell short. The 1,000 hectares promised for new investment was not allocated, and although training and financial support for projects like poultry keeping were planned, little more than training was delivered.

A more contentious aspect of compensation involved household and economic assets that were to be assessed and compensated on a case-by-case basis. Responsibility for asset valuation was delegated to the Ministry of Local Government. Inventory registers were agreed with affected individuals, and were countersigned by village heads, mine officials and district administration officials. However, the financial valuation criteria used by the ministry were not made known, nor were the levels of financing available, the processes by which valuation assessments were made, or the means by which appeals might be made to challenge officials' findings. Basic elements of compensation assessments were not disclosed; for example, whether the market or replacement value of assets would apply. Few villagers reported they were aware of commitments made by Mbada around asset compensation. By their own valuation, displaced families reckoned they had lost US$25-30,000 as a consequence of displacement and resettlement. Five months after the first phase of relocation, the results of the asset assessment had still not been communicated to villagers or mine officials in order that valuation amounts could be compiled and used for the purposes of budget formulation. Among relocated families, scepticism was growing about the likelihood of fair compensation ever being paid in full. As one village head observed,

We do not know if we will ever be compensated for the land, property and animals that we lost when we came here. The so called disturbance allowance of $1,000 was not enough to help us start a new life. There is not enough land here for farming and other income generating projects compared to the place we were before.

Ministerial pronouncements on the impact of the Kimberley Process ban on diamond exports from Marange compounded villagers' pessimistic stance on compensation. 'We will only get the money to compensate the villagers when our diamonds are sold freely', mining minister Obert Mpofu said in May 2011, thereby making the promised compensation of community losses contingent upon the decisions of a treaty organisation which had decried both the poor treatment of artisanal miners and communities, and the shady management of mining contracts and diamond trading by the very forces on whom villagers were depending for their payouts.[4]

The question of compensation for 'non-economic' and cultural assets also emerged as source of conflict. Under the scheme implemented by the government and Mbada, natural resources that supported livelihoods, and some immovable natural infrastructure – including non-cultivated fruits and plants, non-husbanded animals and natural water sources – were excluded from economic compensation. Some villagers had sunk deep wells at their homesteads, had well-tended gardens, mature fruit trees and woodlots to meet fuel wood needs in the future. They also had built granaries and cattle kraals. However, these assets were not included in the official asset inventory, and the logic for excluding them was not

---

4 'No compensation for displaced Chiadzwa villagers-Minister', *ZimEye*, 14 May 2011.

well communicated. Displaced families argued that these assets might not have been evaluated appropriately. For the community these conditions implied considerable losses, particularly with regard to food security and water resources. The extent of the problem is illustrated in Table 1. In this context villagers complained that the short term provision of household food baskets and the slow pace in preparing land for cultivation and grazing at ARDA Transau reflected only part of a much larger food and resource deficit created by their relocation from Chiadzwa.

Table 1. Non-economic Assets Lost	
Asset type	**Percent of respondents**
Fruit trees	70
Deep wells/boreholes	50
Fences	58
Crops not harvested	60
Eggs that won't hatch	10
Vegetable gardens	80
Forest resources	100
Ancestors' graves	100
Valuation of non-economic assets and resource lost by respondents	
US$ 500-600	10
US$ 700-800	30
US$ 900-1,000	60

'Cultural assets', such as ancestors' graves, were not initially included in inventories and were a source of additional tension. Displaced people regretted leaving behind such graves. They complained that Mbada had not communicated information regarding dates for exhumation, reburial sites and the degree and timing of compensation, fuelling speculation that villagers would have to bear the cost themselves. Many agonised over the fact that they had not yet performed the necessary cultural rites at these sites. These uncertainties weighed heavily on displaced villagers' minds and were a focus of community anxiety and frustration: being forcibly moved from one's ancestral home, respondents observed, is like casting away one's identity. Mbada subsequently bore the costs for exhumations and reburial, albeit on land to which access was limited.[5] Once the villagers had been displaced, access to their original area was tightly restricted and return for the purpose of important cultural practices was difficult to arrange due to the heavy security presence in Chiadzwa. In some instances disruption by mining and excavation made this permanently impossible.

Relocation also disrupted social support systems. The families relocated were a collection of people not necessarily related by lineage or village. Displacement was determined by the mine's geological footprint and development phases, so that people were displaced not as intact villages but rather as individual households: proximity to mine works was the key factor in the phased relocation and allotment of housing and plots at ARDA Transau. The process of social disarticulation was worsened by the fact that displaced families' names were listed randomly on the house allocation list at the resettlement farm, without due regard to the villagers' social organisation structures; for example, houses were assigned according to the order in which names had been recorded at the point of displacement. Therefore communities were fractured from the outset. As a consequence displaced people were separated from or placed in competitive, antagonistic relations with their traditional leaders, relatives, neighbours and social support systems, at a time when they were in critical need of them.

A final and vital form of disruption cited by many respondents concerned livelihoods going into the future. The majority of displaced people were subsistence farmers. Before the advent of mechanised mining, the extensive and growing presence of artisanal diamond miners in Chiadzwa had presented the displaced villagers with alternative forms of livelihood. While some were engaged in diamond extraction, others sold a variety of goods and services to the artisanal miners. There was a trade market in small livestock, vegetables and other agricultural products. However, with the contraction of mining companies and the start of relocations, such options came under pressure. Employment and agricultural opportunities were severely limited in the new settlement area, and back in Chiadzwa, Mbada did not offer many jobs to the local population. The

---

5   A total of 143 graves spanning the period 1959-2013 were exhumed, with relatives of the deceased given US$ 1,500 and two heads of cattle for each grave moved. Exhumations were done by a funeral undertaker contracted by the company.

company engaged little with displaced people around employment provision, apart from keeping a record of their names for future consideration. The community's expectation was to get an inheritable employment quota, but it soon became apparent that diamond mining was caught up in a larger dynamic of patronage involving other parts of the country and other interests, and that the displaced were not high up on the list of constituencies attracting government or corporate favour. Informants felt that jobs were being filled by ZANU-PF party loyalists ahead of local residents, and that diamond mining companies were complicit in this arrangement. One community leader recalled:

> *We talked to mine officials and we asked them to employ our sons and daughters who had left school; they simply wrote their names down but up to now nothing has been done. Those people are employing their relatives from different parts of the country.*

The web of patronage extended overseas when it came to labour. Anjin, one of the larger mining operations with a major Chinese shareholding, brought Chinese workers in large numbers into the country to work the company's Chiadzwa claim.

Chinese labourers at Anjin: local benefits for whom?

Conclusion

All told, diamond mining in Marange would result in the displacement of hundreds of families and several thousand people over a three-year period. In both its planning and execution by government in co-oper-ation with the diamond mining companies in Marange, the relocation and resettlement of villagers was undertaken in highly untransparent, unfair and disruptive ways. While various promises and mechanisms for displacement-related compensation were put in place, villagers found it increasingly difficult to access information, communicate with companies and government, and actively lobby for the delivery of compensation. A crisis of expectation tinged with frustration emerged from the first wave of relocations and inspired heightened wariness in both Chiadzwa and ARDA Transau about the promised 'new start' for villagers. The reality was rather one of torn-up communities; substan-tial loss of economic, social and cultural assets; inadequate and unde-livered compensation; and profound disempowerment.

For Chiadzwa's displaced, the first-hand experience of mining 'de-velopment' raised important questions about government's strategy for managing the resource, and the ascendancy of mining companies in the shaping and making of critical decisions around community impacts of mining. If the government claimed that Marange diamonds would be the source of funding for national development and associated local benefits, as Chiadzwa's villagers understood, it was not clear why even the initial manifestations of development remained hard to see, and why relocat-ed communities were poorer and less stable after diamond mining than before it. Moreover, for a sector in which the state had claimed such a large role in organising and redistributing benefits, the reasons for the strengthened role of mining companies in managing relocation and com-pensation arrangements were not apparent. The hidden power of mining companies, shielded by secretive concession contracts and underpinned by government's dependency on their success, was felt directly by villag-ers and was severely disabling. Government had been effective in forcing compliance from villagers with regard to displacement; its willingness and power in forcing compliance from companies in paying compensa-tion to those whose land they now occupied was weak in comparison. In Chiadzwa and ARDA Transau the uneven and unfair approach by gov-ernment in managing and balancing the interests of Chiadzwa's residents and its new mining investors set the stage for new forms of engagement among local diamond stakeholders. In the face of challenges from above, Chiadzwa's communities and villagers emerged to assert alternative visions and demands around development of a different kind. In the years ahead, the lessons from the first wave of relocations would help to animate discussions within Chiadzwa about how to resist the government's notions of 'development' and promote the community's own visions of sustainable diamond and community growth.

9

Holding Ground: Community, Companies and Resistance in Chiadzwa

Melanie Chiponda and Richard Saunders

Introduction

Diamond-related 'development' descended on Marange like a terrible storm, upending homesteads and livelihoods, scattering communities, ripping through the natural environment and profoundly disrupting the social and economic landscape. In its midst, Marange's villagers struggled to survive, defending their livelihoods and rights by mobilising and mounting challenges to the imposition of an unwelcome new order. As traditional structures were corroded through forced evictions and relocations to make way for mining operations, old and new forms of community organisation emerged and became intertwined. The globalisation of the Marange problem through growing national and international attention provided new opportunities for the community in its campaign to secure its rightful benefits from local diamond wealth – but also raised new obstacles. A decade later, both the power and limits of communities and companies in mounting competing forms of resistance are increasingly clear, raising important questions about the role and effectiveness of civil society in contesting, re-imagining and shaping resource governance and development.

This chapter follows the experiences and responses of Marange's communities as they engaged and tried to mediate the powerful diamond mining forces in their midst. The main focus falls on the period of formalised mining beginning in 2009, when government oversaw the establishment of large scale mechanised extraction and the restructuring of local communities to accommodate miners' needs. The discussion follows the impact of forced relocations, damaged livelihoods and broken promises on local society, and charts the emergence of resistance through new forms of community organisation that took up the linked issues of human rights and development as a starting point for community participation. It explores how the community and its organisations were transformed through engagement with larger scales of power and interests, and assesses the potential and pitfalls of Marange villagers' evolving strategic engagement with miners, government and civil society allies. Where, the chapter asks, was the centre of gravity of social and economic power in the case of Marange; and what did this imply for communities as they engaged government and mining companies with the aim of securing more equitable, participatory and locally sustainable forms of minerals-based development?

Origins of a Community's Trust

Long before the diamond rush of the 2000s the community of Marange was aware of the unusual qualities of some local soils. Local folk knew that the diamond-bearing stones had something special about them, but they did not place a market value on them or define them in any scientific form. It was common knowledge that the stones at Zengeni, Chirasika and Betera were very strong. They could make lasting and strong foundations for houses and were often used when constructing graves. The Mwashita family's homestead in Zengeni was well known for using the 'strong stones' for decorating their foundations as the stones were found in abundance in their area. Diamond-bearing stones were moved freely in the villages as people often picked them up when they were building their houses in order to strengthen their foundations. There were no restrictions in gathering stones for building. Similarly, the stones had no market value, beyond the fact they were recognised for their structural strength. People did not fight over the stones; no one claimed them as their own; they belonged to the village. This would change dramatically

Pondering the next move: displaced villagers at ARDA Transau resettlement area

Demanding a share: demonstration by members of Chiadzwa Community Development Trust, 2012

and irreversibly in the 2000s. While the De Beers diamond company had had a presence in the community for many years, most people in the Marange community did not bother about what the company was doing. Their exploration activities were not very pronounced. The De Beers trucks often transported the spotted stones and other non-spotted stones and soil, but their exploratory work was low-key and for the most part villagers' subsistence farming and their daily lives were unimpeded by De Beers. People moved freely; there were no fenced-off areas; there were no army or police in the village. There had been occasional rumours of the existence of diamonds – but there were always rumours, and few paid attention or took them seriously. However, when De Beers left Marange in March 2006 and a new company, African Consolidated Resources (ACR), arrived soon after, the rumours were confirmed by the new title holder. ACR officials seemed willing to engage the community. They visited the traditional leaders, and members of the community were invited to meetings. ACR promised the community a range of benefits; above all, they promised to compensate for the disturbances that they would cause.

Shortly thereafter, without warning, what appeared to be a promising engagement was turned upside-down by the sudden intervention of government. In May 2006, government publicly announced the 'discovery' of diamonds in Marange, and soon senior officials invited the people of Zimbabwe to come to the district to mine freely – as long as they sold their diamonds to government. It was the beginning of an unprecedented diamond rush in the country, and the beginning of the end of life in Marange as the community had known it. Thousands had descended on fields and homesteads by late 2006. At first, the community tried to bar people from entering their homesteads, but as the number of people increased it became impossible to control anything, particularly in the diamondiferous fields in Wards 29 and 30 where there was digging on every plot of land. An entirely new economy and society – violent, chaotic, disrespectful and wholly disruptive – forced itself into the middle of the Marange community.[1]

---

1 There is a growing literature on this 'free-for-all' period of mining in Marange. See for example, contributions by Nyamunda and Ruguwa in this volume; see also, Centre for Research and Development (2009); Global Witness (2010); Human Rights Watch (2009); Martin and Taylor (2010); Katsaura (2010b); Towriss (2013).

By early 2008, this new order, compounded by the national economic meltdown, was overwhelming communities in Marange. Government was not helping the situation or providing leadership to solve these problems; in many ways it was making them worse, and its adherents were profiting from the chaos at the expense of locals. Government's manipulations were on display in its strategic handling of the Marange chieftaincy succession. When exploration for diamonds first began, the then Chief Marange was forcefully and publicly opposed to any development which proceeded without consulting traditional authorities, and which did not directly benefit the local community. When he passed away on 16 November 2007, the rightful heir to the chieftaincy – who was also opposed to development without local approval and engagement – was pushed aside by government, which instead appointed Gilbert Marange as Chief without proper consultations and procedures involving the Marange chieftaincy. Gilbert, a passive supporter of government from his first days in the post, was installed in 2007. He would later be bestowed with new assets including an impressive house; as a result, there was much talk amongst Marange folk about compromises and rewards and the chieftaincy.

All of this contributed to a strong challenge to ZANU-PF in the 31 March 2008 elections and, later, to the formation by community members of an organisation to lobby on their behalf around the new development challenges facing them. The Movement for Democratic Change (MDC) put forward a strong candidate, Shuah Mudiwa, a former executive at the Reserve Bank of Zimbabwe, to stand against the prominent ruling party MP, Christopher Mushowe, in the March poll. There was a lot of harassment by ZANU-PF and government of the MDC and its potential supporters; for example, during the campaign Mudiwa was arrested on charges of kidnapping for the purposes of witchcraft.[2] Despite this, he narrowly won the Mutare West parliamentary constituency, notably with strong support from voters in Wards 29 and 30, the diamond-affected areas.[3]

---

2 Mudiwa was initially convicted and sentenced to seven years' incarceration, but on appeal was fully exonerated. 'Mudiwa granted bail', *The Zimbabwean*, 8 July 2009.

3 Mudiwa's margin of victory was only 20 votes; when he appeared to be gaining votes in the course of a recount, the recount figures were abandoned and the official result reverted to the earlier narrower win. It was clear that

Having an MDC MP representing Marange opened the door to more discussion in the community about how to deal with the continuing problems associated with mining, but it also presaged an intensification of attacks from government. Mudiwa began convening community meetings in order to gather information and grievances which he hoped to bring to government's attention through parliament. These complaints were mounting in the post-election period, in the wake of the growing political and diamond-related violence. After the election, violence was unleashed on the MDC and many activists fled the community for safety in the forests along the Odzi River or to stay with relatives in urban areas. At the same time, the state's clampdown on the community was worsening. Vending was criminalised and women's vending stalls were closed; security agents stated that the stalls posed a security threat to the diamond fields. Cropping fields were taken over. Violence intensified sharply in late 2008 and culminated in 'Operation Hakudzokwi', which saw 1,500 security officers deployed into the area, camping in schools, crèches, shopping centers, and open spaces. By this time, many villagers had lost their homes, jobs, and schools. Scores of people were killed during the diamond fields 'clean-up' by security forces, and many more were subjected to harassment, personal indignities and other human rights abuses. Buses were barred from entering Marange and the few that were allowed only went up to Mutsago. As a result, communities from wards 29 and 30 had to walk more than 20 kilometres to get to the bus stop in order to reach their homes.[4] Body and car searches were introduced at all major entry points into Marange. At Bambazonke shopping centre and 22 Miles Entry Point, tents were pitched for body searches. Women were commanded to take off their clothes in the tent so that female officers could search their private parts. Only the elderly were spared.

While many in the community hoped Mudiwa would be able to draw attention to these alarming issues, the MDC struggled to be effective in its challenge to ZANU-PF after the 2008 elections. Control over Marange was especially important to ZANU-PF and Mudiwa was personally targeted. He was soon facing removal from parliament and a long term prison sentence after his initial conviction on trumped-up kidnap-

---

without the higher levels of support he obtained in Wards 29 and 30 Mudiwa would have been defeated.

4   The situation still pertained in 2014; see, 'Villagers trapped in Marange diamond fields', *Bulawayo 24 News*, 24 February 2014.

ping charges.[5] The new MP did help mobilise new support for those who had been victimised by violence and abuse or were affected by mining and links were made with Harare-based organisations. The Counselling Services Unit (CSU) assisted victims of violence and rape to access free medical services and counselling; Zimbabwe Lawyers for Human Rights (ZLHR) offered free legal representation, training and advice to the Marange community; the Zimbabwe Environmental Law Association (ZELA) started training and teaching on environmental issues; and Dewa Mavinga of the Crisis Coalition came to offer solidarity with the community. However, the larger challenge of getting government to acknowledge and redress the problem of violence and rights abuses seemed to be beyond the MDC's capacity, as government had politicised the Marange issue and blocked all opposition efforts.

In late 2008, local women, who were bearing the brunt of the harassment, deepening economic deprivation and personal indignity and hardship, grew more vocal in complaining about the situation. They pushed Mudiwa to do something to protect their rights and interests. A woman whose field was taken and homestead divided in two by a mining fence took the initiative in organising locally and approaching Mudiwa. After consulting ZLHR, ZELA and other NGOs, the MP raised the idea of setting up a community organisation to collect and disseminate information, train and support villagers and lobby government. In the event that the MP could no longer function as their representative, he argued, such an organisation might prevent the community's voice from being silenced. This marked the start of the Chiadzwa Community Development Trust (CCDT). Community meetings convened in early 2009 discussed the aims and objectives of the organisation and initiated the process of selecting its board. With advice and help from ZLHR and ZELA a Deed of Trust was drawn up and the CCDT was formally registered as a trust on 30 June 2009.

From the outset, the CCDT attracted a large and diverse membership. People living in the diamond fields, political activists, people whose land had been grabbed by government and the mining companies, women who were survivors of abuse and those who were disgruntled with gov-

---

5   Mudiwa was suspended from Parliament in July 2009, but following his successful appeal against conviction and sentence in 2010 he resumed his parliamentary seat; see, 'High Court quashes MP conviction', *The Legal Monitor*, 6 December 2010.

ernment's poor management of Marange, participated in the formation of the Trust. So did community businessman whose businesses had been affected by diamond mining and the state security agencies. At first people filled in forms to join, but this became burdensome as more people came and it was decided that new members would only have to read and sign forms in order to join. Later, a public meeting resolved that the CCDT would represent anyone in Marange who needed representation, and would assist any member of the community who had been physically abused in accessing free medical treatment and legal representation.

Unfortunately, but not surprisingly, the founding leadership of the CCDT did not fully reflect the bulk of its membership. Communities in Marange are traditional, hierarchical and deeply patriarchal in their organisation and allocation of leadership authority. As a result, even if women were very active in the mobilisation that led to the Trust's formation and remained active members of it, their voice was marginalised in the jostling for positions when the Trust's board was formed. The leadership structure was heavily dominated by local elites, including traditional authorities and businessmen. Only one woman was selected as a trustee; youth, who had also been energetic activists, were entirely excluded. Yet, even with its narrower elite membership, the Board of Trustees still reflected political diversity, and it was clear that political sympathies differed at the elite level. To prevent partisan politics from getting in the way of the CCDT's mandate to help the whole community – and to avoid compromising situations for party activists who might be forced through the CCDT to defend the rights of people belonging to another political party – the Trust's constitution explicitly banned partisan activism. While these measures failed to prevent the departure of some founding board members politically aligned with government, they did prove important in maintaining the CCDT's formal non-partisan status, and made it possible to engage government, the mining companies, donors and others as the Trust began its lobbying, advocacy and community support work.

The rapidly changing situation in Marange and the country at large in 2009 brought a number of challenges and opportunities for the Trust. Government announced that it had formally contracted mining companies to start preparations for mechanised mining in late 2009, and that this would involve the forced relocation of thousands of villagers to new areas. A Government of National Unity (GNU) was formalised in early 2009, bringing the MDC into a power-sharing agreement with ZANU-PF. This seemed to present new opportunities for engaging government more effectively, particularly around concerns about violence, security and human rights abuses. Both of these changes helped place CCDT at the centre of debates about managing Marange's development and protecting its communities, and brought it into closer contact and co-operation with national organisations and interests. The Trust became an important link between Marange and the outside world, in both directions: given security restrictions on entering the district, CCDT became a critical player in the collection and dissemination of information; a provider of training and support for human rights, environmental and relocations monitoring; and the local co-ordinator for a range of related work. Even government officials like mining minister Obert Mpofu, who had been hostile towards those campaigning for social justice in Marange, started to engage the CCDT. Government adopted the paradoxical position of requesting information from the CCDT on human rights violations, complaints of abuse and related matters, while simultaneously working to politically undermine it.

Outside organisations also benefited greatly from the CCDT's work and had a strong interest in helping build its capacity and reach. Investment in training, institutional and financial support flowed in from civil society and donors. A part-time employee started in 2009 and would become regularly employed within a year; offices were established, recruitment expanded, and training and education projects started. Through linkages with the South Africa-based Bench Marks Foundation, training in community-based human rights monitoring was launched. The CCDT contributed to policy discussions in support of the proposed Diamond Policy and Mines and Minerals Amendment Bill, opened up Community Dialogue Forums on natural resource governance and environmental management, and participated in the Zimbabwe Mining Revenue Transparency Initiative, a tripartite group consisting of government, the private sector and civil society.[6] Meanwhile, its members became im-

---

6   ZMRTI was modeled on the international body, the Extractive Industries Transparency Initiative. Other members included government's ministries of Finance and Mines and Mining Development, the Zimbabwe Revenue Authority and the Zimbabwe Mining Development Corporation. Private sector members included the Zimbabwe Chamber of Mines and some of its member

mersed in various forms of capacity building and training with a view to strengthening skills for monitoring, reporting and defusing violence and conflict, and launched a sustainable livelihoods project in the relocation area aimed at bolstering food security.

From Demilitarisation to Displacement

Initially, the CCDT's work focused on dealing with heightened levels of political and diamond-related violence in the community. One of the first targets of advocacy was the demilitarisation of Marange District in the wake of 'Operation Hakudzokwi'. Attention was drawn to the killings of late 2008, continuing cases of detention and torture, and the establishment of 'Diamond Base', a military camp which many locals came to view as a torture centre. The military seemed to be everywhere, and people felt endangered and frightened. But the focus of the Trust's work would shift dramatically in September 2009, when new mining companies showed up in Marange unannounced. There had been no advance consultation with the community and no information provided. MP Mudiwa explained that although he sat on Parliament's Portfolio Committee responsible for mining, even he was in the dark, and that the committee itself was being prevented from making a research visit to Marange because of 'security considerations'. Rumours were flying and tensions in the community were escalating. Then in November 2009, Christopher Mushowe – the ZANU-PF former MP who had been defeated by Mudiwa only to then be appointed to the powerful post of Governor of Manicaland by President Mugabe – called for community meetings at Zengeni and Mashukashuka. They were attended by a number of government officials and security agents, but the Governor, District Administrator (DA) and the local Chief were the only people the community knew. Armed police and soldiers accompanied the visitors. The atmosphere was extremely intimidating.

It was announced that everyone should stop construction projects and that all agricultural activities should cease, even though the new cropping season was just getting under way. The DA said government feared that the community might dig for diamonds under the pretext of land cultivation, and that mining was now the exclusive right of the new com-

---

mining companies, and the Association of Women in Mining. In addition to the CCDT, civil society representatives included ZELA and the Centre for Research and Development.

panies to whom government had awarded mining licences. Security of the mining concession enclaves was a priority, and therefore 'loitering' was strictly prohibited. People were told to stay at their homesteads and keep their animals close, ensuring they did not wander into nearby mining territories. Finally, the DA announced he would be conducting a census of the district in preparation for the relocation of all households in Wards 29 and 30, which would start in January 2010 – just two months away. At the new unspecified resettlement location, houses, schools and clinics would be built by the mining companies; land would be available for cultivation, including some irrigation facilities; there would be free tap water and electricity available to relocated residents; and there would be some unspecified forms of compensation for forfeited household assets. The DA promised that everything would be put in writing and that the community could access the agreements and conditions through their chiefs and the DA's office. Then the Governor proclaimed in no uncertain terms that people did not have the right to resist relocation. The community was left in a state of shock.

CCDT called an emergency meeting of the community for the next day. There was need for a common position on what to do, and an important step was taken: it was resolved that villagers should not leave their homes without adequate compensation being made. About one month later, the DA and his evaluation team returned and announced that 4,310 families had been identified as living in the diamond fields and would be targeted for relocation. Properties would be evaluated in preparation for individual compensation. The DA and the evaluation team moved around, taking notes and only asking a few questions; sometimes no more than one. Villagers were sceptical about the process and sought to explain what was of value to them, but few were given a chance. It seemed that value was solely attributed by the DA and the evaluation team; what the owners of property felt mattered little. In the meantime, CCDT consulted with civil society partners to strategise on how to slow down the process of forced relocations. ZELA promised to assist with legal issues around relocations and some months later in 2010 lodged an urgent court application, unsuccessfully, to stop the process.[7] ZLHR

---

7   ZELA's application was dismissed because the court did not regard the matter as urgent. The court also raised questions about the legitimacy of the applicant, one of CCDT's board members, since he himself was not listed for relocation.

provided a two-day intensive training of CCDT members on the rights of relocated communities, and how it might be possible to refuse relocation successfully. After the training, Trust members agreed to refuse relocation if there were no houses and other services of sufficient standard immediately available. Those who feared the wrath of the soldiers were encouraged to leave their homes and visit relatives until the resistance was over and government had backed off.

About one month after ZELA's application was dismissed, the first twelve families were relocated from Marange to the ARDA Transau resettlement area by Anjin, one of the larger mine operators. Despite CCDT cautions, they had been lured out of Marange by promises of compensation, new houses, land, education and health services. They soon discovered that the reality at ARDA Transau was something quite different. They were housed in old farm buildings not fit for human habitation; there was no tap water and no clinic or health facility; there was an old farm primary school but no secondary school. When CCDT members first visited the resettled families two months after their relocation, the Trust found them living in destitution, with little to eat and nothing to do. The mining company had dumped them with no food. They urged CCDT to inform their relatives back in Marange to refuse relocation and certain destitution. When this information was shared with the CCDT and ordinary members there was initially mixed feelings: after all, the first families relocated had defied the recommendation of CCDT to refuse relocation without first obtaining compensation. But in discussion, it was decided not to abandon the displaced villagers; they had been deceived by the DA's promises, they had been intimidated, and in any event, hundreds of Marange families were slated to join them in ARDA Transau, and all community members needed to share information and strategies to avoid a common fate. CCDT resolved to continuously engage with ARDA Transau's families and take up their cause as part of the plight of those left behind in Marange.

When news of the situation at ARDA Transau was brought to Marange, resistance to relocations became stronger. In August 2010 the DA informed 60 families they would be moved during the school holidays, in the first week of the month. But when trucks arrived to carry people and their property to ARDA Transau no one boarded. The police told people to start packing to leave, but all of the families who were supposed to be relocated remained in their homes doing their daily chores as if nothing was happening. Soldiers came and intimidated the community but this did not work either, and people ignored them. The moving trucks were parked in Marange for a month. The school holidays came and went, and the community still resisted relocation. The CCDT followed up this success by organising a community meeting in Mutare with relocated families and those who had said no to relocation. The DA and the Provincial Governor were invited, with the aim of negotiating a more transparent, fairer process, with guarantees of compensation and provision of services and infrastructure for the relocated. The families came but the DA and Provincial Governor did not, so a list of demands was sent to their offices. Trust members met with the Provincial Administrator and informed him of their grievances and concerns over the relocation process. He promised to act on the issues and appeared to have understood the problems with the forced removals.[8]

It soon became clear that community resistance and public campaigning by the Trust around the rights of the relocated was prompting contrasting responses. The DA with whom the community had fractious relations was withdrawn from his post and replaced in 2010; at the same time, a large-scale house-building project began in ARDA Transau, and about 100 houses were built by December 2010. However, both these gains were ambiguous. The new DA proved to be no more co-operative than his predecessor, and seemed constrained by the same political pressures and top-down decision-making processes. He continued to fail to honour pledges made to relocated families around compensation, quality of infrastructure and transparency of process. Meanwhile, the new housing at Transau was less than ideal, as revealed by monitoring overseen by CCDT: many houses were of poor quality and in inappropriate locations, and services were wholly insufficient.[9] When CCDT complained, the new DA said his duty was to avail land to the mining companies, and that the building and certification of houses was beyond his authority: it

---

8   'Govt seeks land to relocate villagers', *The Herald*, 28 March 2013.

9   CCDT monitoring revealed that many houses were shoddily built, often made with wet bricks. The result was cracked walls and rising damp from the floor during rainy season. The roofs of at least 89 houses built by Anjin were blown off in the wind.

was the companies which had the mandate to build as they saw fit – and if the companies refused to engage with the community, they would not be pressured to do so by government.[10] Nevertheless, government put this 'development' on display for the media and Marange community with some degree of success, to counter the CCDT's arguments and campaign against forced relocations.

Towards the end of 2010 the DA and mining companies hired a bus and invited the Marange community to come and see the new homesteads. They consisted of four-roomed houses under asbestos, each with an outside thatched kitchen, outside toilet and bathroom. The DA promised that clearing of land for cultivation was underway and that irrigation equipment was being worked on as well. He told the community that they would receive groceries until they had their first harvest. With a fresh outlook, and in the face of some scepticism on CCDT's part, the community accepted the offer, and relocations to ARDA Transau ramped up quickly in 2011. In that year each of the main diamond mining companies moved people off their land. By December 2012 nearly 700 families had been moved; within a year 1,100 were relocated, the total reaching 1,400 by the end of 2014.

The rapid growth of households at ARDA Transau placed new pressures on the community and those meant to be providing the new infrastructure, and revealed deep flaws in the relocation process. Government had adopted a hands-off approach to overseeing development at the relocation site, giving companies extensive powers to manage and fund the process. Some companies were more generous and more open than others when it came to solving problems by engaging with the community and the CCDT. As a result, a hierarchy of better-offs and worse-offs emerged in the resettlement area, depending on which company was responsible for the household concerned. Anjin, the large Chinese-run firm, was particularly problematic, and for some time refused to deal with the CCDT or complaints from others; Mbada Diamonds and Marange Resources, on the other hand, were more approachable, and some-

---

10 In a further twist, the DA was later accused of corruptly extracting payment from villagers at ARDA Transau for access to small farming plots, reportedly demanding $100 per family for farming rights; see, Centre for Natural Resource Governance, 'Mutare District Administrator demands payment from displaced ARDA Transau Villagers'; http://teamzimbabwe.org/govt-attacks-chiadzwa-villagers-again/

times more amenable to solving logistical and other problems brought to their attention. Even then, what companies like Mbada saw as a matter of corporate social responsibility (CSR) – that is, a voluntary contribution to community development – the community viewed as contractual obligation. For example, Mbada listed its building of resettlement houses in its CSR report, when these were in fact a contractual undertaking implicit in its acquisition of villagers' land and homesteads. This approach adopted by companies meant that the CCDT was repeatedly forced to agitate and haggle for what it took as the due right of the community under government's relocation promises.

The community's conflictual relations with companies were underpinned by an essential problem: government's refusal to intervene and force companies to live up to guarantees and equitable standards for relocated households. Government continued to resist demands by the community for the publication of its agreements with the mining companies, particularly those sections concerning removals, compensation and environmental degradation back in Marange. Most important of all, it failed to live up to its commitment to divulge the findings of the original household asset evaluations, or explain why only a fraction of the more than 4,000 households slated for removal had been evaluated. Companies insisted that they could not pay compensation until they were notified by government of its assessment findings; on their part, villagers had no information on the amount of compensation they were entitled to seek from the companies. The tragic result was that five years after the first removals villagers had yet to be compensated for the loss of their homesteads and livelihoods, while fortunes were made by the companies mining their former fields.[11]

By 2014, ARDA Transau was approaching its full carrying capacity of 1,800 families, and government announced it was considering new sites for relocation – again, without consulting the community, or acknowledging continuing social and economic problems in both Marange and the relocation area.[12] Among the relocated, an environment of misery

---

11 On the other hand, compensation was paid to some businesses that had been closed down in Zengeni, and to prominent traditional figures and political elites. But such compensation was the exception, and only underscored the ad hoc, partisan and secretive nature of compensation under government's mandate.

12 'Relocation at Chiadzwa hits snag', *The Financial Gazette*, 13 June 2013.

and dependency took root, fuelling rising social tension; back in Marange, where resistance to relocation was stiffening in the wake of the ARDA Transau reality, there was a pervasive climate of violence, coercion and constrained subsistence. A 2015 survey of villagers' experiences of forced removals underscored the severity of the continuing crisis: 69 per cent of those surveyed reported being coerced or threatened with violence by companies and government security forces to get them to relocate; arrests, torture and murder were reported as being amongst the tools deployed by soldiers to this end.[13] The testimony of a 61-year-old woman about her forced eviction was compelling and representative of a wider experience:

> *They came in the dead of the night. A Chinese man and three soldiers told me that I had a death wish. They asked what makes me so important that I refuse to move when all the others had gone. I told them that my husband, my son, and my ancestors were buried here. They said if I want to follow them to the world of the dead, I should just do so without disturbing the diamond mining. I was scared and they told me to start packing. I did in a hurry. I left a lot of things behind—my cattle, my garden, my field, my orchard but most importantly, my son and my husband. Who does that to a human being? Who destroys a grave that does not belong to his relative?[14]*

Of those relocated to ARDA Transau, two-thirds reported that their lives were 'worse' or 'much worse' than before their eviction. Only 24 per cent indicated they had received the land promised for subsistence farming, and none had been provided with gainful employment. Other accounts of dispossession in Marange and later destitution at ARDA Transau came to similar conclusions, noting the particular vulnerability of women, widows, the elderly and households with multiple wives. The experience of one elderly woman was instructive:

> *My story is a riches to rags ordeal. I had over fifty cattle, seventy goats and 300 free range chickens. When we were relocated, I brought some of my livestock here but they succumbed to diseases and died. I sold some of my livestock to make ends meet... Most of the older persons here are wid-*

---

13 Chiponda (2015).
14 Ibid., p. 58.

owed women and taking care of orphaned grandchildren who
still need our care. Some children are now dropping out of
school as we are in school fees arrears at the schools dating
back to 2011.[15]

Many at ARDA Transau remained dependent on food handouts. For those who resisted moving, mine operators used coercion of new kinds; for example, mining directly on homestead land and blasting next to homes, sometimes late into the night. The noise and dust made many homes uninhabitable. Livelihoods were deliberately destroyed, watering holes were removed, schools and health clinics were bulldozed, and pollution made it unhealthy to stay. Livestock ran away or drowned in mining pits. Those who held out – including the Chairman of the CCDT – paid the price. After 2010, villagers were prevented from growing crops and many lived on the edge of starvation, dependent on food from political parties, or scavenging in the canteen bins of the mining companies. CCDT advised Marange villagers to continue farming and some did, but those were the brave. Most sat idle, dependent on handouts from family and well-wishers, while they waited for some version of justice to be served.

Community, Trust and Politics

The arrival of the mining companies seemed set to permanently transform Marange's social and environmental landscape in ways that were hard to predict. To meet these threats and mediate their impact on the community, it would be necessary to build local capacities to engage meaningfully – with government at different levels, diverse mining companies, allies and potential allies in civil society, and donors and diplomats who were key figures in the KP side of the Marange story. All of this would require resources, capacity-building support, new skills and perhaps most of all, strong support from the community. There were new opportunities for strengthening community activism but also potential pitfalls, as communities faced powerful interests in government and the diamond industry in setting the agenda for 'development' in Marange.

For the CCDT, building capacity through training links with other civil society organisations continued and expanded in new directions,

15   Zimbabwe Environmental Law Association (2015: 27), quoting Elisha Matanguro.

including not only community-based monitoring of environmental and human rights but also skills development around risk management for human rights monitors. Training of Trust members by ZLHR on human rights monitoring, by ZELA on pollution, monitoring and environmental rights, and the engagement of Trust members directly with the constitutional outreach process in 2010-2012, helped the CCDT and the community to respond more powerfully to abuses and other problems, especially with additional legal and professional assistance from civil society partners. Community members were trained to monitor and record abuses, how to respond to them, who to call on for assistance, and how to convey formal complaints. Systematic reporting of human rights and environmental abuses was put in place and produced important results. CCDT members' monitoring and reporting of abduction, torture and murder involving three local men led to the unprecedented situation of soldiers being arrested and the conviction and sentencing to eighteen years of a policeman for the murder of a villager.[16] It became clear that the more extensive and regular the monitoring, the lower the occurrence of abuse by security personnel and companies.[17]

A contributing factor in reducing abuses was the capacity of civil society to channel monitoring reports and complaints into national and international fora, including media, government and civil society platforms. Especially important were intergovernmental organisations, like the African Union and World Bank. The CCDT built on its initial role in the KP's Civil Society Local Focal Point in Zimbabwe sharing its findings from the human rights monitoring in Marange, and sought to engage more widely with international civil society partners and donors. It participated in a number of international meetings armed with first-hand, well-researched, professional reports on the situation in Marange, at a time when both government and the mining companies were anxious to project a clean image of Marange in the wake of severe criticism by the

---

16   'Killer cop jailed for 18 years', *The Herald*, 6 July 2012. The case reflected the intrigue and violence that continued sporadically in the diamond fields, and the continuing involvement of state security personnel. While it was claimed by government that the men were illegally panning for diamonds, they were in reality digging a well at their homestead when they were seized by soldiers. Although the soldiers claimed that the murdered man had stolen from them, the two were well-known diamond dealers in Marange, and it is suspected that it was a diamond deal gone wrong.

17   Chiponda (2015: 61).

KP and continuing critical NGO reports. Companies especially wished to avoid the tarnishing of their reputations, and recognised the Trust's capacity to bear well-informed witness. This focus of international attention emboldened the CCDT and afforded its members a degree of protection on the ground in Marange. But expanded advocacy and heightened profile also led to new challenges from government. On the one hand the Trust's work was targeted for disruption and interference; on the other, there were attempts to undermine its representatives and its connection with the community. Following the suspicious theft of sensitive CCDT data in 2012 and ominous threats from government shortly after, it was decided that the risk management capacity of the Trust's human rights monitoring programme required strengthening. Training was undertaken to improve security management for monitoring work, data collected and not least, the monitors themselves.[18]

The second challenge was more difficult to confront directly. It involved moves by ZANU-PF and sections of government to establish several parallel, competing 'community trusts' in Marange and ARDA Transau. There were two objectives: first, clouding the waters of diamond activism by introducing conflicting points of view and undermining the broad community representativeness claimed so successfully by the CCDT; and second, supporting ZANU-PF's campaign for the critical 2013 national elections, in an effort to take back the Mutare West seat from the MDC. In Marange alone, seven trusts were formed in 2011-2012. Some were clearly sponsored by ZANU-PF or ZANU-PF youth, and closely paralleled local party structures and activists; others seemed to be formed directly by ZANU-PF wings of government, notably the Ministry of Mines and Mining Development, whose minister, Obert Mpfou, was responsible for the establishment of at least one trust. Their language and agenda reflected a sharp partisanship: there was much talk of 'sell-outs' and 'regime change agents' among diamond advocacy groups, but they expressed little interest in raising questions of human rights abuses, or the lack of fairness or transparency by government and mining companies. They claimed their objectives were to focus on 'development' issues, not 'rights' or 'environmental' issues. The CCDT countered that rights and environmental issues were development issues, and that there could be no development if past and current rights abuses were not

18 With support from the Human Rights Defenders' Facility, 60 CCDT members were trained by the ZLHR in 2012-2013.

acknowledged and addressed.

The highly partisan and politically-expedient nature of the trusts was most clearly seen in the case of the Marange-Zimunya Community Trust (MZCT). Launched with great fanfare in July 2014 at a ceremony attended by President Mugabe, the MZCT was the fifth Community Share Ownership Trust (CSOT) to be initiated by government since 2011. It featured as a component of ZANU-PF's flagship 'indigenisation' policy, and was a key plank in the party's 2013 election platform.[19] At the launch it was announced that the Trust would receive a founding investment from Marange's mining companies totalling $50m – $10m from each of the five companies operating in Marange – for community development projects. A board would be appointed consisting of community leaders, including traditional authorities and others, to manage the Trust's funds. The whole process would be overseen and regulated by government. The only significant difference between the Marange trust and previous CSOTs was the absence of shareholding transfers to the community: in other cases foreign companies ceded 10 per cent of their shares to a community trust and 10 per cent to employees as part of indigenisation-related asset transfers, but in the Marange case government already owned a a stake in each mining company through the Zimbabwe Mining Development Corporation (ZMDC), and therefore the state presumed to manage the community's share in local mining directly.[20]

The community and its CCDT members were sceptical from the outset. As if to highlight the MZCT's partisan origins, government did not invite the CCDT to the launch – the DA claimed that there were so many trusts operating in the area they could not invite them all. It was not long before the MZCT's weak foundations were revealed. A 2014-2015 parliamentary inquiry in response to community anger over the shortcomings of several CSOTs found that many were neither legally constituted nor functional; in reality, hardly any funds had been transferred to them. In the case of the MZCT, there appeared to have been no formal or legal undertaking by the mining companies to provide funds to the Trust; indeed, the companies concerned would later deny ever being consulted

---

19   The first CSOTs were focused around foreign-owned platinum mines: Tongogara (Unki mine), Zvashavane (Mimosa mine), and Gwanda and Mhondoro-Ngezi (Zimplats mines). 'Mugabe To Launch Marange Zimunya Community Trust', *Radio Voice of the People*, 26 July 2012.

20   Mawowa (2013: 22).

about the MZCT, its operations and their expected contributions to it.[21] Despite all the fanfare around the MZCT's launch, it is likely that no more than $400,000 was actually deposited with it by the mining firms. By 2015 the MZCT – along with most of the other trusts established under ZANU-PF sponsorship in competition to the CCDT – was not functioning, and Marange's mining companies, with government's tacit acceptance, had distanced themselves from any real or imagined obligations to it. This situation of 'confusion,' noted Walter Chidhakwa, the new Minister of Mines and Mining Development in 2015, required a re-thinking and renegotiation of the whole process surrounding the Trust.[22] For the CCDT, there was less confusion and greater clarity about what the focus of community development should be in Marange: the redressing of abuses associated with the grabbing of their land and forced relocation; compensation for the community's loss of livelihood; and pursuit of justice for those who had suffered human rights violations at the hands of government and company agents, including, not least, the many who had been killed in 2008.

New Ground and Shifting Sands

If ZANU-PF's victory in the 2013 elections brought challenges to Marange, it also opened new opportunities for community engagement around core issues. The new 2013 constitution, ratified by referendum in advance of the July elections, included important provisions for local community participation in natural resource governance. The 'Founding Principles of the Constitution'[23] mandated the 'equitable sharing of national resources, including land'; Section 13(4) specified that, 'the

---

21 Parliament of Zimbabwe, Thematic Committee on Indigenisation and Empowerment (2015). See also, 'Chaos mars share ownership trusts', *Zimbabwe Independent*, 17 April 2014; 'Marange-Zimunya Community Share Ownership Trust under fire', *The Herald*, 13 February 2014.

22 'Marange-Zimunya Trust to be renegotiated,' *The Herald*, 13 March 2015. The Minister, testifying before the Parliamentary Portfolio Committee on Youth, Indigenisation and Economic Empowerment, was damning in his assessment of the MZCT's establishment: 'I took the opportunity to talk to the mining companies when I went to Marange... when the [MZCT] was formed, there was not a single meeting that was held to invite them to talk about not just the amount that would be deposited into the account, but the manner and the purpose of the Community Share Ownership Trust and how that links with the day to day social responsibilities of any company.'

23 See Section 3(2) (j).

State must ensure that local communities benefit from the resources in their areas'. The constitution also provided for the establishment of a Human Rights Commission (HRC); as one of the new constitutional-ly-mandated Independent Commissions (Section 242), it was given key 'general objectives' to 'support and entrench human rights and democ-racy', 'promote transparency and accountability in public institutions', and 'ensure that injustices are remedied'. The space appeared to be opening for more active constitutionally-mandated challenges around the turmoil in Marange. At the same time, ZANU-PF's resumption of power in government, and its eagerness to re-engage donors (and vice-versa) in charting a path to national economic recovery, held some promise in terms of normalising what had been highly polarised forms of engagement around Marange. However, the shifting sands of politics, diplomacy and the diamond industry also presented new and in some ways unexpected challenges that further complicated the terrain for community activists.

Political turbulence during the electoral period, and the transition to a new government, brought into sharp focus some important issues. It became clear that government was unwilling, even during an election campaign, to force companies to honour their pledges of full and fair compensation for the 1,400 families evicted from Marange or the busi-nesses that had been displaced and shut down. It was also evident that some traditional leaders, including those who participated listlessly in the MZCT and seemed little interested in actively consulting and pro-tecting their people, could be obstacles to the community's progress in obtaining social and economic justice. In the first instance, the CCDT needed to develop new tools to apply pressure for the resolution of con-tinuing problems at ARDA Transau and back in Marange. Some of these were on display at a well organised protest, including a march and sit-in at the gates of Mbada Diamonds, called to protest against 'greed and cor-ruption' and 'lack of transparency' in the allocation of commercial min-ing rights in Marange, the exclusion of community stakeholders from the MZCT and the lack of compensation for families and businesses.[24] The protest resulted in large payouts by Mbada of $35-$75,000 to the affected businessmen. Chief Newman Chiadzwa, then Chair of the CCDT, was later revealed to have received a total of $724,000 from the company.

24 'Community protest over Marange diamonds', *Daily News*, 25 September 2012.

Ordinary evicted villagers, meanwhile, received nothing. Consequently, another outcome of the protest and its resolution was a change in the Trust's leadership: in 2012 the rules for election and representation on the board changed, in advance of the AGM and elections at the end of that year. New mandated representation of women and men was put in place so that the trustees more closely reflected the wider membership.[25]

It became apparent that tackling the problem of fragmented and compromised traditional authorities was also important. The traditional leadership, and the cohesion it had once afforded Marange, had been disrupted by both the forced removals to ARDA Transau and government's strategic intervention in imposing a Chief commonly seen as passive and compliant with government's wishes. The combined result was a gaping hole in local power structures which needed to be filled if the community was to take full advantage of traditional authorities' power to engage higher levels of government on issues of resource governance and to address past human rights abuses. Against this backdrop, in 2014 the CCDT helped to organise a challenge to the current Chief Marange's legitimacy, led by the son of the previous Chief Marange and members of the community.[26] The Trust argued that restoring legitimacy and order to the chieftaincy was an important step in strengthening local autonomy through political structures now empowered with resource governance rights under the 2013 Constitution. Some of CCDT's civil society partners provided technical and other support to this challenge.[27]

Another point of engagement was the HRC, which the Trust petitioned for an official inquiry into what happened in Marange during the most violent years of the diamond rush. The objective was to reveal who was responsible, identify the victims, make public the findings of wrong-doing and arrive at recommendations for compensation and other forms of redress. The initial response from the HRC underscored familiar difficulties of dealing with government institutions which promise one thing and do another: it was made clear to the Trust that the Marange rights

---

25   Under the new procedures, equal numbers of men and women would be nominated from each of Marange's 11 Wards and from ARDA Transau. There were also provisions for four youth representatives, two of each gender. Some of the old leadership of the CCDT, including Chief Chiadzwa, lost their positions.

26   'Plot to dethrone Chief Marange thickens', *Daily News*, 27 March 2014.

27   At time of writing in 2015, this challenge to the Marange chieftaincy remained unresolved.

issue was a 'sensitive' one, and that an official commission of inquiry would require the approval of government structures. The government argued that it bore no responsibility for the actions of individual agents of government, including members of the state security forces. It was a sobering lesson: despite the promising language of the 2013 Constitution, it was the political practicalities that mattered. The HRC had been appointed by the President; it was therefore far-fetched to expect it to investigate human rights violations in Marange perpetrated by the same government and executive which had appointed it. In broad terms, the new Constitution's enshrinement of community resource rights – a response by constitutional drafters to the clearly expressed desire in resource-rich areas for greater participation – was admirable. However, in the absence of government's commitment to facilitating the pursuit of such rights they faced the risk of rapid withering. The blame did not fall entirely on government: its lethargic response was predictable, but civil society, too, was slow in getting off the mark to inform local communities of their rights and how to access them. As a result, local communities, as key prospective beneficiaries of the new constitutional order, remained largely non-conversant with their rights in principle and practice.

The weak engagement by civil society of the rights opportunities that came with the new constitution reflected a broader dynamic emerging after 2013: the shift by donors towards accommodation of government. This had important implications for donor funding of civil society programmes.[28] If in the recent past donors had been enthusiastic supporters of capacity building for rights monitoring and advocacy around diamonds, the new political dispensation saw them shift their focus to issues of economic development and 'normalisation' of mining. The pursuit of rights appeared to fall from the top of their priorities list; some seemed to suggest that human rights were a luxury in a country in severe economic stress. They shied away from conflict over 'non-core' issues, and displayed increased willingness to compromise with government in order to make progress on re-engagement of development co-operation. The CCDT and several partners sensed donor support becoming more contingent; gaps were emerging between what civil society and communities wanted to do, and what donors were keen to continue funding.

For the Trust, donors appeared less interested in pushing for greater

28 See for example, 'Civil society strategises on engaging government', *Southern Eye*, 26 November 2013.

transparency and accountability around Marange, particularly when it came to community grievances. It did not seem to register with them that government had failed to honour its assurances that the lifting of export and trading sanctions on Marange's diamonds would result in 'legitimate' money flowing into Marange through the payment of compensation to relocated villagers and infrastructure development. In reality, after the legal trade in diamonds resumed no mechanisms for the transparent management of diamond revenues were put in place, and corruption, tax evasion and prejudicing of the government treasury persisted. For civil society, transparency of diamond management was the first step in economic recovery and development; without new structures, bad habits would continue. While donors sought accommodation, communities were becoming wary of engaging with government. In Marange, many felt confrontation rather than compromise was the best way forward, and lost faith in the prospect of gaining ground through engagement with institutions like parliament and the DA's office. The CCDT and some other civil society partners wondered if it would be more productive to link with and work through other, less politicised, more 'professional' channels where individuals were more understanding of and sympathetic to community issues and less directly invested in the entrenched interests at play in diamond mining. There was little enthusiasm for engaging with politicians or administrators who would likely toe the party line. All the while, it was still necessary to maintain pressure on government to compensate for villagers' relocation, environmental damage and livelihood losses in Marange.

The mining companies posed additional obstacles, especially when production and profitability dipped after 2012. The large-scale and illegal retrenchment of workers in 2012 by Anjin and two years later by Mbada, for example, threw many households into poverty. Companies' claims of loss-making operations diminished the likelihood of timely payment of outstanding relocation compensation and further community investment. Both issues prompted new forms of intervention by CCDT. In the first instance, the Trust sought to assist 1,200 workers fired by Anjin by helping them to sue the company for reinstatement, or for the retrenchment packages to which they were entitled. But while court cases against Anjin and Mbada were successful, the problem lay in compelling the companies to abide by the courts' orders, and pay. Government refused to enforce the law and rather protected the companies, which were suddenly claiming poverty and inability to pay. Information on government's secret contracts with mining companies – and what obligations they had to compensate and invest in communities – continued to be concealed from the public, despite repeated information requests by the CCDT and others. Government argued that the agreements were private business deals that had the right of protection from public prying.

A further twist in 2014-2015 raised new fears that these issues might never be resolved, when the mining minister announced that all diamond mining companies in Marange would be merged into one entity under the control of government's ZMDC. Government argued that poor performance and declining state revenues from the diamond mines had led to the decision. But just how the mines would be merged, and who would control the assets – and crucially, who would assume responsibility for outstanding contractual liabilities to Marange's communities – was unclear. Some suspected the merger process was a way to close the books and exonerate companies of their social debts, now that they had mined out Marange's most accessible, cost-efficient deposits. For the community, the prospect of a mining company merger posed new challenges and questions. Where would the communities go to claim their compensation? If diamond revenues were suddenly falling, who would pay it? It was difficult to imagine how government's 'clean-up' of the diamond sector would resolve either the problem of mining firms' transparency and accountability, or the outstanding issues of unpaid compensation and local livelihood support.

Conclusions and Lessons: Saying 'no' to 'normal'

Of the many cruel ironies arising from the Marange community's experience of profound impoverishment amid production of great wealth, perhaps the most painful was that despite powerful and dedicated mobilisation by villagers in defence of their communities, rights and livelihoods, very few concrete gains were won. The primary grievances which fuelled community anger and led to the formation of the CCDT remained outstanding in 2015. Seven years after 'Operation Hakudzokwi's' horrific killings and gross human rights abuses, five years after the first forced relocations to ARDA Transau, and four years after the 'legalisation' of the diamond trade, Marange's communities were still waiting for compensation for the loss of their homes, communities and livelihoods, and for the redress of other human rights abuses and social injustices. The community's campaign for social justice and equitable diamond-driven development – a campaign which stretched from Wards 29 and 30 of Marange District to across Zimbabwe, and subsequently around the world – had made a lot of noise, attracted global attention and engaged governments and the diamond industry at the highest levels. Back in Marange, it nurtured determined, well-informed resistance to exploitation. So its defeat raised difficult questions. How were government and companies able to deflect the communities' legitimate, legal, and morally powerful demands? What elements were missing from civil society's engagement that might have made a difference to the outcomes? What were the realistic chances of other communities mounting successful claims to resource governance in the future, in the wake of Marange's toxic experience? There were no simple answers.

One lesson emerging from Marange involved the capacity of government to absorb and deflect problematic social demands in a relatively straightforward way: by ignoring them, repeatedly and consistently; and in the process, wearing down the will, patience, energy and coherence of the aggrieved critics. Silence, inaction and avoidance became very effective tactics deployed by ZANU-PF in dealing with demands from Marange for the implementation of apparently agreed obligations, such as compensation and infrastructure investment for relocated communities. Unfortunately, the capacity of government to remain silent and wilfully ignorant far exceeded that of communities to protest, organise, mobilise and energise constituencies who were impoverished, desperate and physically disaggregated. Meanwhile government demonstrated a willingness to use parallel tactics to actively disrupt its critics. Legal and extralegal harassment and threats, organisational infiltration, generating donor chill, the setting up and patronising of alternative social organisations, and more: these were some of the 'soft weapons' in the state's arsenal in its dealings with less compliant components of civil society. All of these were deployed in Marange, and confronting them meant taking on a well-resourced, politically savvy state and its strategy for gaining secretive control over Marange's diamonds. It was not obvious in the first years of the diamond rush how critical this project was to the survival of ZANU-PF, but this became clear early in the life of the GNU. The funding of a parallel government through secret revenues from illicitly traded diamonds subject to sanctions and export bans was not to be interfered with, and Marange's villagers and their demands stood in the way.[29] Without a more open government and state, demands for greater transparency and community benefit in Marange were unlikely to make headway. A civil society strategy which assumed government's shared good intentions around diamonds and development was therefore misplaced.

Under a post-GNU government and with diamond mining in decline, some in civil society called for greater engagement and compromise with government around resource issues. These voices noted the opportunities for local participation in resource management under the new constitution, by engagement with the Environmental Management Agency (EMA) and through other means. In the case of the Marange community's unresolved grievances, the implicit suggestion was that the CCDT and others should 'move on', and explore positive ways in which the authorities could be engaged for future development. In Marange this position attracted little support: it was not clear how and why the community should move forward, when the key issues from the turbulent recent past remained unaddressed. Moreover, some practical forms of new engagement were not encouraging. For example, the EMA invited communities to participate in dealing with the environmental mess generated by mining in Marange, even though the agency was nowhere to be seen when degradation was in full swing and villagers were laying complaints with it. The CCDT rejected the EMA's invitation, arguing that the community should not be asked to take responsibility and assume the liabilities for pollution when it had derived no benefit from the mining which produced it. Similarly, while some civil society organisations urged communities to take up their rights to resource governance under the new constitution, the CCDT held that government had demonstrated little interest in upholding those rights in Marange and elsewhere; indeed, in practice, government's record was one of delaying and deferring legislation that might enable improved resource governance. Therefore, placing a focus on training and capacity building of civil society for engagement with an uneven, unfair and untransparent governance regime, was seen by the CCDT as misplaced.

Beyond the question of government's sincerity in its stated commit-

---

29 See chapters by Saunders, Martin and Mtisi in this collection.

ment to sharing resource governance with civil society and mining-affected communities, a broader point of division within civil society emerged around the drive towards a 'sustainable mining' policy. There was much talk – by government, donors, mining companies and several local NGOs – of how to domesticate the 'African Mining Vision' (AMV), a set of proposals for mining development, beneficiation, and maximising investment in minerals, endorsed by the African Union and several member countries. The experience of Marange suggested that such propositions were highly premature, if not wrong-headed. There was little to suggest that a local version of the AMV would provide the kinds of protections, mechanisms and guarantees for community and environmental sustainability that was desperately lacking in Marange and elsewhere in Zimbabwe. Without such safeguards, mining would simply mean more displacement, community disruption and impoverishment. In reality, when communities mined for a livelihood – as with artisanal mining in the early years of the diamond rush – government had criminalised their activities, raining violence, intimidation and new poverty on them in the name of 'law and order' and 'national interest'. Without explicit consideration and protections given to local communities, the AMV's vision seemed to be dominated by the likelihood of more land grabs and environmentally harmful, business-as-usual mining.

The turn towards re-engagement of government and the mining industry by some civil society groups underscored a broader political gap which opened up after the 2013 elections. Some groups were increasingly comfortable engaging government on its own terms, for example in the context of the AMV. They typically pursued low-risk arenas for contestation – the court system, public briefings, the media and so forth – while remaining broadly supportive if sometimes mildly critical of state initiatives like CSOTs. Others were less accommodating in stance, and these included the CCDT. The engagement of government on its own terms under conditions that were often unevenly balanced – for example, the judicial system, and the administration of local government under the DA – was tantamount to enabling the 'normalisation' of a profoundly abnormal, unfair situation. For the Trust, contestation around the terms of government's agenda for mining development was a necessary first step in a process leading to meaningful engagement. Thereafter, careful consideration needed to be given to the most appropriate tactics for dealing with government under different circumstances, particularly during disputes. Experience suggested that 'consultation' and court challenges were often less effective in producing outcomes than more confrontational forms of engagement, like sit-ins, demonstrations and the publication of human rights monitoring reports. Similarly, risk aversion could lead to passivity, compromises and a derailed agenda; risk taking that took government or companies by surprise, could be highly effective. And telling communities what training they needed in order to plug into the state's new minerals dispensation, could be less empowering than asking communities what training they wanted.

The Marange experience provides sobering evidence of the limits to what can be achieved through repeated compromises and compliance, and the real dangers in accepting unjust situations as 'normal'. At the same time, Marange also calls attention to the scale and diversity of the obstacles confronting those who insist on charting a more equitable, sustainable approach to mining. Perhaps above all, Marange illustrates that the struggle for development and social justice around resources for those who are most directly and deeply affected by them is an arduous, enduring and sometimes lonely one.

EPILOGUE:

BACK TO THE BEGINNING...

Richard Saunders

Less than a decade after the first wave of the diamond rush and four years after Zimbabwe's re-entry into the legitimate global diamond trade, new revelations about the looting and plunder of Marange were brought to public attention. This time, news of the theft and its staggering scale – perhaps as much as $13 billion since 2010, it was claimed – was revealed not by the usual sources of reliable critical commentary like civil society and the KP, but by the most senior official in the government which had overseen the mess in Marange.

In March 2016, President Robert Mugabe announced that the mining companies his ministers had licensed and whose concessions he had personally approved, had acted like robbers, engaging in 'swindling' and 'smuggling', and making off with the lion's share of Marange's diamond wealth. Less than $2 billion of the more than $15 billion which was estimated to have been earned by diamond mining firms since 2012 had been remitted to government, the President said. On his telling, government had been shocked to learn of the missing funds, had no idea of the scale of the systematic subterfuge and was therefore moving to take charge of the situation. The lesson learned, President Mugabe concluded, was that private companies could not be trusted with valuable public resources, and that direct state control of mining was the solution. Thus government's announcement in 2016 that it was nationalising all mining operations in Marange and bringing them under a single entity, the Zimbabwe Consolidated Diamond Company, in which the state would maintain a 50 per cent controlling shareholding.

For veteran Marange observers it was difficult to determine which was the most incredulous claim in this latest spin on the situation: that government had known nothing about the looting of the diamonds; that it was unaware of where billions in diamond wealth had been parked, and by whom; or that direct state control of the diamond fields was the solution to the problem of corruption and theft.

Since the June 2013 publication of a report by Parliament's Portfolio Committee on Mines and Energy led by ZANU-PF MP Edward Chindori-Chininga, detailed knowledge of what had gone wrong in Marange, who was responsible and what should be done to redress the problems, had been in government hands and the public sphere. The Committee's four-year study, unprecedented in its depth of investigation, carefully detailed systematic malfeasance at the highest levels of the state – only to be studiously ignored by senior officials, several of whom were implicated in the report's findings. Despite compelling corroborating evidence of state-condoned criminal activity and extensive governance failures in Marange provided by the KP, civil society organisations, independent researchers and the popular media, ZANU-PF officials categorically refused to acknowledge the plunder they oversaw in the diamond fields; much less, take meaningful steps to redress it.

So government's sudden turn in 2016 towards acknowledgement of wrong-doing – even if it was attributed to others – begged the question: why now?

Here, Marange once again served as a lens into the morass of contesting interests, accumulation agendas and elite power calculations that had come to define Zimbabwe's troubling political transformation in the 2000s. Some speculated that the forced merger of Marange's firms was an efficient way to 'close the books' on years of systematic looting involving tax evasion and unremitted shared earnings at a time when production levels and profitability were sinking; others observed that the winding up of individual company stakes relieved firms of their unfulfilled financial, developmental and environmental management obligations to both government and local communities in Marange. Few found government's justification of nationalisation in the interests of strengthening transparency, accountability and revenue flows to be convincing; to the contrary, many saw its poor record of transparency in Marange as suggesting that state meddling had been a key factor in the dismal performance of the mining firms. From this perspective, the latest moves toward the merger of companies under the state represented a step backward, not forward: having shamelessly plundered many billions of dollars, Marange's key beneficiaries – unnamed, unindicted, untouched – stood to be relieved of liability for their actions by the same government which had irregularly, secretively, and apparently recklessly, licensed them to operate.

Looking back on the trajectory of Marange's mining boom from the vantage point of its implosion provides compelling evidence of the dynamics which continue to animate ZANU-PF's diamond politics and more broadly, the party's strategic re-engagement with donors, civil society and the private sector. As several authors in this collection have shown, refracted in the political economy of Marange's bloodied stones were elements of state capture, elite predation and private sector collusion. These dynamics coagulated in a toxic flow of systematic, shared profiteering. There is now little doubt about the highly lucrative nature of the diamond ventures overseen by a secretive coalition of forces, this having been confirmed by President Mugabe himself – if not yet by government's own formal record of accounts. However, the implications of elite embedding have been less well understood by some popular groups and other stakeholders in their recent turn to engage with government. This represents a challenge to meaningful reform of the diamond sector, and to wider initiatives aimed at leveraging greater transparency and participation from government through processes of re-engagement.

In the wake of the July 2013 elections which saw ZANU-PF resume unilateral control of government, some mining stakeholders argued that closer co-operation with the state was the most appropriate way to pursue reform of the diamond sector; a view echoed and reinforced by donors' calls for re-engagement with the ZANU-PF government. Some optimistically saw government's 2016 Marange merger announcement in this context, taking at face value government's assertion that nationalisation would enable greater transparency and public benefit from diamond resources; and seizing upon provisions in the 2013 Constitution pertaining to community rights to resource sharing, as the basis for fruitful future engagement with the state. Others, including some community organisations based in Marange, and groups and individuals who have led challenges to government's handling of Marange since the early days of the diamond rush, were more sceptical. They suggested that the transparency and accountability required to authenticate government's good faith in the current period needed to start with full transparency and accountability about the recent past: without full disclosure of past wrongdoing, including notably a convincing account of how $13 billion went missing on government's watch, there was little reason to expect there would be full transparency and good faith moving forward. Moreover, some organisations argued, without the redress of important outstanding grievances arising from 2006 to 2015, including compensation for lost properties, livelihoods and lives, there could be no meaningful engagement of government as a development 'partner'. Others argued that it was illogical, if not fantastical, to expect elites embedded in highly profitable forms of accumulation to simply abandon them by choice: promises of transparency needed to be measured against the reasonable likelihood that they could be delivered upon, not the appeal of the rhetoric by which they were made. In the emerging diversity of opinion on the best way forward, splits and divisions among and within key civil society constituencies – reinforced by the funding prowess of donors and the patronising power of the state – threatened to unwind the coherence and power of a civil society sector which had been forged and hardened in the long struggle for diamond justice.

Marange's recent past provided a number of important illuminations for the road ahead. If the arc of the alluvial diamond experience demonstrated the creative capacity of an elite to preserve and expand its power in opportunistic coalitions with partners, it also underscored the importance of challenging that elite on terms of one's own construction. Over several years of confrontation with government and mining companies – in the KP, Marange, ARDA Transau and elsewhere – civil society and community organisations repeatedly achieved important gains by strategically defining their own terms of engagement, and challenging government and companies to agree to these criteria as a means for demonstrating good faith and moving forward. The Marange experience suggested that engagement unaccompanied by solid evidence of transparency and good faith on the part of elites risked a backslide by civil society and community negotiators into concession and appeasement. The flip side of this observation was equally important: the setting of criteria for good faith, making of demands derived from one's own agenda and offering of concessions in demonstration of one's own commitment to engagement, were constructive, creative and empowering processes in their own right. Evidence from both facets of engagement with elite interests in Marange pointed to a final critical lesson: community trust in future engagement cannot be built without a meaningful, transparent, actionable account of the recent past. In Marange, illuminating the shadows of the past will be needed before the rocky path ahead can be seen; we must return once again to the beginning, to chart the best way forward.

BIBLIOGRAPHY

Bates, R. (2012), 'Financing Terror: Zimbabwe and the Return of the Blood Diamond', Speech given at the African Policymakers Meeting, Cape Town, 14 February.

Berdal, M. (2005), 'Beyond greed and grievance – and none too soon', *Review of International Studies*, 31(4) (October), pp. 687-698.

Bieri, F. (2010), *From Blood Diamonds to the Kimberley Process: How NGOs Cleaned Up the Global Diamond Industry*, Burlington, VT, Ashgate.

Botswana, Precious and Semi-Precious Stones (Protection) Act (Chapter 66:03).

BusinessMap (2001), *SADC Investor Survey 2001: Opportunities in Waiting*, Johannesburg, BusinessMap SA.

Centre for Research and Development (2009), 'A Preliminary Report of the Atrocities Committed by the Police and Army in Mutare and Chiadzwa under 'Operation Hakudzokwi' (You Will Not Return) in 2008', Mutare, Centre for Research and Development.

Centre for Natural Resource Governance (2013), 'An Analysis of Zimbabwe's Diamond Policy', April.

Chamber of Mines of Zimbabwe (2009), Annual Report 2008, Harare, May.

Chiadzwa Community Development Trust (2010), 'Petition on Diamond Mining Activities in the Community', Document submitted to the Parliamentary Portfolio Committee on Mines and Energy and the Ministerial Task Force on Marange, 29 March.

Chikane, A. (2010), 'Second Fact Finding Mission Report', Kimberley Process, 24-28 May.

Chimonyo, G.R., Mungure, S. and Scott, P.D. (2012), 'The Social, Economic and Environmental Implications of Diamond Mining in Chiadzwa', Mutare, Centre for Research and Development.

Chiponda, M. (2015), 'Community documentation and mobilization around diamond mining in Zimbabwe', in *Back to Development: A call for what development could be*, Washington, DC, International Accountability Project.

Cleveland, T. (2014), *Stones of Contention: A History of Africa's Diamonds*, Athens, Ohio University Press.

Collier, P. and Hoeffler, A. (2004), 'Greed and Grievance in Civil War', *Oxford Economic Papers*, 56, pp. 563-595.

Cross, E.G. (2012), 'Diamond Production and Sales from the Marange Fields in Eastern Zimbabwe', Paper presented to Parliament, Harare, 23 November.

Dhliwayo, M. and Mtisi, S. (2012), 'Towards the Development of a Diamond Act in Zimbabwe: Analysis of the Legal and Policy Framework on Diamonds and Zimbabwe's Compliance with the Kimberley Process Certification Scheme (KPCS) Minimum Requirements', Harare, Zimbabwe Environmental Law Association.

Duffy, R. (2005), 'Global Environmental Governance and the challenge of shadow states: The Impact of Illicit Sapphire Mining in Madagascar', *Development and Change*, 36(5), pp. 825-843.

Ernst & Young (2010), 'Forensic Report to the Office of the Comptroller and Auditor General in Respect of the Marange Diamond Reconciliation', September.

Gibbon, P. and Ponte, S. (2005), *Trading Down: Africa, Value Chains, and the Global Economy*, Philadelphia, Temple University Press.

Global Witness (2010), 'Return of the Blood Diamond: How the crisis in Zimbabwe is undermining international efforts to eradicate conflict diamonds', London, Global Witness.

Global Witness (2011), 'Why we are leaving the Kimberley Process - A message from Global Witness Founding Director Chairman Gooch,' 5 December.

Global Witness (2012a), 'Diamonds: A Good Deal for Zimbabwe?', 13 February.

Global Witness (2012b), 'Financing a Parallel Government? The involvement of the secret police and military in Zimbabwe's diamond, cotton and property sectors.' London, Global Witness, 11 June.

Government of Zimbabwe, Ministry of Mines and Mining Development (2012), 'Zimbabwe Diamond Policy'.

Hammar, A., Raftopoulos, B. and Jensen, S. (2003), *Zimbabwe's Unfinished Business: Rethinking Land, State and Nation in the Context of Crisis*, Harare, Weaver Press.

Hawkins, T. (2009), 'The Mining Sector in Zimbabwe and its Potential Contribution to Recovery', Harare, United Nations Development Program.

Hujo, K. (ed.) (2012), *Mineral Rents and the Financing of Social Policy*, New York, Palgrave Macmillan.

Human Rights Watch (2008), '"Bullets for Each of You": State-Sponsored Violence since Zimbabwe's March 29 Elections', June.

Human Rights Watch (2009), 'Diamonds in the Rough: Human Rights Abuses in the Marange Diamond Fields of Zimbabwe', June.

International Crisis Group (2008), 'Negotiating Zimbabwe's Transition', *Africa Briefing* 51.

Jones, J. (2010), '"Nothing is Straight in Zimbabwe": The Rise of the Kukiya-kiya Economy, 2000-2008', *Journal of Southern African Studies*, 36(2), pp. 285-299.

Kaplinsky, R. and Morris, M. (2001), 'A Handbook for Value Chain Research', Paper prepared for the IDRC.

Katsaura, O. (2010a), 'Socio-cultural Dynamics of Informal Diamond Mining in Chiadzwa, Zimbabwe', *Journal of Sustainable Development in Africa*, 12(6), pp. 101-121.

Katsaura, O. (2010b), 'Violence and the Political Economy of Informal Diamond Mining in Chiadzwa, Zimbabwe', *Journal of Sustainable Development in Africa*, 12(6), pp. 340-353.

Kimberley Process Certification Scheme (2003), 'KPCS Core Document'.

Kimberley Process Certification Scheme (2007), 'Report of the Review Visit of the Kimberley Process to the Republic of Zimbabwe', 29 May - 1 June.

Kimberley Process Certification Scheme (2009a), 'Kimberley Process

Certification Scheme Review Mission to Zimbabwe, 30 June - 4 July, 2009: Final Report'.

Kimberley Process Certification Scheme (2009b), Administrative Decision on Marange adopted at Swakopmund, Namibia, 5 November.

Kimberley Process Certification Scheme (2010), 'Report of the Review Mission to Zimbabwe', August.

Kimberley Process Certification Scheme (2011), 'Final statement from KP Intercessional Meeting', Tel Aviv, 14 June.

Kimberley Process Certification Scheme (2012), 'Final Communiqué from the Kimberley Process Plenary Meeting', Washington, DC, 30 November.

Kimberley Process Civil Society Representatives in Zimbabwe (2010), 'Report submitted to the KPCS', December.

Kimberley Process Civil Society Coalition Representatives in Zimbabwe (2012a), 'Report on Visit to Marange and Other Matters Observed in the First and Second Quarter of 2012', Report submitted to the KPCS Working Group on Monitoring, 10 May.

Kimberley Process Civil Society Representatives in Zimbabwe (2012b), 'Report to the Working Group on Monitoring', presented to the KPCS 2012 Plenary Meeting, Washington, DC, 29 November.

Le Billion, P. (2001), 'The Political Ecology of War: Natural resources and armed conflicts', *Political Geography*, 20, pp.561-584.

Lujala, P, Gleditsch, N.P. and Gilmore, E. (2005) 'A Diamond Curse? Civil War and a Lootable Resource', *Journal of Conflict Resolution*, 49(4) (August), pp. 538-562.

Mabhena, C. (2012), 'Mining with a "Vuvuzela": Reconfiguring artisanal mining in southern Zimbabwe and its implications to rural livelihoods', *Journal of Contemporary African Studies*, 30(2), pp. 219-233.

Machonachie, R. (2008), 'Diamond Mining, Governance Initiatives and Post Conflict Developments in Sierra Leone', BWPI Working Paper No 50, University of Manchester.

Mailey, J.R. (2015), 'The Anatomy of the Resource Curse: Predatory investment in Africa's extractive industries', ACSS Special Report

No.3, Africa Center for Strategic Studies, Washington, DC.

Martin, A. and Taylor B. (2010), 'Diamonds and Clubs: The Militarized Control of Diamonds and Power in Zimbabwe', Report by Partnership Africa Canada, Ottawa.

Martin, A. and Taylor B. (2012), 'Reap What You Sow: Greed and Corruption in Zimbabwe's Marange Diamond Fields', Partnership Africa Canada, Ottawa.

Mawowa, S. (2014),'The Political Economy of Artisanal and Small Scale Gold Mining in Central Zimbabwe', *Journal of Southern African Studies*, 39(4), pp. 921-936.

MDC, Movement for Democratic Change (2013), 'Minister Biti concerned over missing diamond revenue', 28 May.

Mitchell, J., Shepherd, A. and Keane, J. (2011), 'An Introduction', in J. Mitchell and C. Coles (eds), *Markets and Rural Poverty: Upgrading in Value Chains*, London, Earthscan.

Mpofu, O. (2010), 'Speech by the Honourable Minster of Mines and Mining Development at the World Diamond Council 7th Annual Meeting Held in Saint Petersburg, Russia', 15 July.

Mtisi, S., Dhliwayo, M. and Makore, G.S.M. (2011), 'Analysis of the key issues in Zimbabwe's mining sector: Case study of the plight of Marange and Mutoko Mining Communities', Harare, Zimbabwe Environmental Law Association.

Mukumbira, R. (2006), 'AIM listed Zimbabwe diamond miner evicted from its claims', *Mineweb*, 12 December.

Mukwakwami, N. (2013), 'Formalising Zimbabwe's Artisanal Mining sector', Project 263, available at: http://projekt263.wordpress.com/2013/09/24/formalising-zimbabwes-artisanal-mining-sector/

Nyamunda, T. (2014), 'Cross Border Transport Operators as Symbols of Regional Grievance: The Malayitsha Remittance System in Matabeleland, Zimbabwe', *Africa Diaspora*, 7(1).

Nyamunda, T. and Mukwambo, P. (2012), 'The State and the Bloody Diamond Rush in Chiadzwa: Unpacking the Contesting Interests in the Development of Illicit Mining and Trading, c. 2006-2009', *Journal of Southern African Studies*, 38(1), pp. 145-166.

Nyamunda, T., Mukwambo, P. and Nyandoro, M. (2012), 'Navigating the hills and voluntary confinement: Magweja and the socio-economic and political negotiation for space in the diamond mining landscape of Chiadzwa in Zimbabwe, 2006-2009', *New Contree*, 65, pp. 111-138.

Nyota, S. and Sibanda, F. (2012), 'Digging for Diamonds, Wielding New Words: A linguistic perspective on Zimbabwe's "Blood Diamonds"', *Journal of Southern African Studies,* 38(1), pp. 129-144.

Parliament of Zimbabwe, Portfolio Committee on Mines and Energy (2013), 'First Report on Diamond Mining (with special reference to Marange Diamond Fields) 2009-2013', presented to Parliament June 2013.

Parliament of Zimbabwe, Thematic Committee on Indigenisation and Empowerment (2015), 'First Report of the Thematic Committee on Indigenisation and Empowerment on the Operations of the Community Share Ownership Trusts and Employee Share Ownership Schemes', presented to Parliament February 2015.

Partnership Africa Canada (2005), 'The Failure of Good Intentions: Fraud, theft and murder in the Brazilian diamond industry', Ottawa, May.

Partnership Africa Canada (2006), 'Fugitives and Phantoms: The diamond exporters of Brazil', Ottawa, March.

Partnership Africa Canada (2009a), 'Zimbabwe, Diamonds and the Wrong Side of History', Ottawa, March.

Partnership Africa Canada (2009b), 'Diamonds and Human Security: Annual Review 2009', Ottawa, October.

Pigou, P. (2010), 'Zimbabwe's Transition: Fact or Fantasy?', *The Thinker*, 17, pp. 36-39.

Pilossof, R. (2009), '"Dollarisation" in Zimbabwe and the Death of an Industry', *Review of African Political Economy*, 36(120), pp. 294-299.

Poverty Reduction Forum Trust (2013), 'Study on Rural Poverty in Manicaland: The Case of Mutare Rural', Harare, PRFT.

Raftopoulos, B. (2009), 'The Crisis in Zimbabwe, 1998-2008', in B.

Raftopoulos and A.S. Mlambo (eds), *Becoming Zimbabwe: A History from the Pre-colonial Period to 2008*, Harare, Weaver Press.

Raftopoulos. B. (ed.) (2013), *The Hard Road to Reform: the Politics of Zimbabwe's Global Political Agreement*, Harare, Weaver Press.

Research and Advocacy Unit (2010), 'What are the options for Zimbabwe? Dealing with the obvious!', Harare, RAU.

Roitman, J. (2005), *Fiscal Disobedience: An Anthropology of Economic Regulation in Central Africa*, Princeton, NJ, Princeton University Press.

Rosser, A. (2009), 'Natural Resource Wealth, Development and Social Policy: Evidence and Issues', in Hujo, K. and McClanahan, S. (eds.) *Financing Social Policy: Mobilizing resources for social development*, Basingstoke, Palgrave Macmillan.

Ruguwa, M. (2013), 'A History of the Social Impact of Diamond Mining on Schools in Marange, 2006-2013', BA dissertation, University of Zimbabwe.

Sachikonye, L. (2007) 'Diamonds in Zimbabwe: A Situational Analysis', *Resource Insight*, 1.

Samset, I. (2002) 'Conflict of Interests or Interests in Conflict? Diamonds & War in the DRC', *Review of African Political Economy*, 93/94, pp.463-480.

Saul, J.S. and Saunders, R. (2005), 'Mugabe, Gramsci and Zimbabwe at 25', *International Journal,* 60(4), pp. 953-75.

Saunders, R. (2007), 'Mining and Crisis in Zimbabwe', Amsterdam, Niza/Fatal Transactions.

Saunders, R. (2008), 'Crisis, Capital, Compromise: Mining and Empowerment in Zimbabwe', *African Sociological Review*, 12(1), pp. 67-89.

Saunders, R. (2009), 'Briefing Note: Conflict diamonds from Zimbabwe', Amsterdam, Niza/Fatal Transactions.

Saunders, R. (2010), 'The Modern Face of Conflict Diamonds: Lessons from Zimbabwe', Paper presented at Pathfinder 2010 Conference, 'Illegal Trade in Natural Resources: What Can Brussels Do?', Brussels, 30 September.

Saunders, R. (2011), 'Zimbabwe: Liberation nationalism – old and born-again', *Review of African Political Economy*, 38(127) (March), pp.123-134.

Saunders, R. (2014), 'Geologies of Power: Blood diamonds, security politics and Zimbabwe's troubled transition', *Journal of Contemporary African Studies*, 32(3), pp. 378-394.

Sibanda, M. (2014), 'Analysis of ZMDC'S 2012 Audited Financial Statements', Zimbabwe Environmental Law Association, Harare.

Sibanda, M. and Makore, G. (2013), 'Tracking the Trends: An Assessment of Diamond Mining Sector Tax Contributions to Treasury with Particular Reference to Marange Diamond Fields', Zimbabwe Environmental Law Association, Harare.

Smillie, I. (2010a), *Blood on the Stone, Greed, Corruption and War in the Global Diamond Trade*, London, Anthem Press; Ottawa, IDRC.

Smillie, I. (2010b), 'Ian Smillie addresses human rights, diamonds and the Kimberley Process', *Rapaport News*, 10 September. http://www.diamonds.net/news/NewsItem.aspx?ArticleID=27951

Smillie, I. (2014), *Diamonds*, Cambridge, Polity Press.

Solidarity Peace Trust (2008), 'Punishing Dissent, Silencing Citizens: The Zimbabwe Elections 2008', Johannesburg.

Solidarity Peace Trust (2010), 'What options for Zimbabwe?', Johannesburg.

Taylor, I. and Mokhawa, G. (2003), 'Not Forever: Botswana, Conflict Diamonds and the Bushmen', *African Affairs*, 102(407), pp. 261-283.

Towriss, D. (2013), 'Buying Loyalty: Zimbabwe's Marange Diamonds', *Journal of Southern African Studies,* 39(1), pp. 99-117.

Tsvangirai, M. (2010), 'PM This Week.' Edition 45, 2 June.

United Nations Security Council Resolutions 1173 (1998), 1295 (2000), 1306 (2000), and 1343 (2001) United Nations General Assembly Resolution 55/56 (2000).

Vambe, M. (ed.) (2008), *The Hidden Dimensions of Operation Murambatsvina*, Harare, Weaver Press.

Vircoulon, T. (2010), 'Time to Rethink the Kimberley Process: The Zimbabwe Case', International Crisis Group, 4 November.

Zimbabwe Environmental Law Association (2015), 'Untold Stories from

Mining Communities: A collection of stories of mining impacts, community resilience and their commitment towards defending their environmental, economic social and cultural rights', Harare, ZELA and ActionAid.

Zimbabwe Lawyers for Human Rights, Centre for Research and Development, Zimbabwe Environmental Lawyers Association, Counselling Services Unit and Zimbabwe Association of Doctors for Human Rights (2009), 'Submission to the KP Review Mission', June.

Zimbabwe, Minerals Marketing Corporation of Zimbabwe Act (Chapter 21:04).

Zimbabwe, Mines and Minerals (Minerals Unit) Regulations, 2008 Statutory Instrument 82 of 2008.

Zimbabwe, Mines and Minerals Act (Chapter 21:05).

Zimbabwe, Mining Development Corporation Act (Chapter 21:08).

Zimbabwe, Precious Stones Trade (Amendment) Regulations (SI 282 of 2002).

Ziyera, E. (2007), 'A Handful of Dust: the diamond saga in Zimbabwe', *Break Free: Monthly Newsletter of Zimbabwe Coalition on Debt and Development*, March.

Printed in the United States
By Bookmasters